Working the Sea

Working the Sea

Historic Images from *National Fisherman*

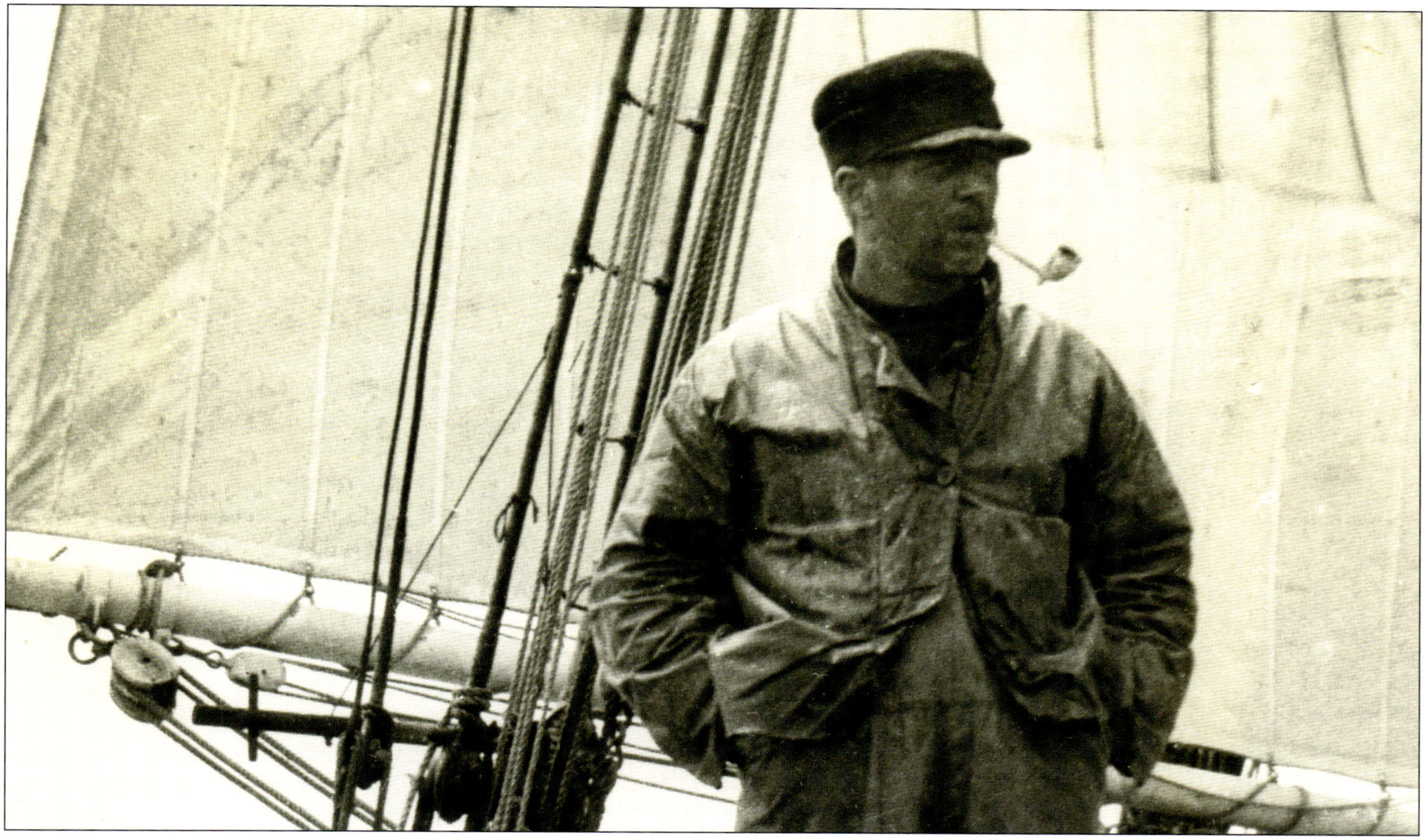

By *Michael Crowley* and the
Penobscot Marine Museum

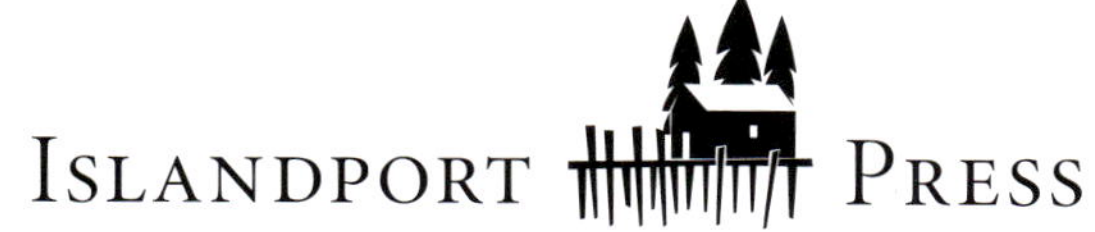

ISLANDPORT PRESS

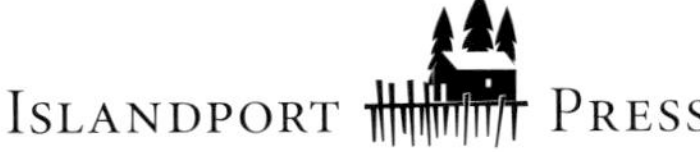
ISLANDPORT PRESS

Islandport Press
P.O. Box 10
Yarmouth, Maine 04096
www.islandportpress.com
info@islandportpress.com

First Edition: December 2024
ISBN: 978-1-952143-51-9
Library of Congress Control Number: 2022937846

Dean L. Lunt | Editor-in-Chief, Publisher
Shannon Butler | Vice President
Marion Fearing | Assistant Editor
Grace Caselden | Editorial Assistant
Dylan Andrews | Graphic Designer
Emily Lunt | Assistant Editor, Design

Front Cover Image: Unloading sardine catch from a small boat to be loaded into the hold
of the *Allan McLean* sardine boat, where they will be packed in salt to be returned to port at
Blacks Harbour, New Brunswick.

Title Page Image: Doug McLean, captain of 92-foot mackerel schooner *Pinta* (see page 37).

Author's Note

I first encountered *National Fisherman* years ago in a bar in Kodiak, Alaska, when I was between halibut longlining trips. More than once, the chance to work on this book and put together this collection of photographs took me back to that time. This book and those memories would not have been possible without Penobscot Marine Museum's tremendous photo archive collection of *National Fisherman* and *Atlantic Fisherman* images. Thanks especially to Kevin Johnson, Matt Wheeler, and Cipperly Good, who all work for the museum, for all their needed guidance and help. —Michael Crowley

The National Fisherman Collection

National Fisherman is the nation's preeminent publication in the commercial fishing industry, originally a consolidation of earlier, regional fisheries' trade papers including *Atlantic Fisherman*, *Pacific Fisherman*, and *Maine Coast Fisherman*. In 2012, Diversified Communications of Portland, Maine, donated the magazine's entire pre-digital photographic archive to the Penobscot Marine Museum. Over the next three years, Museum staff and volunteers processed, digitized and cataloged the collection with grant support from the Institute of Museum and Library Services and the National Maritime Heritage program, administered by the National Park Service, U.S. Department of the Interior. Diversified Communications has also continued to provide crucial support for the collection, exhibits created from it and other associated projects including this publication. This extraordinary photographic archive offers a comprehensive visual timeline of American fisheries from the middle to the end of the twentieth century, with all the grit, drama, resourcefulness, practical minutiae and sometimes epic feats that characterize the industry. —Penobscot Marine Museum

Photographers

The talented photographers who made the amazing images that appear in *Working the Sea* are credited below when known. Unfortunately, many of the photographs did not include photo credits. It is hoped that this publication will help link photographers with their work to give them credit for their historical contributions.

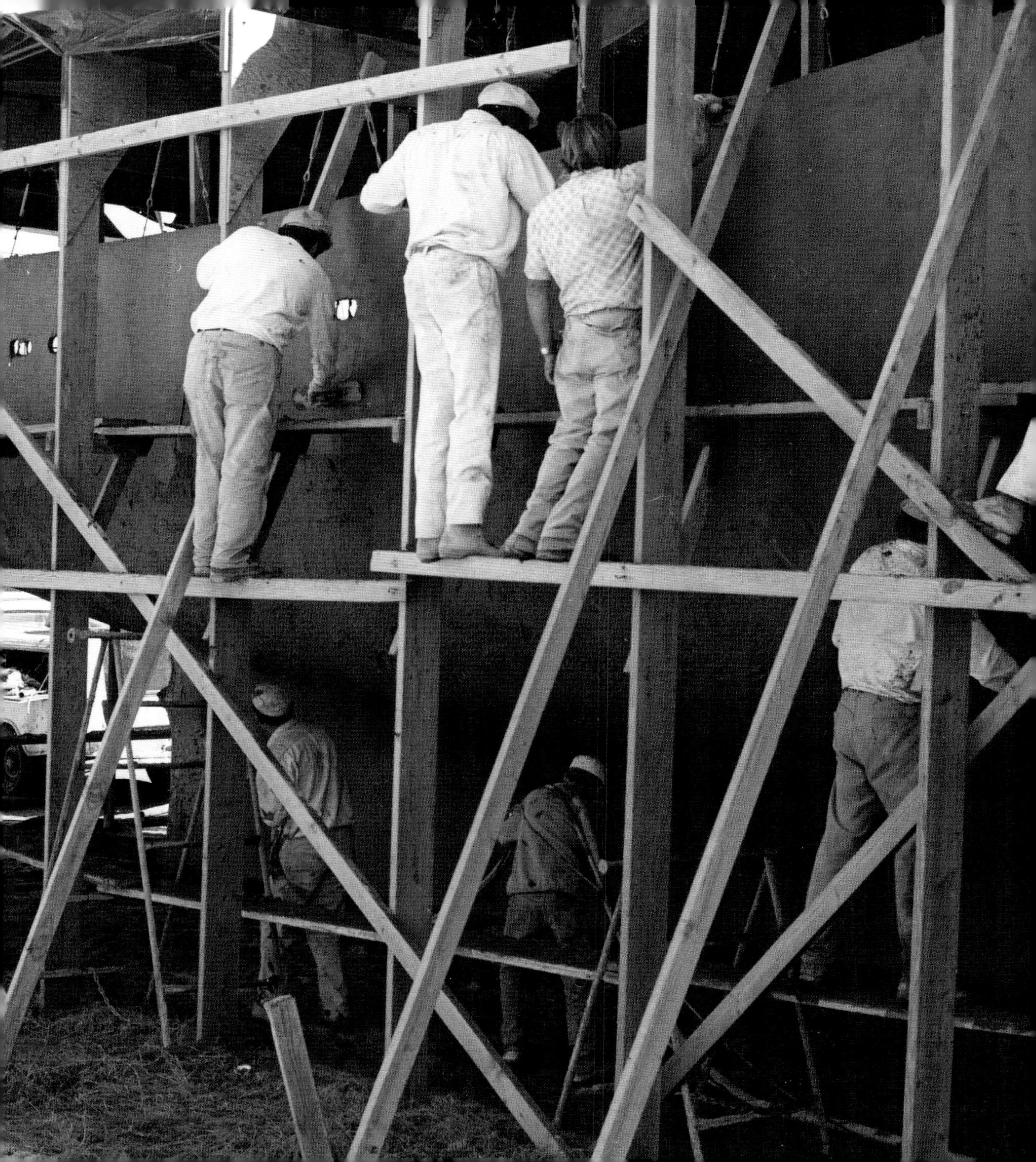

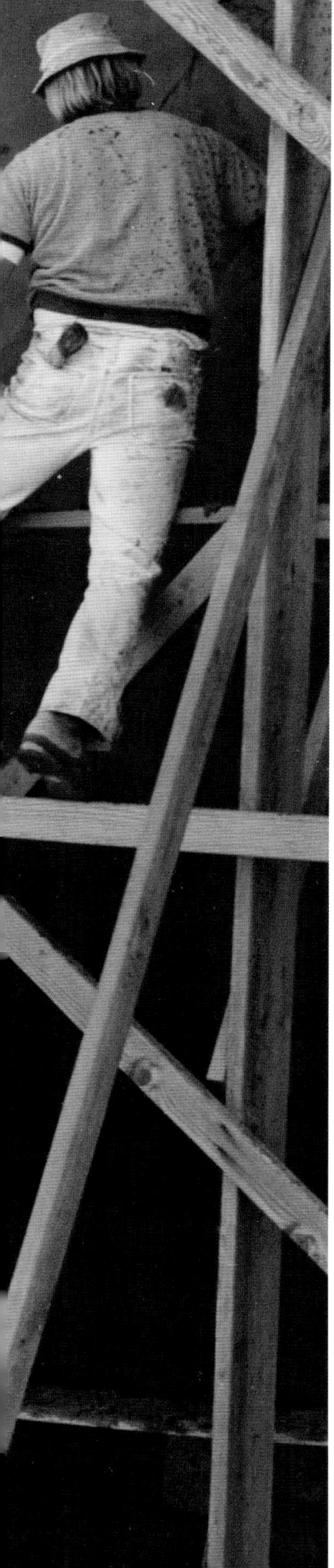

Table of Contents

Plasterers hard at work on side of vessel in 1974.

"The saltiest magazine on the newsstand."

Introduction

National Fisherman, which traces its roots to the early twentieth century, has been a critical and influential voice for commercial fisherman and the fishing industry for more than one hundred years. Its editors, reporters, and photographers have chronicled the industry, its growth, and its changes. The magazine and its predecessor, *Atlantic Fisherman,* have always focused on commercial fishermen—the industry that surrounds them, the boats they fish, and the gear they rely on to harvest the bounty of the sea.

Atlantic Fisherman was first published in February 1921 and was dedicated to the Atlantic fisher-folk—a "vast army, who contributes so richly to the life-blood of the North American nations."

Atlantic Fisherman moved north to Goffstown, New Hampshire in 1929 and then renamed itself *National Fisherman* in 1954. It increased its coverage area by adding the Pacific Coast coverage. The name change reflected the fishing industry's need for a more in-depth magazine that provided a national perspective regarding fishing practices, processing, boat design, regulations, and resources.

For many years, *National Fisherman* was known as "the saltiest magazine on the newsstand." While it was a trade publication, fishermen haven't been the magazine's only audience. A good portion of its readers owned pleasure boats, wanted to build their own boats, or were simply interested in the commercial fishing way of life and maritime history. Before the rise of competing magazines, *National Fisherman* ran articles on such topics as building and repairing small pleasure boats, the latest maritime equipment, and the days when two-, three-, and four-masted schooners ruled the sea.

In 1960, *National Fisherman* consolidated with *Maine Coast Fisherman,* a monthly publication that started in 1946 and was based in Belfast, Maine. The merger allowed for even wider coverage of commercial fishing and boatbuilding, while the increased number of pages provided more space to run articles and display photos. *National Fisherman,* and before that *Atlantic Fisherman,* were seven-by-eleven-inch publications, but the combined *National Fisherman/Maine Coast Fisherman* was much larger, measuring eleven-by-seventeen inches.

The cover included both the *National Fisherman* and *Maine Coast Fisherman* names until December 1967, when the *Maine Coast Fisherman* name was dropped. For that same issue, *National Fisherman* absorbed *Pacific Fishing,* which was published for sixty-three years out of San Francisco. This allowed *National Fisherman* to say it presented "the broadest coverage in the industry ever offered to U.S. fishermen." The magazine's geographic coverage now included the Atlantic, Pacific, and Gulf Coasts; the Great Lakes; and Alaska.

The period from the late 1960s through the 1990s is considered *National Fisherman*'s heyday. A measure of its growing importance and influence was the number of pages in each issue. *Atlantic Fisherman* generally offered a 26-page issue, although it sometimes stretched to 40 pages. The combined *National Fisherman/Maine Coast Fisherman* issues weren't much bigger, ranging from 36 to 48 pages, maybe even hitting 64 pages. But *National Fisherman* was often more than 100 pages, with some *Year Book* issues running more than 200 pages. *Working the Sea* is a collection of more than one hundred of those images, taken from the 1920s to the 1990s.

The images made their way to the Penobscot Marine Museum in Searsport beginning in 1992 when Gardner Lamson, who had been *Atlantic Fisherman*'s editor, gave the museum about 1,000 prints from the magazine's photo files, along with printed copies of *Atlantic Fisherman*.

National Fisherman's parent company, Diversified Communications in Portland, donated *National Fisherman*'s entire pre-digital photographic archive of about 2,100 prints to the museum in 2012. Both of those photo collections have been digitized and cataloged, and most of the images are now available on the museum's website: penobscotmarinemuseum.org.

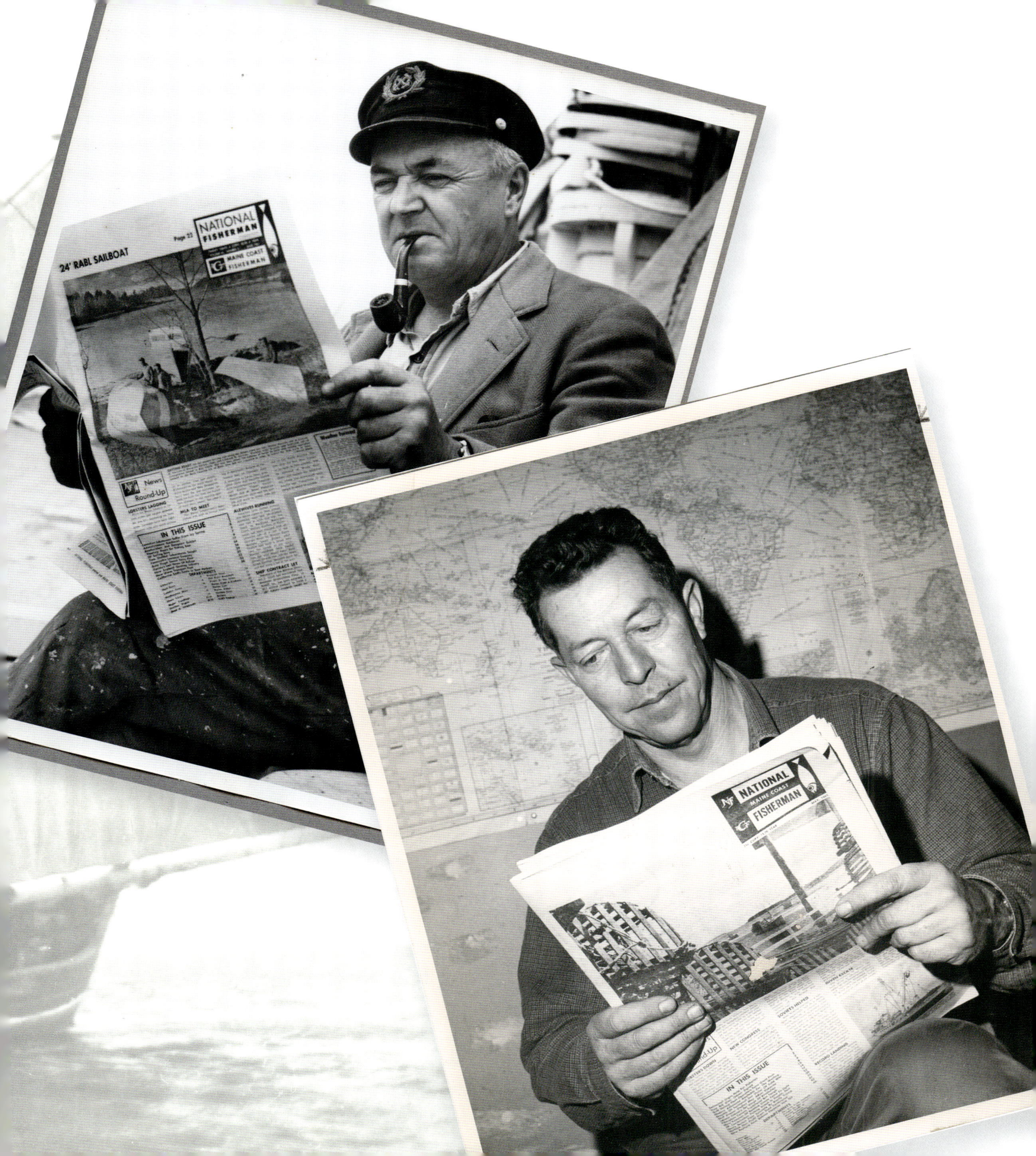

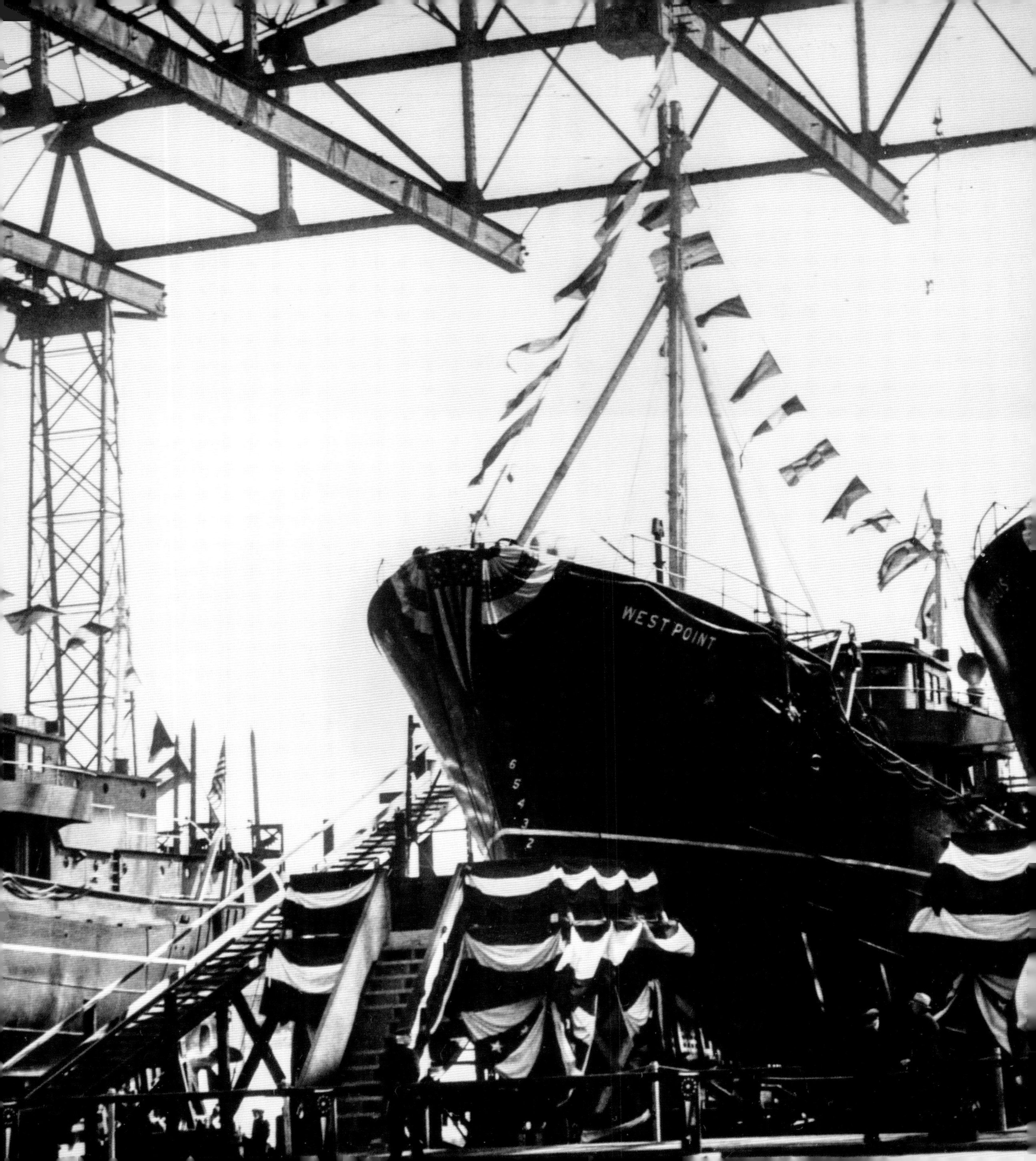

WEST POINT
6
5
4
3
2

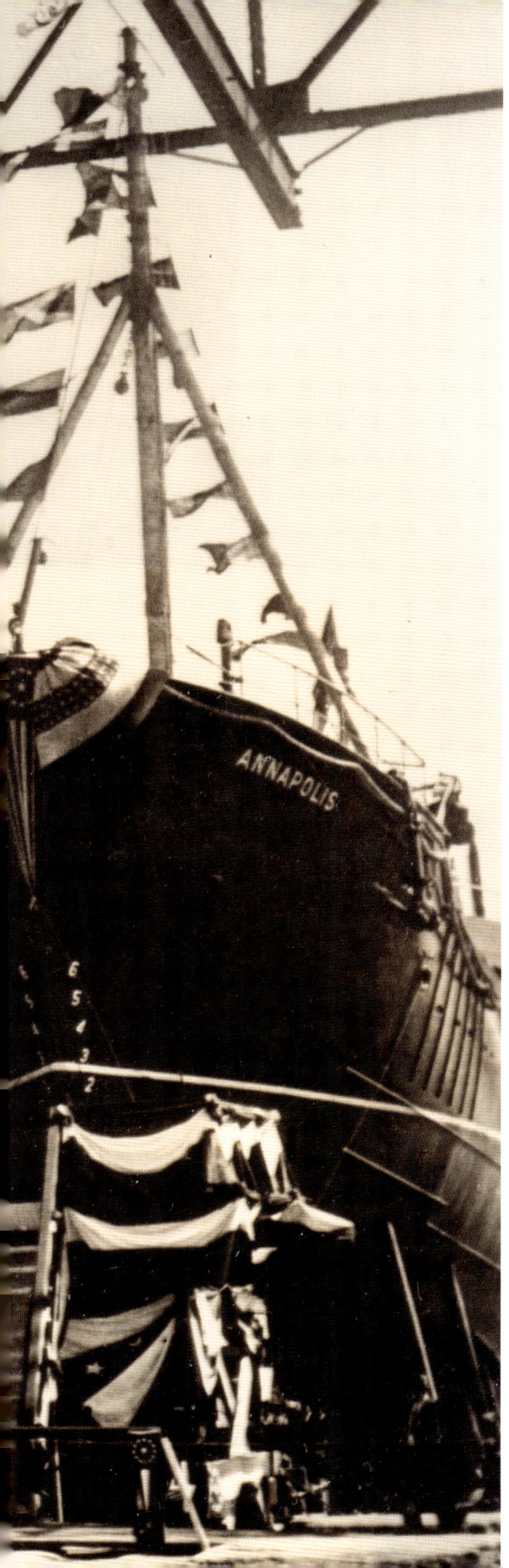

Launch Day

For people to work the sea, It all starts with the boat. Humans have been building vessels for thousands of years, allowing them to take to the waters for transport, for food, for pleasure, or for discovery.

In coastal communities, building those boats may require just a person or two, or perhaps hundreds—depending on whether the boats are large or small, sail or power, simple or elaborate. And as long as boats have been built, people have found ways to make them faster, safer, more efficient, more powerful—or simply better.

Whether building a five-masted schooner, a huge tuna seiner, or a small dory, boat builders and designers have always worked as vital cogs in maritime communities.

And when the building of a boat is complete, that is a cause for celebration. When larger vessels, or even smaller ones, were launched "down the ways" into the water, entire communities came out to watch, cheer, and enjoy the festivities.

Three-masted Schooners

The *Methebesec* (below), a three-masted schooner, is ready for launch on April 25, 1896, at Snow Shipyards in Rockland. Meanwhile, the eight-year-old *John I. Snow* (below, right) is in dry dock for an overhaul. Both schooners were owned by I.L. Snow & Company. Three-masted schooners were prevalent during the second half of the nineteenth century. They nearly monopolized coastal trades during that era, particularly in the lumber business.

The 136-foot *Methebesec* started her voyage on July 8, 1896, bound for Richmond, Virginia, with a load of ice. While on a routine journey, bound for Martinique with a load of fertilizer, she wrecked between St. Kitts and St. Thomas on January 26, 1920. The *Methebesec*, which had no insurance, was valued at $35,000. She was declared a total loss.

The *John I. Snow*, the first three-master built by Snow Shipyards, ended her sailing days in 1907 on a run from New York City to Miami. She sank while carrying a load of general cargo after running ashore on Portsmouth Beach, North Carolina, in foggy weather. The *John I. Snow* was valued at $7,500 (she cost $16,000 to build), and the cargo was valued at $10,000.

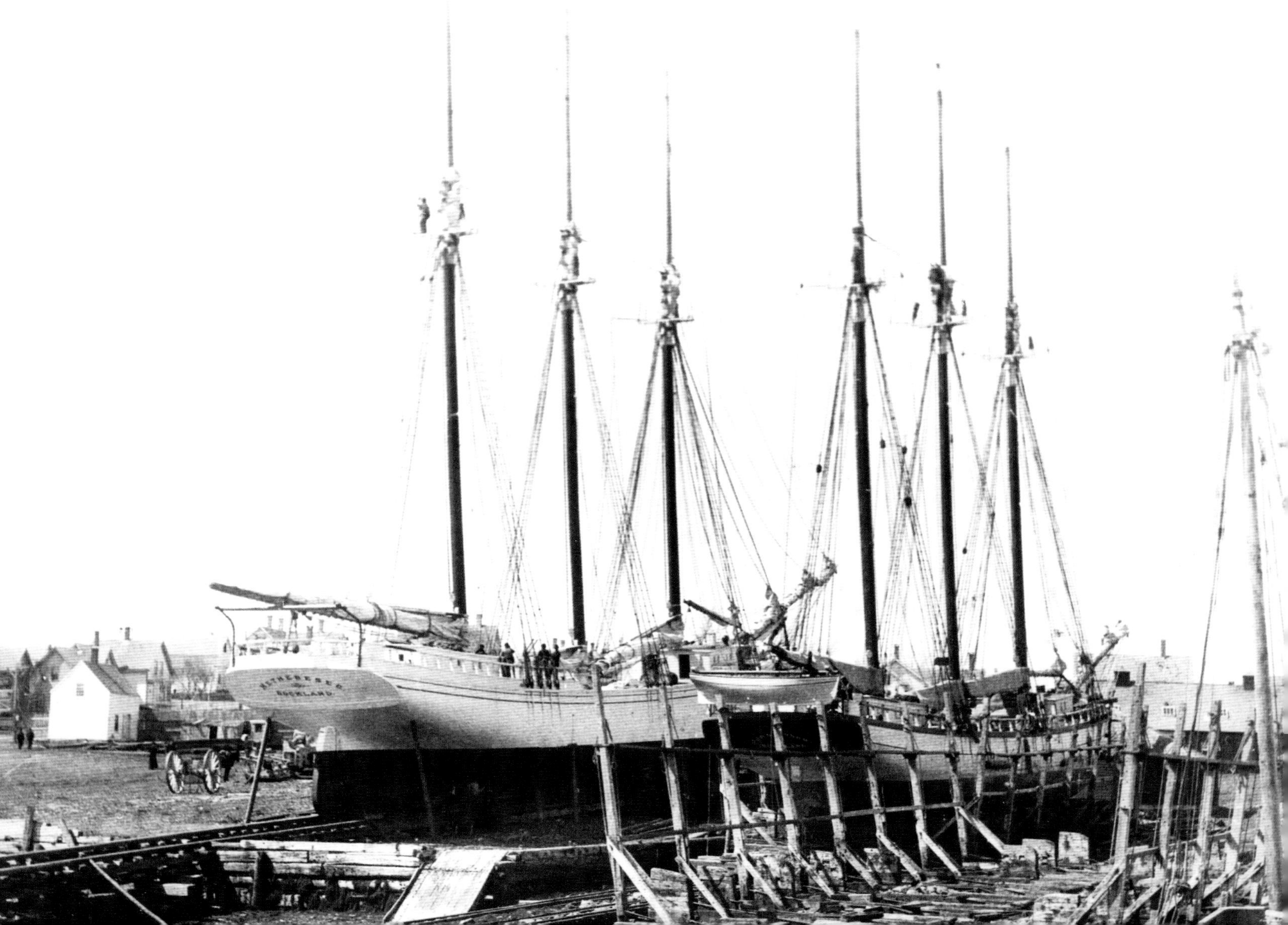

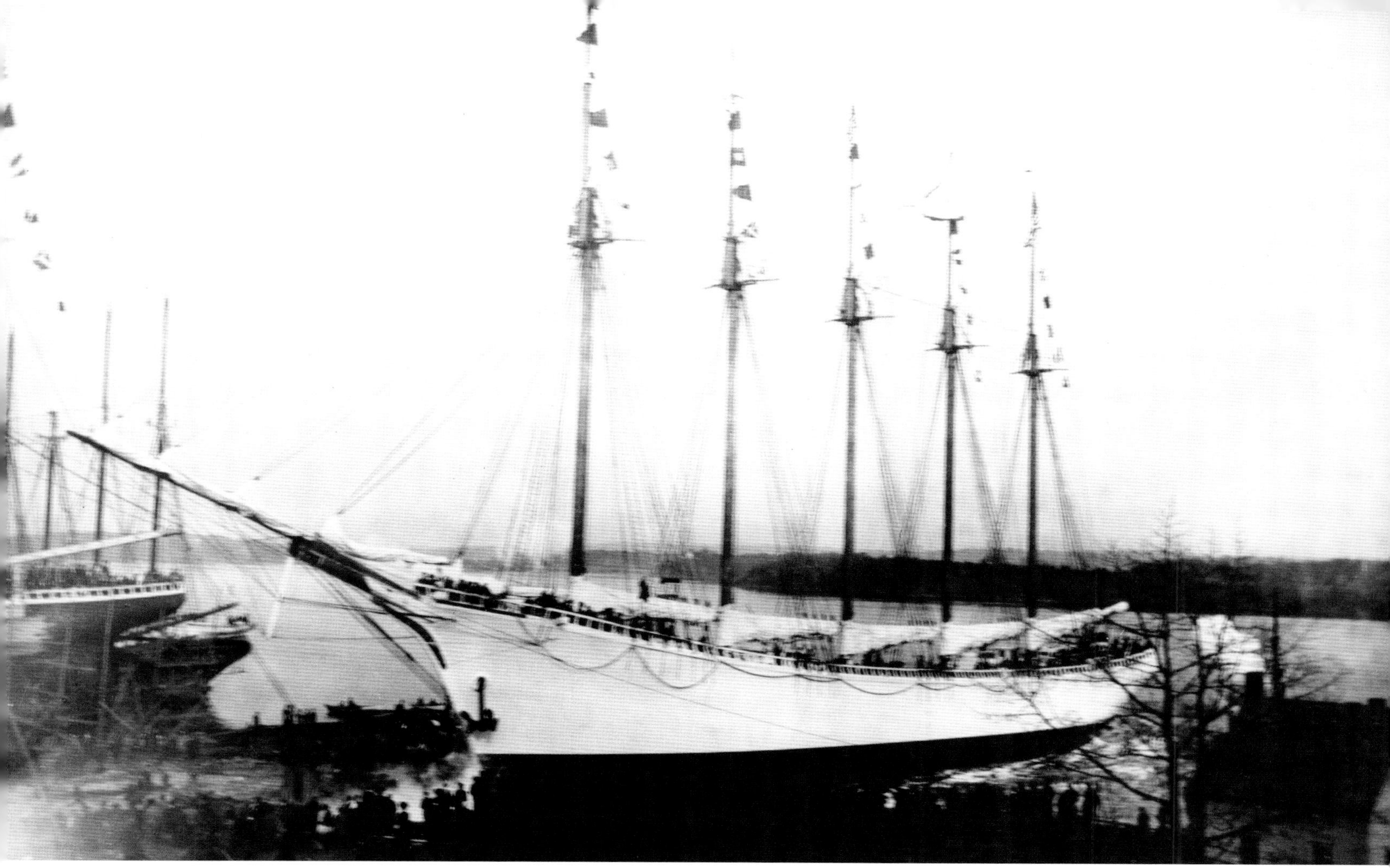

Five-masted Schooners

The five-masted *Fuller Palmer* slides into the Kennebec River on launch day, November 10, 1908, at the Percy & Small shipyard in Bath, Maine. The 309-foot by 49-foot schooner, with a 5,000-ton capacity, was designed to carry coal along the East Coast for Boston-based William F. Palmer.

Percy & Small built fifteen of the East Coast's fifty-six five-masted schooners; four of them for the Palmer fleet. The *Fuller Palmer*, which was built on a $141,000 contract, did not have a long career. Less than six months after launch, she collided with the Italian steamer *Taormina* off New Jersey and had to be towed to port. Eight months later, a rogue wave smashed her rudder, requiring a tow to Portland, Maine.

Finally on January 4, 1914, loaded with coal and bound for Portland, the *Fuller Palmer* and three other five-masted coal schooners were caught in a winter gale. Heavily iced over and pumps frozen, the *Fuller Palmer*, the *Prescott Palmer*, and the *Grace A. Martin* all sank. Fortunately, only one life was lost.

Biloxi Luggers

Schooners, similar to those whose masts are standing tall in the background of this photo, dominanted Mississippi's oyster and shrimp fisheries from the 1800s to the 1930s. However, by the thirties, the Biloxi Lugger, like the one shown being built here in 1936 at the Jules Galle boatyard in Biloxi, had emerged as the fishing boat of choice.

The Biloxi Lugger had a couple of things going for it—it was one of the first gasoline-powered fishing boats in the Gulf of Mexico and it drew only three feet of water while a schooner's much deeper hull prohibited it from working in shallow water.

The Biloxi Lugger could easily slip into the Mississippi marshes chasing after shrimp, and its engine allowed it to tow a 30- to 35-foot otter trawl, all the while not relying on the wind's vagaries.

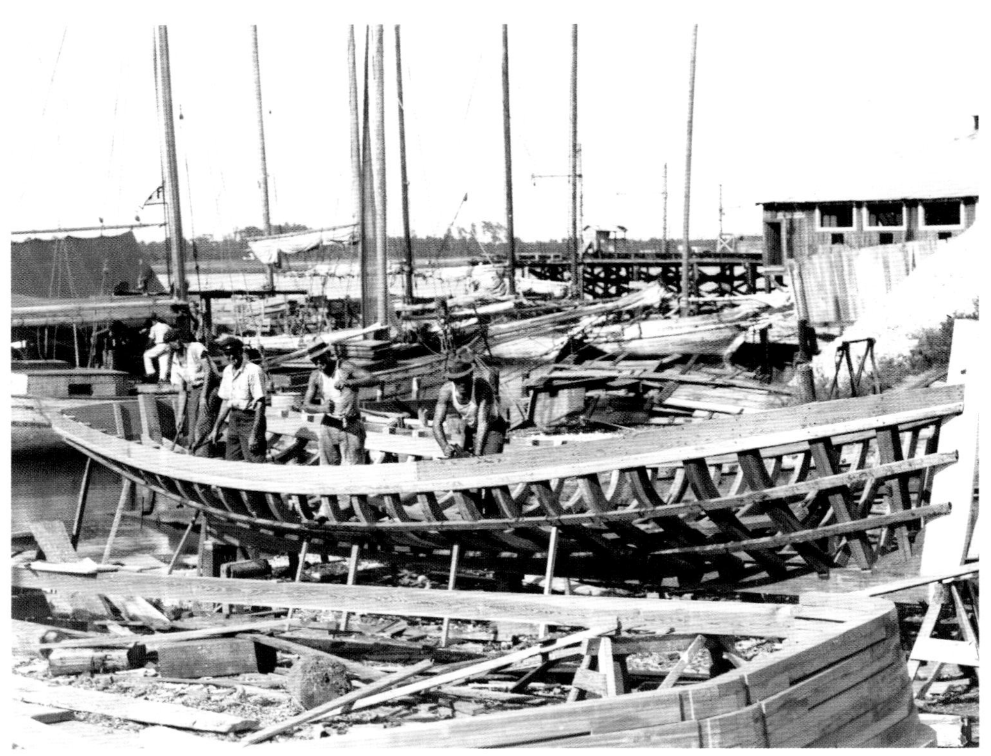

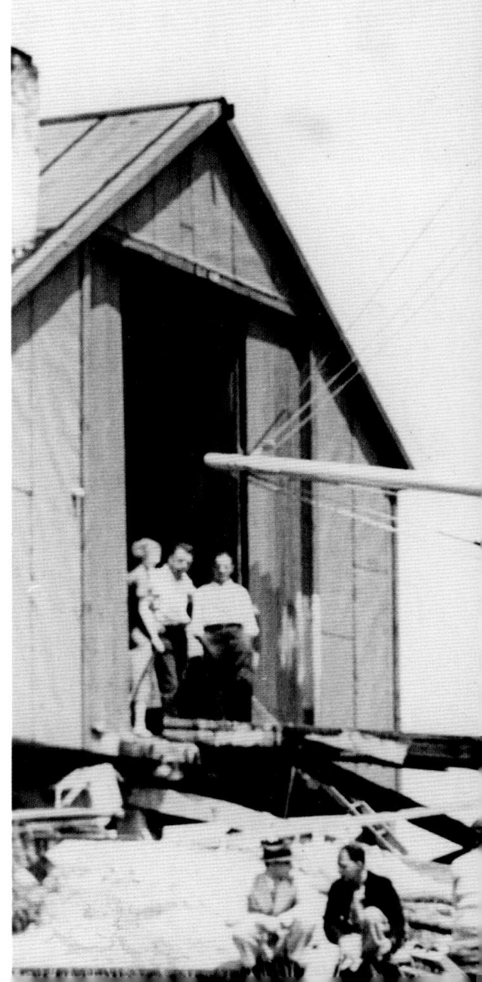

Pinky Schooners

Pinky schooners ruled the New England fishing fleet from about 1815 to 1840, when they were replaced by faster and larger Gloucester schooners. However, even after they fell out of favor in the fishing industry, Pinky schooners remained popular as pleasure boats because of their stability and grace.

Howard Chapelle, a naval architect and historian who wrote at least ten books about America's maritime tradition, was particularly enamored by the Pinky schooner—so named for its uplifted "pinked" or pinched stern. He believed the vessel was "the most seaworthy and comfortable for deep water work" and he couldn't understand why, with a "wide range of double-ender types in our own front yard [Americans] continued to import types of doubtful value for use in our waters."

Given those words, it's no wonder that when Chapelle wanted a boat to cruise the New England coast from Cape Cod to Nova Scotia, he chose the double-ended pinky schooner. Chapelle's *Glad Tidings* was built by Roger I. Sawyer in Milbridge, Maine, and launched July 12, 1937. The launch attracted onlookers sitting on logs—their backs to the camera—who surely admired the hull's graceful, easy lines.

The 39-foot *Glad Tidings* was constructed with an oak backbone and framing, white cedar planking, and pine deck planking and houses. She carried ballast inside and, like the original pinky schooners, she didn't have an engine, although there was a wood or coal burning stove forward and a galley stove aft for warmth on fall cruises and for cooking.

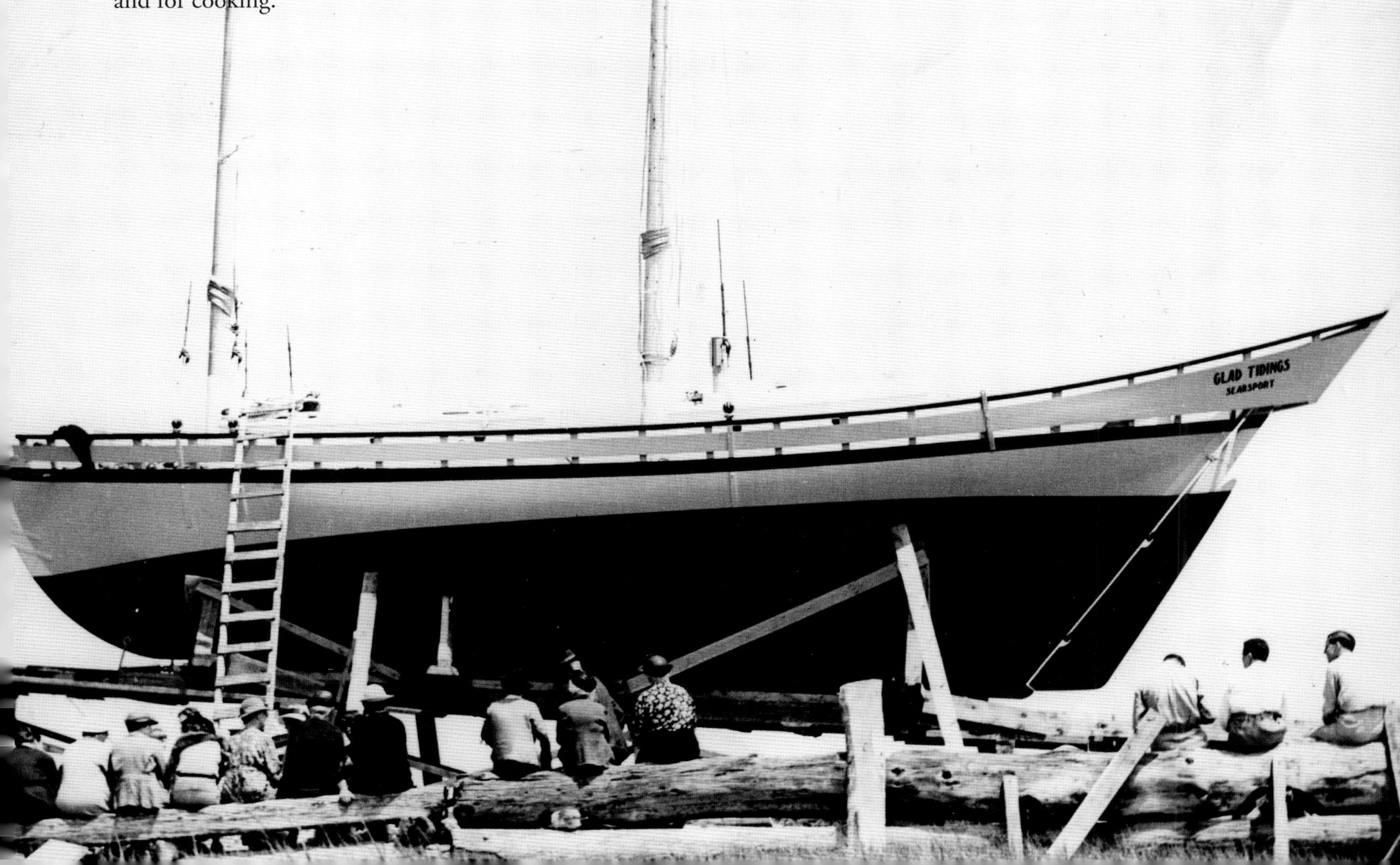

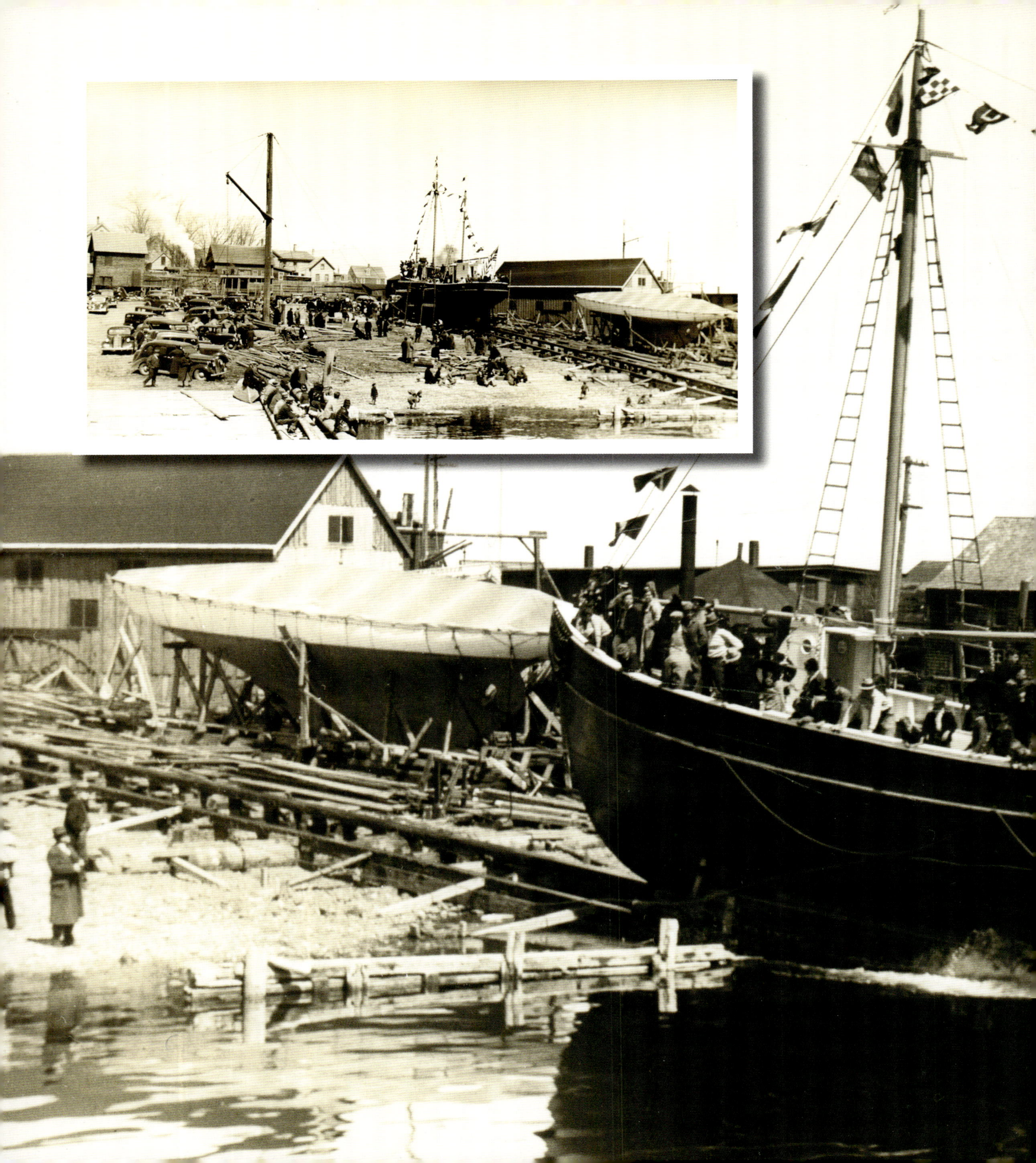

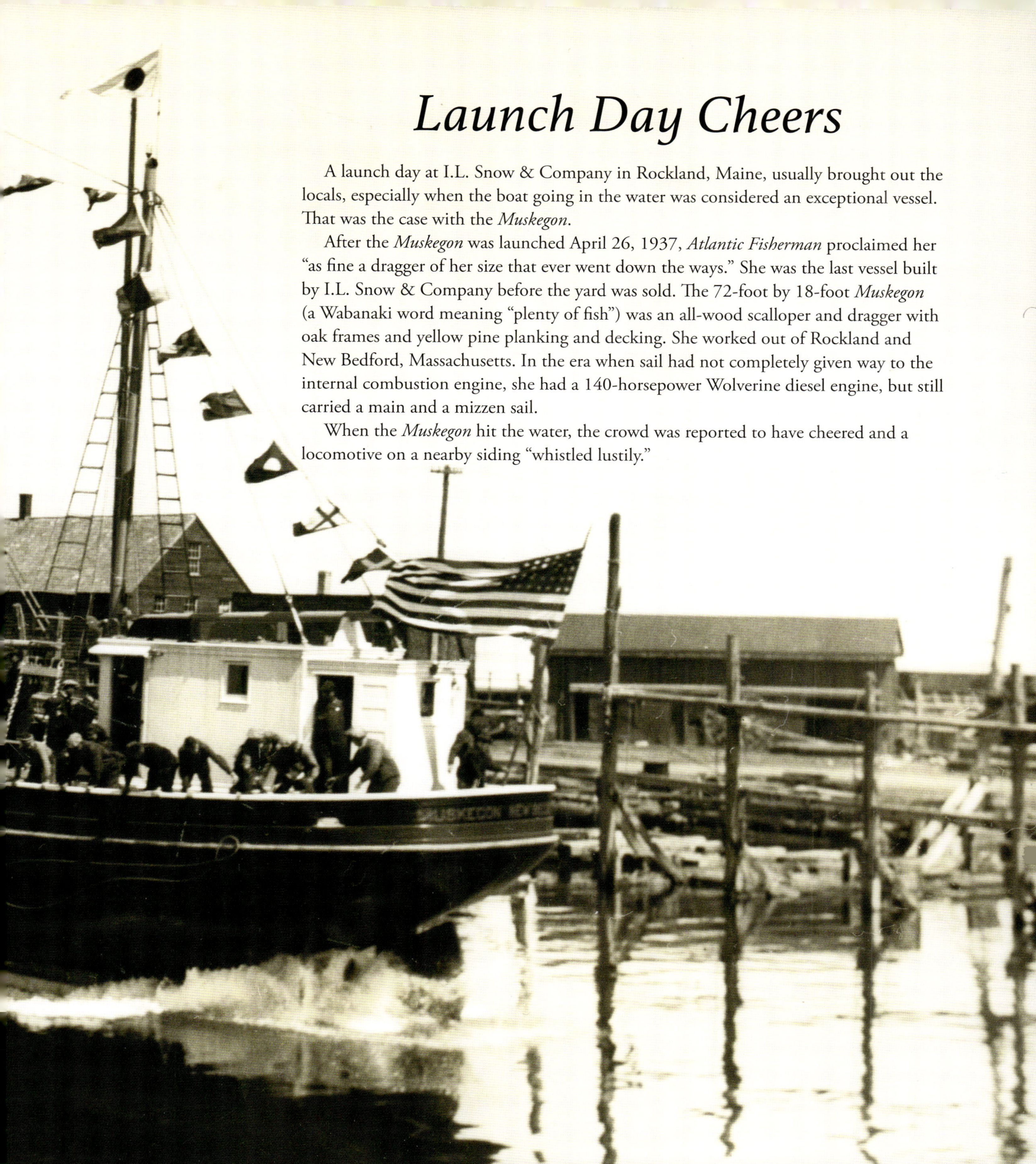

Launch Day Cheers

A launch day at I.L. Snow & Company in Rockland, Maine, usually brought out the locals, especially when the boat going in the water was considered an exceptional vessel. That was the case with the *Muskegon*.

After the *Muskegon* was launched April 26, 1937, *Atlantic Fisherman* proclaimed her "as fine a dragger of her size that ever went down the ways." She was the last vessel built by I.L. Snow & Company before the yard was sold. The 72-foot by 18-foot *Muskegon* (a Wabanaki word meaning "plenty of fish") was an all-wood scalloper and dragger with oak frames and yellow pine planking and decking. She worked out of Rockland and New Bedford, Massachusetts. In the era when sail had not completely given way to the internal combustion engine, she had a 140-horsepower Wolverine diesel engine, but still carried a main and a mizzen sail.

When the *Muskegon* hit the water, the crowd was reported to have cheered and a locomotive on a nearby siding "whistled lustily."

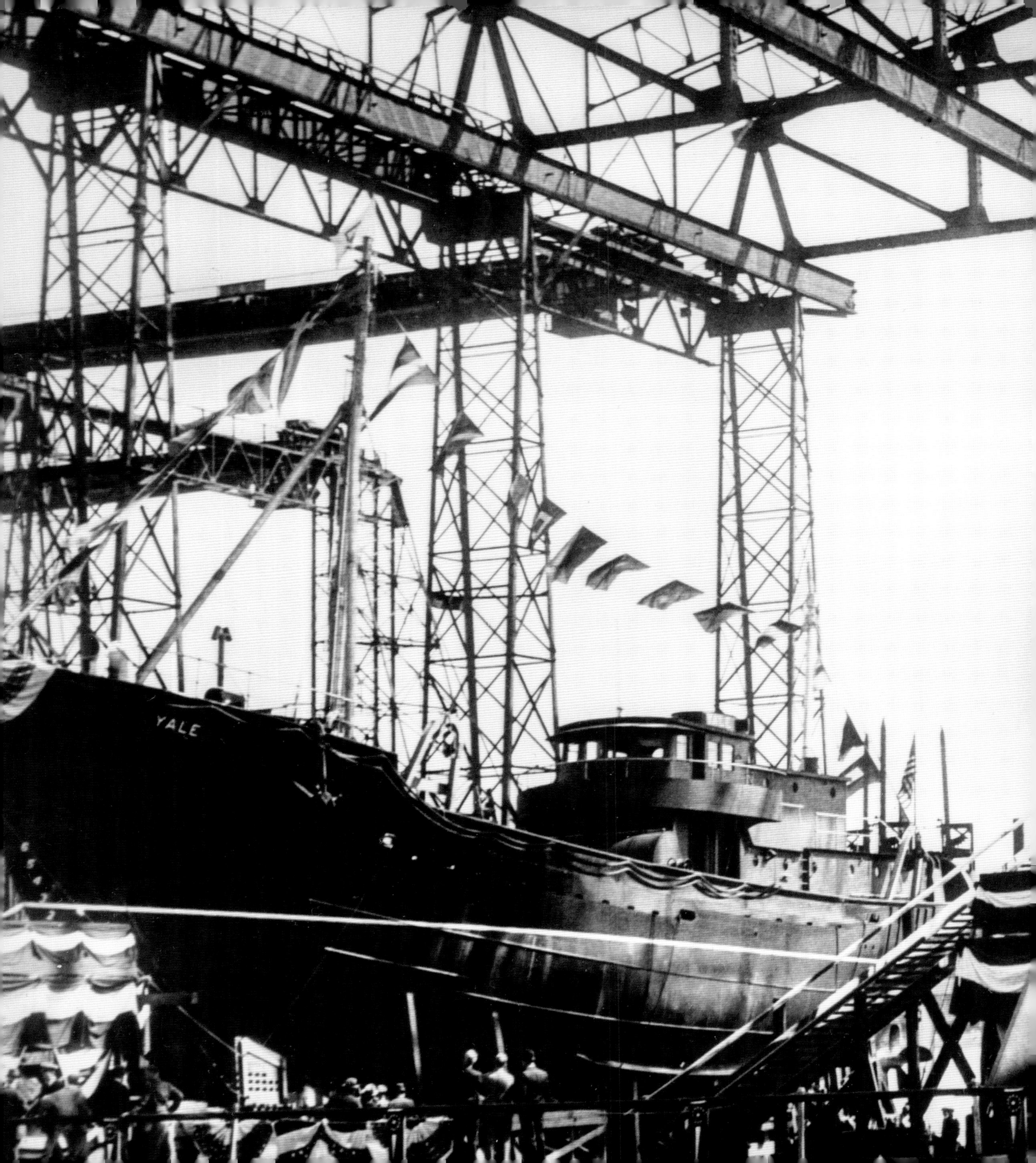
YALE

Super Trawlers

The *Yale, West Point,* and *Annapolis* were billed as "super trawlers" at their September 23, 1937 triple launching at Bethlehem Shipbuilding Corporation's Fore River plant in Quincy, Massachusetts. Several hundred guests attended the event.

The 146-foot trawlers were built for General Seafoods of Boston. Although designed by Boston's John G. Alden, the trawlers were built along what was known as Maierform lines, which originated in Europe. The design resulted in improved seaworthiness and reduced resistance cutting through the water. The steel hulls were built heavier than normal and were almost completely riveted through drilled holes.

In good weather, the trawlers' 650-horsepower Cooper-Bessemer diesel engines could make twelve knots while carrying an average load of 250,000 pounds. A *New York Times* article said the vessels cost about $800,000 each and were expected to fish deeper than normal, reducing the length of a fishing trip from eleven to nine days.

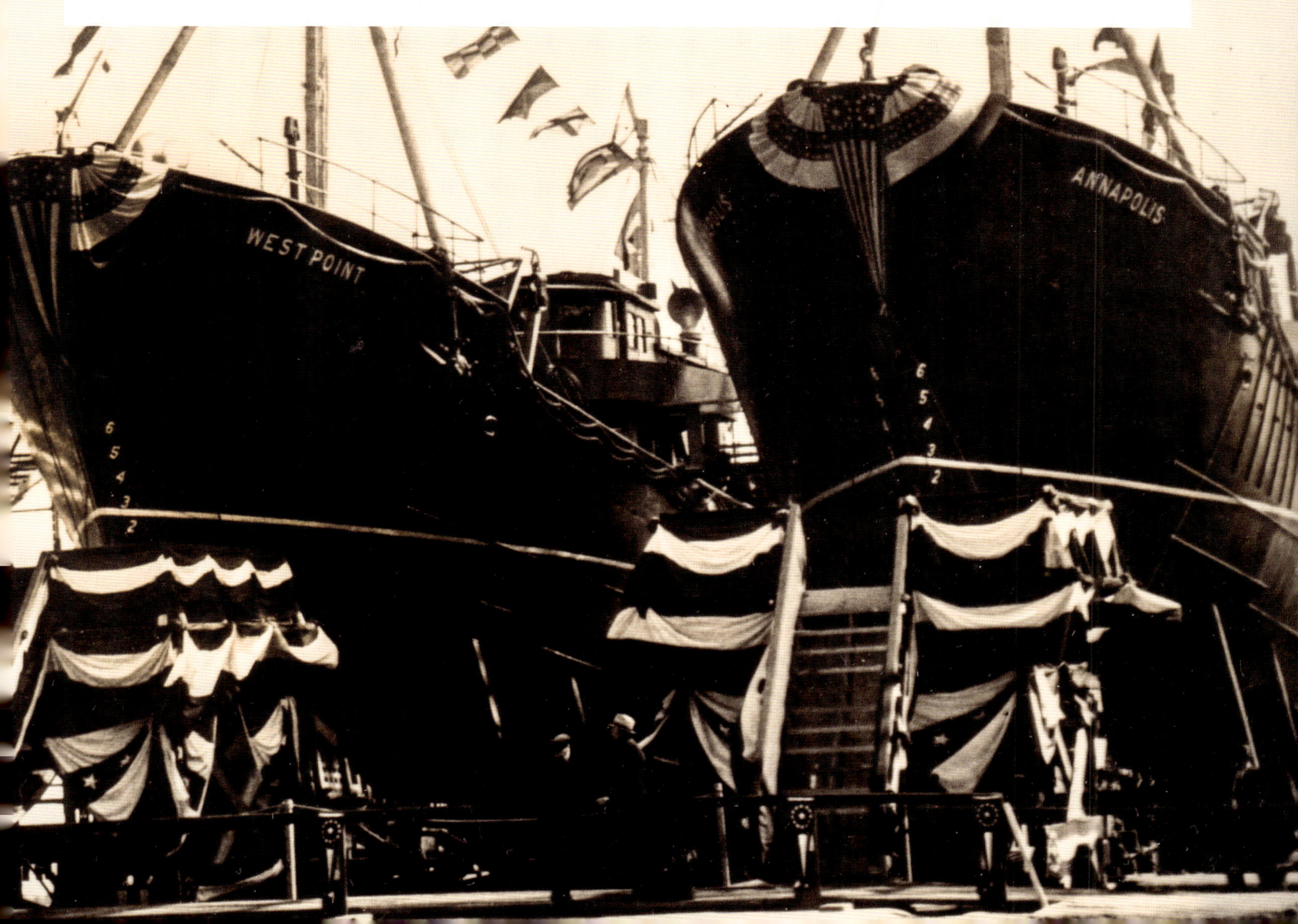

BIW Fishing Trawler

October 21, 1937, was a big day at Bath Iron Works (BIW) in Bath, Maine. On that day, the 136-foot trawler *Villanova* was launched into the Kennebec River for F.J. O'Hara & Sons of Boston. The boat's owner, Francis O'Hara, chartered a special train with six Pullman cars, two diners, and a service car to bring 150 guests from Boston. It was the largest "launching train" to ever visit BIW. A band and professional entertainers came along for the ride.

The *Villanova* and its sister ship, the *Jeanne D'Arc*, which was also built at BIW for O'Hara, were said to be "different from anything now fishing." The hull was particularly noticeable, as it did not look like anything in the fishing service at the time. Its cruiser-style stem, which resembled the superliner *Queen Mary*, was also conspicuous. The pilothouse, with its rounded corners, made the ship more streamlined than other trawlers of the day.

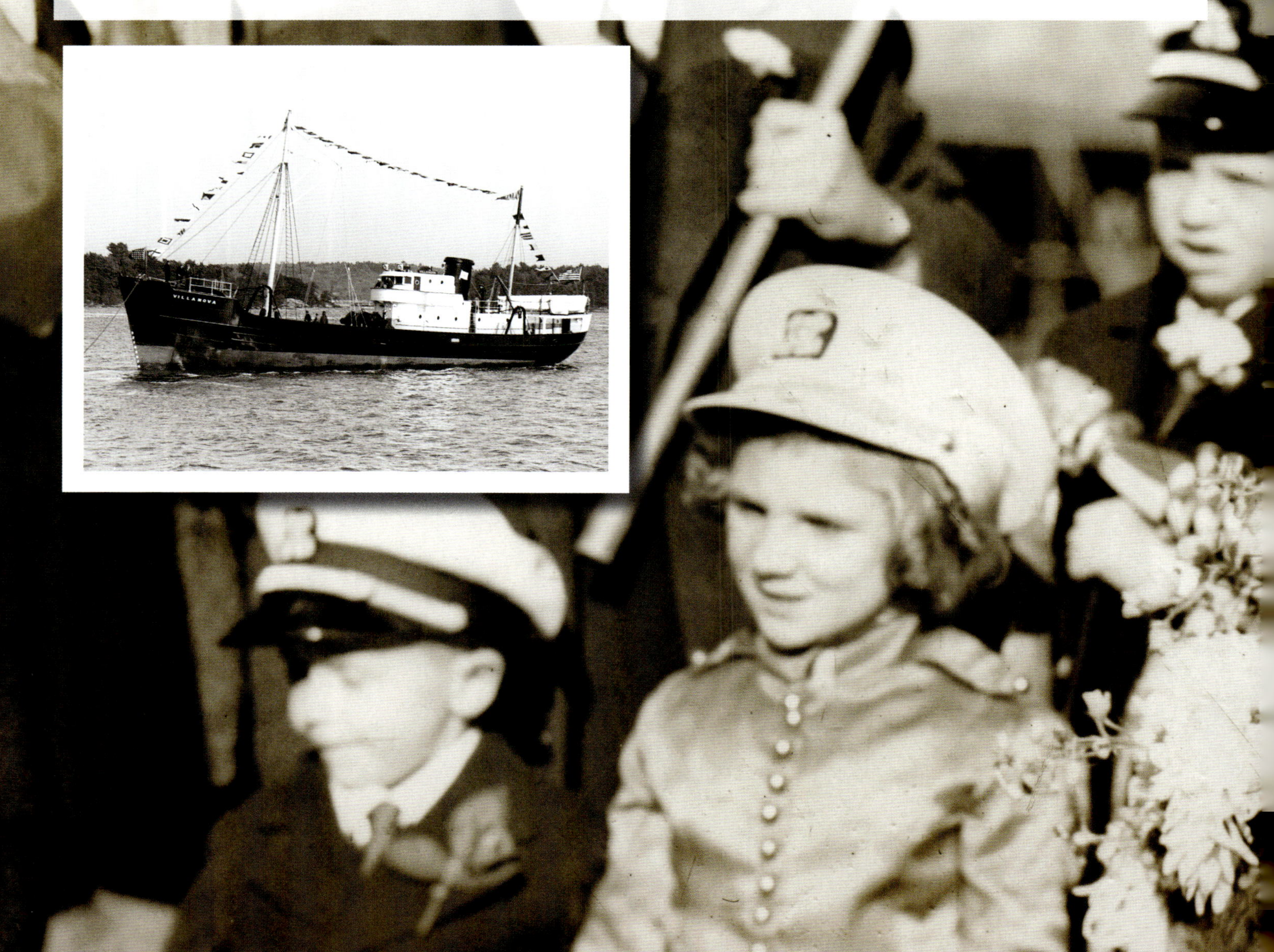

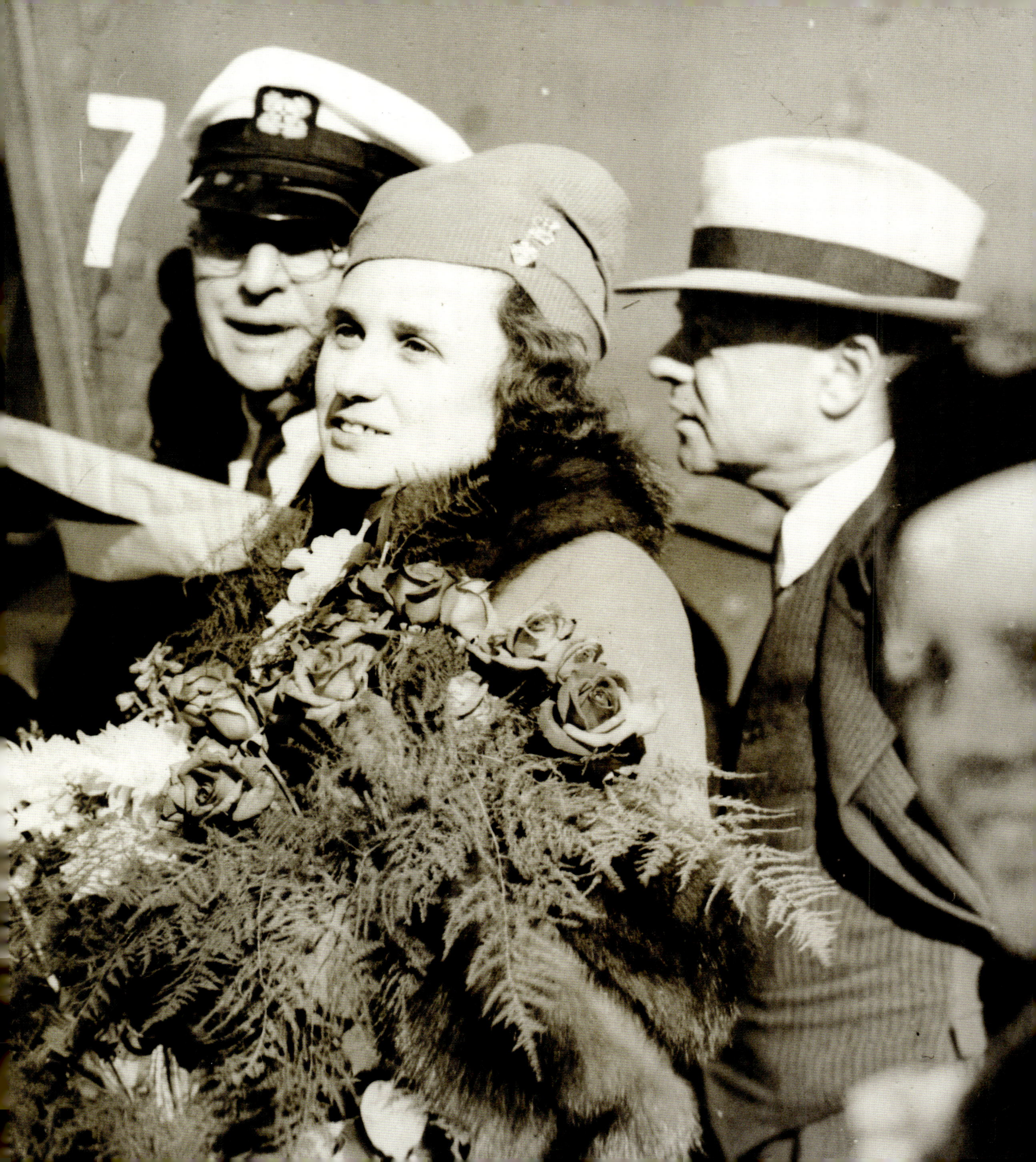

The Halifax Herald Cup

The masters and crews of Gloucester's fishing schooners of the late 1800s and early 1900s loved nothing more than a good race in, as one commentator said, "a fisherman's breeze, everything flying but the cook's drawers."

The most intense competition, however, turned out to be between Gloucester, Massachusetts, and Lunenburg, Nova Scotia. The publisher of Nova Scotia's *Halifax Herald and Mail* initiated the rivalry in October 1920 when he directly challenged Gloucester to engage in "a race for real sailors, for $5,000 and a handsome silver cup." The challenged kicked off a nineteen-year rivalry.

The first event pitted Gloucester's *Esperanto* against Lunenburg's *Delawana*, a competition which the *Esperanto* won handily in two races and sailed home with the silver cup. Almost immediately, the Canadians commissioned the design and construction of a new schooner to restore their pride. The *Bluenose* was launched in March 1921. The following October, under the guidance of skipper Angus Walters, the *Bluenose* brought the trophy back to Lunenburg.

During the next several years, Gloucester failed to win back the international cup. In March 1930, with the financial backing of Louis Thebaud, a Gloucester summer visitor, the *Gertrude L. Thebaud* (right) was launched at the Arthur D. Story Shipyard in Essex, Massachusetts, solely with the aim of beating the *Bluenose* and bringing the Halifax Herald Cup back to Gloucester.

The first race between the *Bluenose* and the *Thebaud* (named after Louis' wife) took place at Gloucester and the *Thebaud* won both races. A year later, in 1931, the *Thebaud* sailed to Halifax and was defeated by the *Bluenose* and her skipper in two straight races.

The next race didn't take place until 1938, but saw the same two schooners going twice around an eighteen-mile triangle outside Boston Harbor (below) in a best-of-five competition. The schooners split the first four races. In the fifth and deciding race, held on October 16, the *Bluenose* crossed the line first, two minutes and fifty seconds ahead of the *Thebaud*. It was the final fisherman's race between the two countries.

In 1946, the *Bluenose* was wrecked off Haiti while working the Caribbean trade. Two years later the *Gertrude L. Thebaud* met a similar fate and ended her days smashed up on the Venezuela coast.

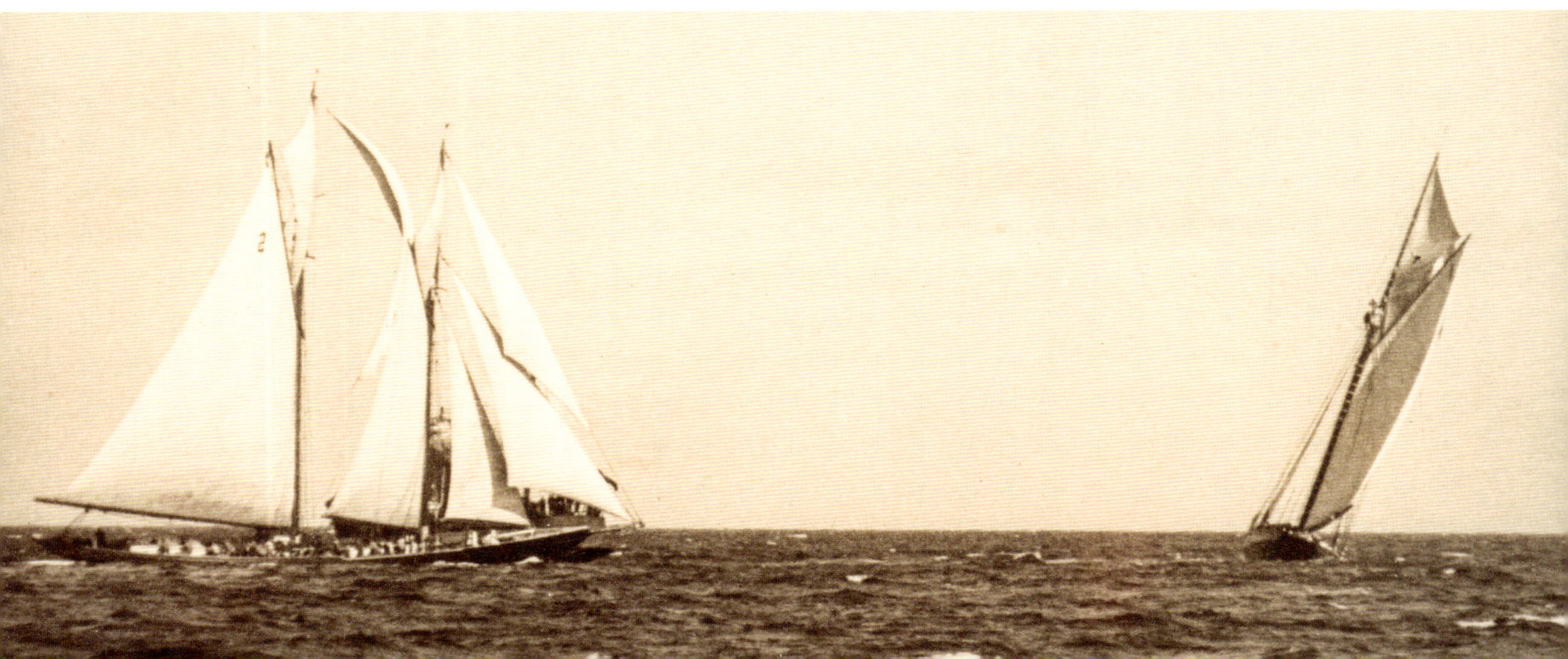

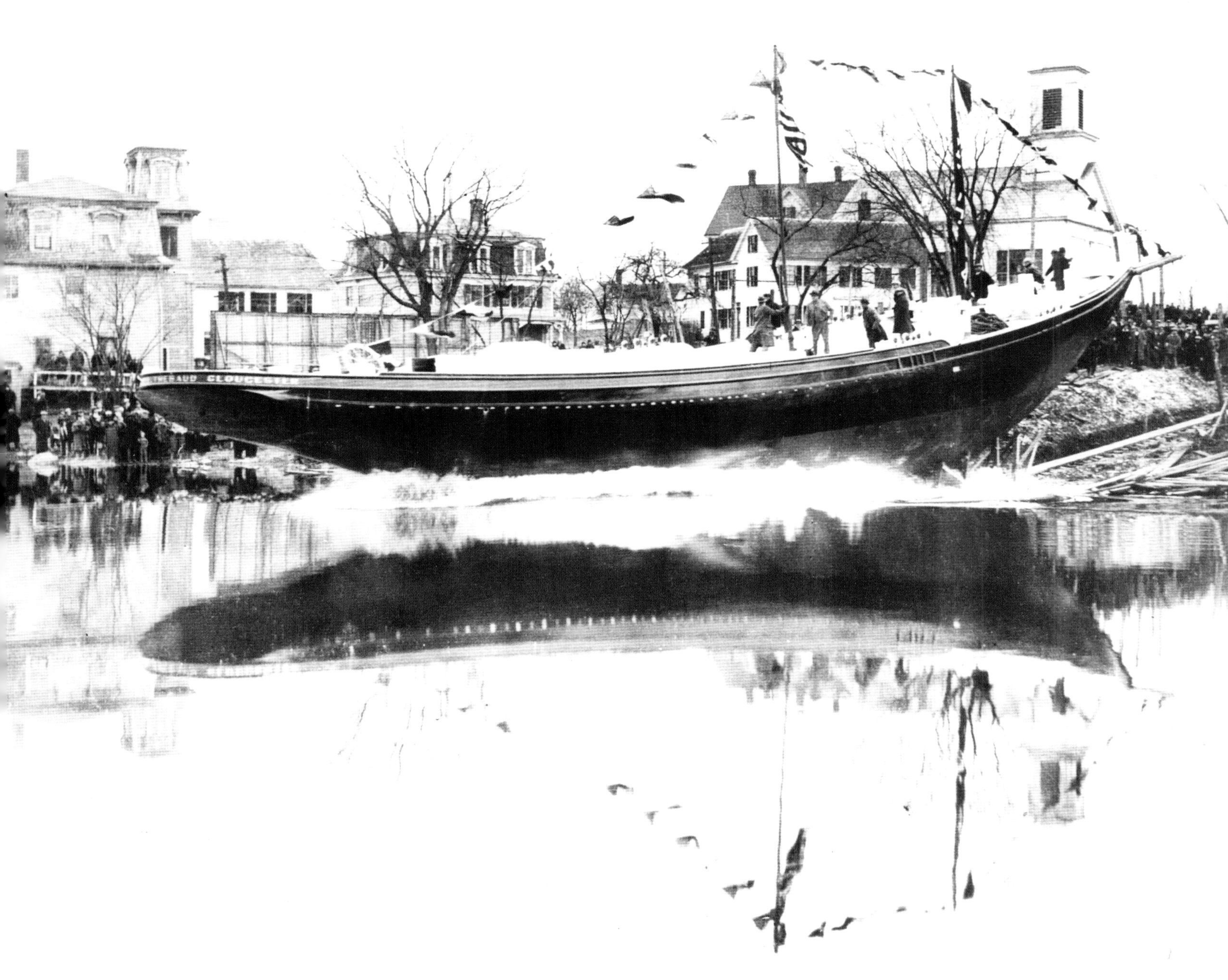
GERTRUD L. THEBAUD GLOUCESTER

The Merilyn Clair

With a deck load of well-dressed passengers and the Canadian flag flying, the 138-foot *Merilyn Clair* slides down the ways at Smith & Rhuland Shipyard in Lunenburg, Nova Scotia, in early fall 1940. She was the 166th schooner built by Smith & Rhuland, started by Richard Smith and George Rhuland in 1900.

In addition to sails, the *Merilyn Clair* had a 300-horsepower diesel engine and, reflecting the increased interest in electronics for fishing boats of that size, boasted the latest electrical equipment including a radio and depth finder.

The *Merilyn Clair*, like many schooners built for commercial fishing, ended up paying her way by carrying cargo instead of iced or frozen fish. While carrying a load of flour from Nova Scotia to Newfoundland, the *Merilyn Clair* wrecked at Port Au Choix, Newfoundland, on September 17, 1962. Smith & Rhuland built hundreds of vessels through the decades, including the *Bluenose* (see page 12), the celebrated fishing and racing vessel that became an important symbol for Nova Scotia and is featured on the Canadian dime.

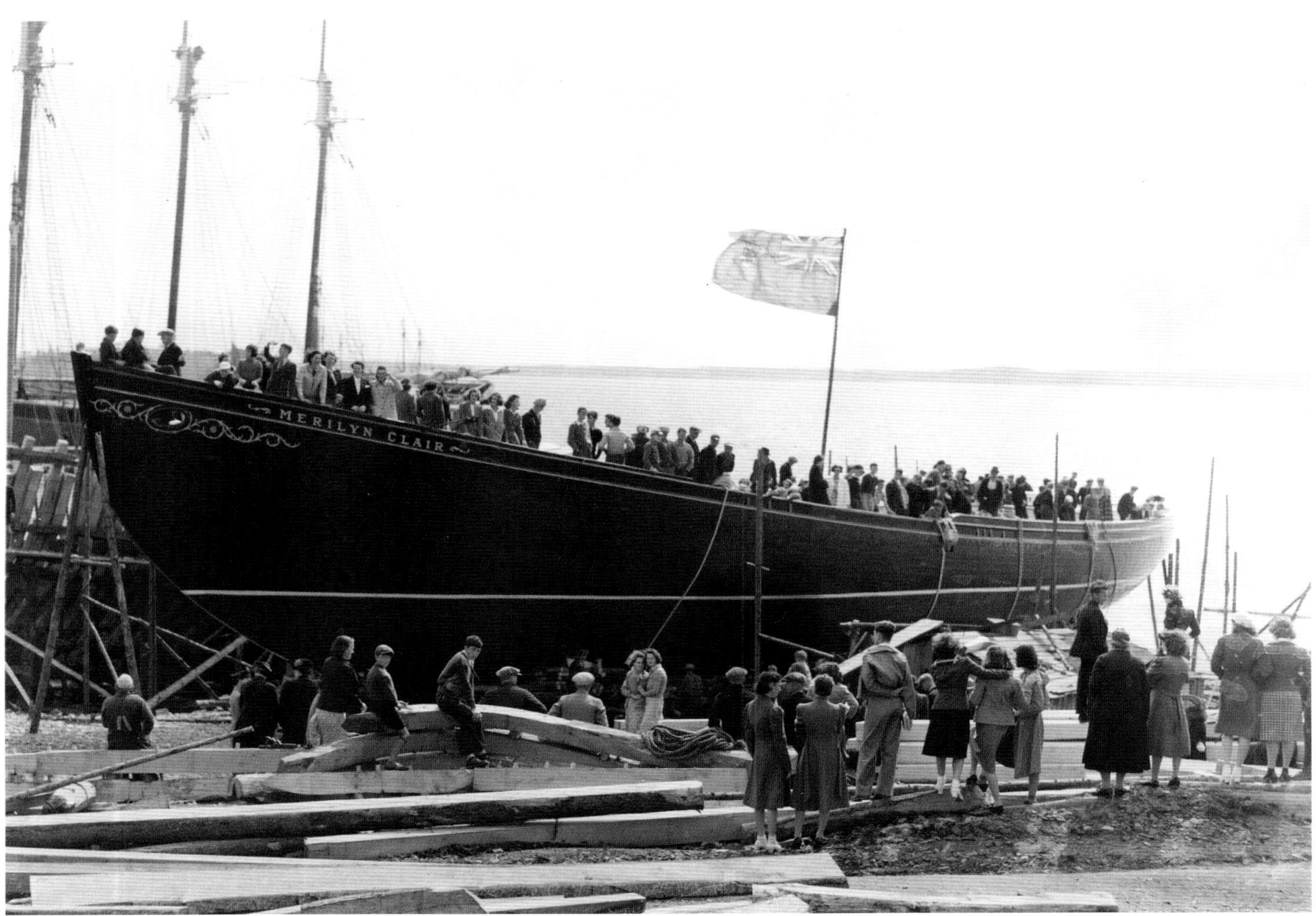

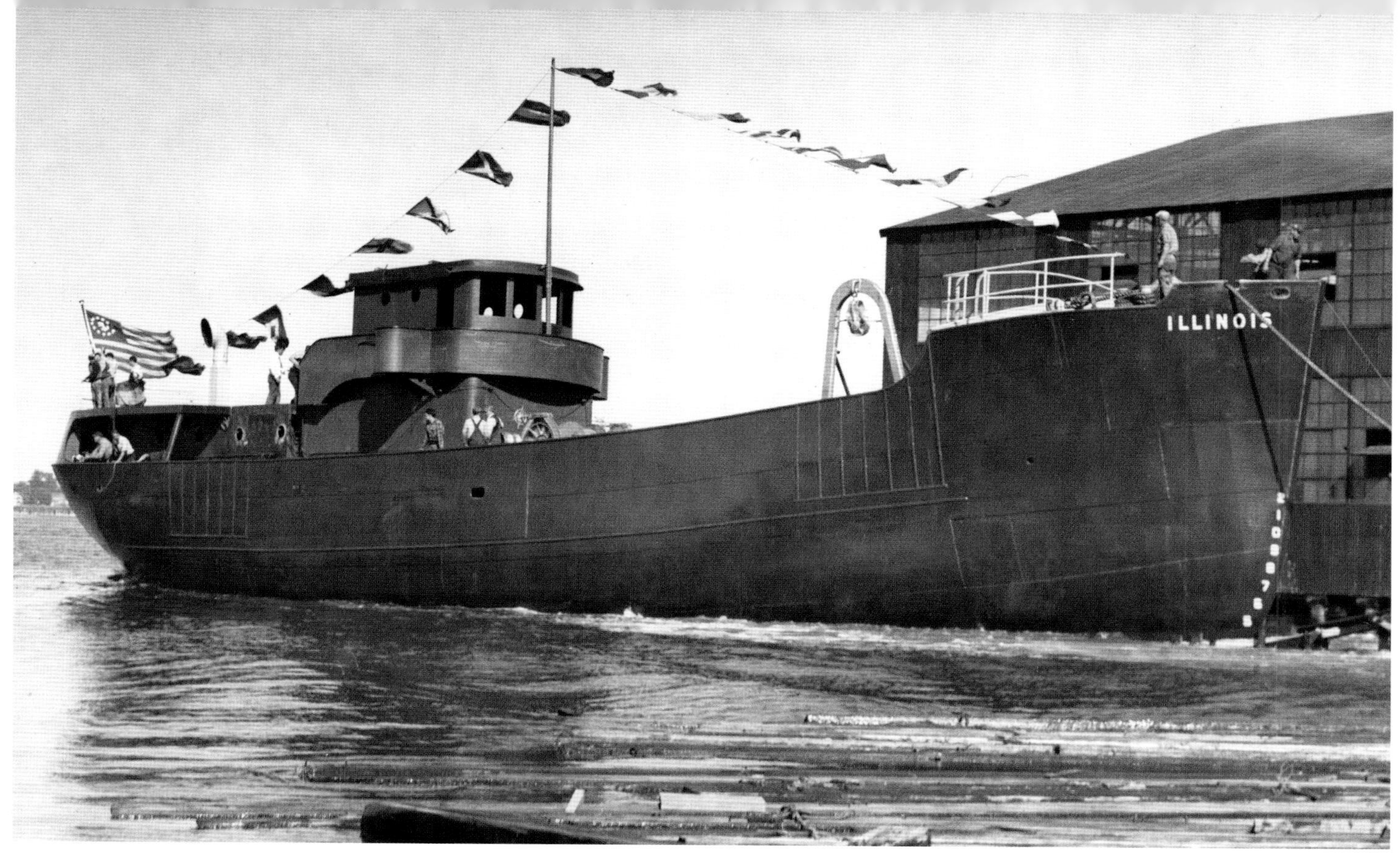

All-Welded Steel Trawler

The *Illinois* was declared "a new milestone in trawler construction" when launched on August 28, 1941, at the George Lawley & Son yard in Neponset, Massachusetts, for Booth Fisheries Corp. The 127-foot vessel was the first all-welded steel trawler—designed to carry a larger load of fish easier, safer, and faster than previous trawlers.

The bow's lack of flare and minimal rake to the stem was an unusual design feature that provided improved buoyancy and reduced its tendency to trim when the vessel was loaded. The stern was described as "entirely new," being well-rounded above the waterline and pointed with very fine lines below the water. The combination of those two features prevented the *Illinois* from dipping in a heavy sea. The design also improved the comforts for the crew, including fully automatic water heating for the entire vessel and air conditioning for the more roomy living quarters.

The *Illinois* was built to carry 300,000 pounds of iced fish in a fish hold insulated with three inches of cork set in hot pitch, covered with two-inch wood sheathing. In the engine room, a 650-horsepower Cooper-Bessemer six-cylinder diesel engine gave the vessel a top speed of twelve knots. It wasn't long after the *Illinois* was launched that a sister ship, the *Maine*, was also launched.

Emma C. Berry

The *Emma C. Berry* was 105 years old when this photo was taken near the end of a two-year restoration project at Mystic Seaport Museum. Launched in 1866 into the Mystic River at the R. & J. Palmer Shipyard in Noank, Connecticut, the *Emma C. Berry* carried a sloop rig with a large mainsail, two headsails, and a gaff topsail for light-weather sailing.

The *Emma C. Berry* was built as a well smack, equipped with a watertight compartment known as a "wet well" in her hold. With holes drilled through the bottom, the wet well allowed ocean water to flow in and out, keeping mackerel alive until the catch was delivered to dockside buyers. By the time the *Emma C. Berry* was donated to the museum, she was the only surviving fishing vessel of this type, though well smack vessels had once plied the waters from Maine to Florida.

A wooden boat that is more than 100 years old and still able to make its way through the water has to have undergone significant changes and experienced some significant luck. That fits the *Emma C. Berry*.

The *Emma C. Berry* was converted to a schooner rig in 1886 and sold a few years later to a Down East Maine owner and used as a bait carrier and lobster smack, for which the wet well was perfectly suited. She also was given a Knox gasoline engine around 1916.

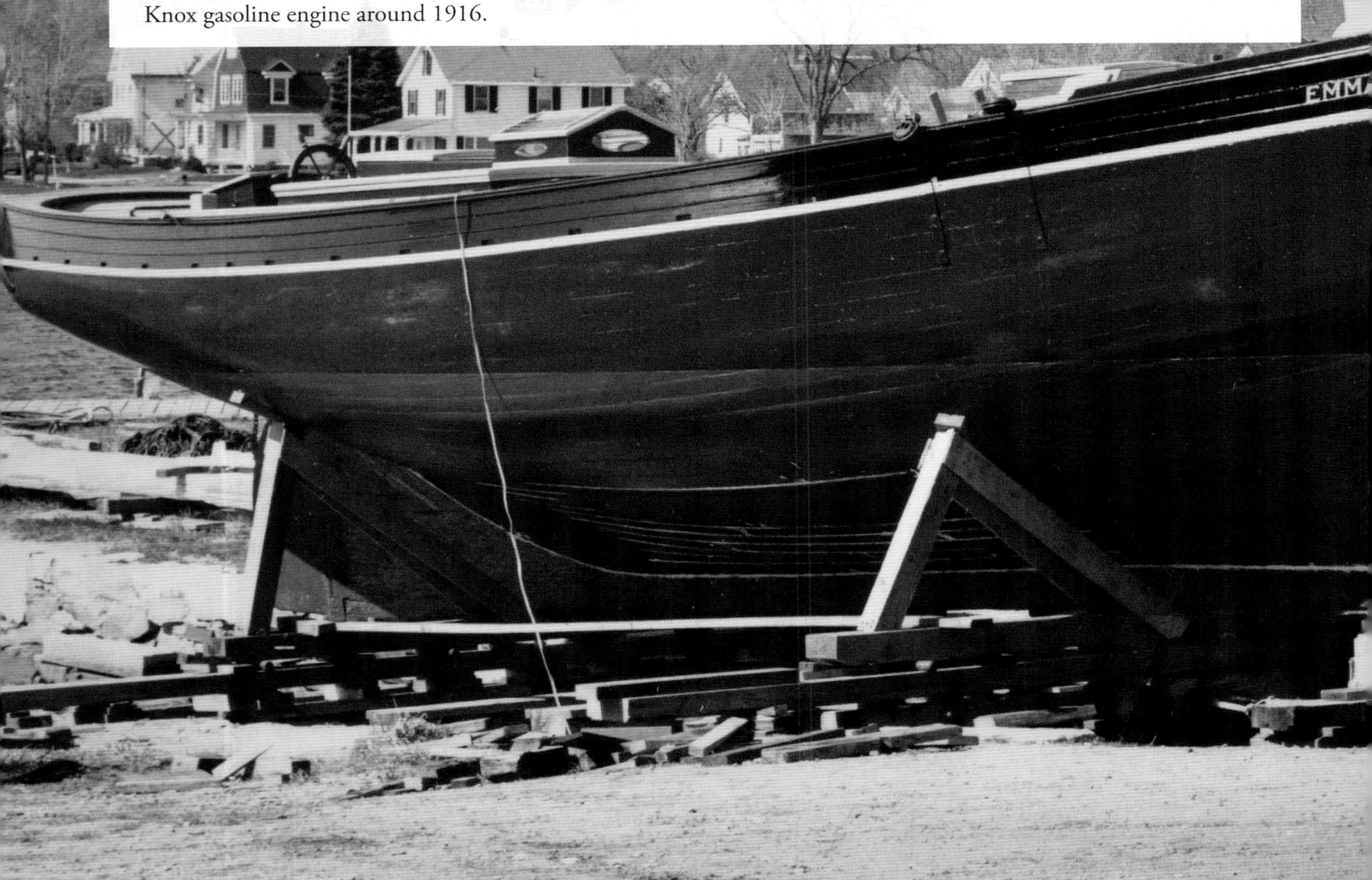

The *Emma C. Berry*'s career as a fishing vessel ended in 1924, and she was abandoned on the mud flats of Beals Island, Maine. Left unattended for a long period of time the *Emma C. Berry* would have rotted and broken up, but in 1926 Milton Beal of Jonesport, across the Moosabec Reach from Beals Island, believed the *Emma C. Berry* still could make a go of it—not as a fishing vessel but as a coastal freighter.

Beal replaced rotten frames and planking and used her to carry salt, coal, and dried fish between Jonesport, Portland, Rockland, and Gloucester. In 1931, F. Slade Dale of New Jersey bought her and partially rebuilt her for use as a pleasure vessel. In 1969, Dale donated the *Emma C. Berry* to the Mystic Seaport Museum where she was restored as one of the oldest surviving commercial vessels in America. In 1994, the *Emma C. Berry* was designated a National Historic Landmark.

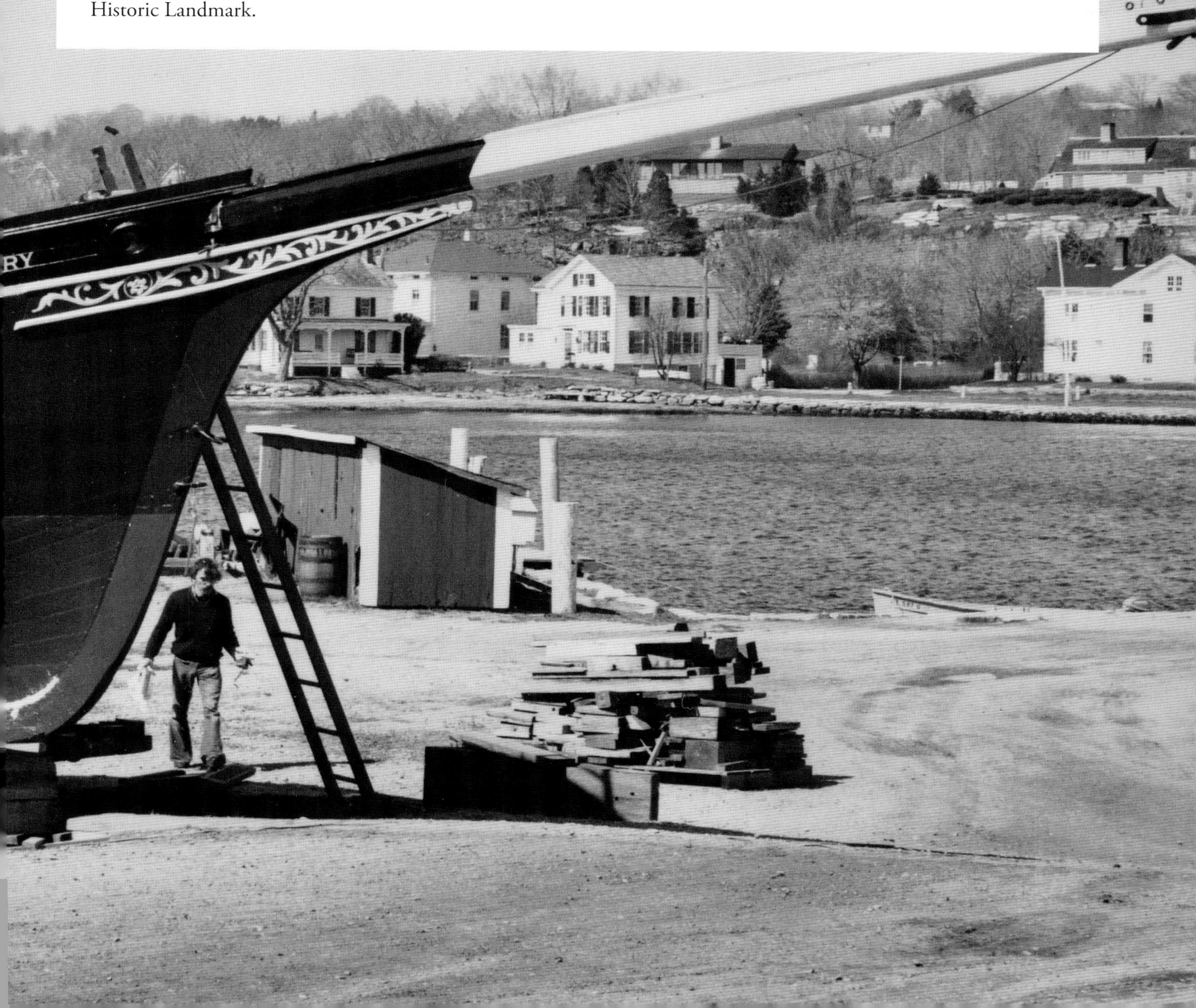

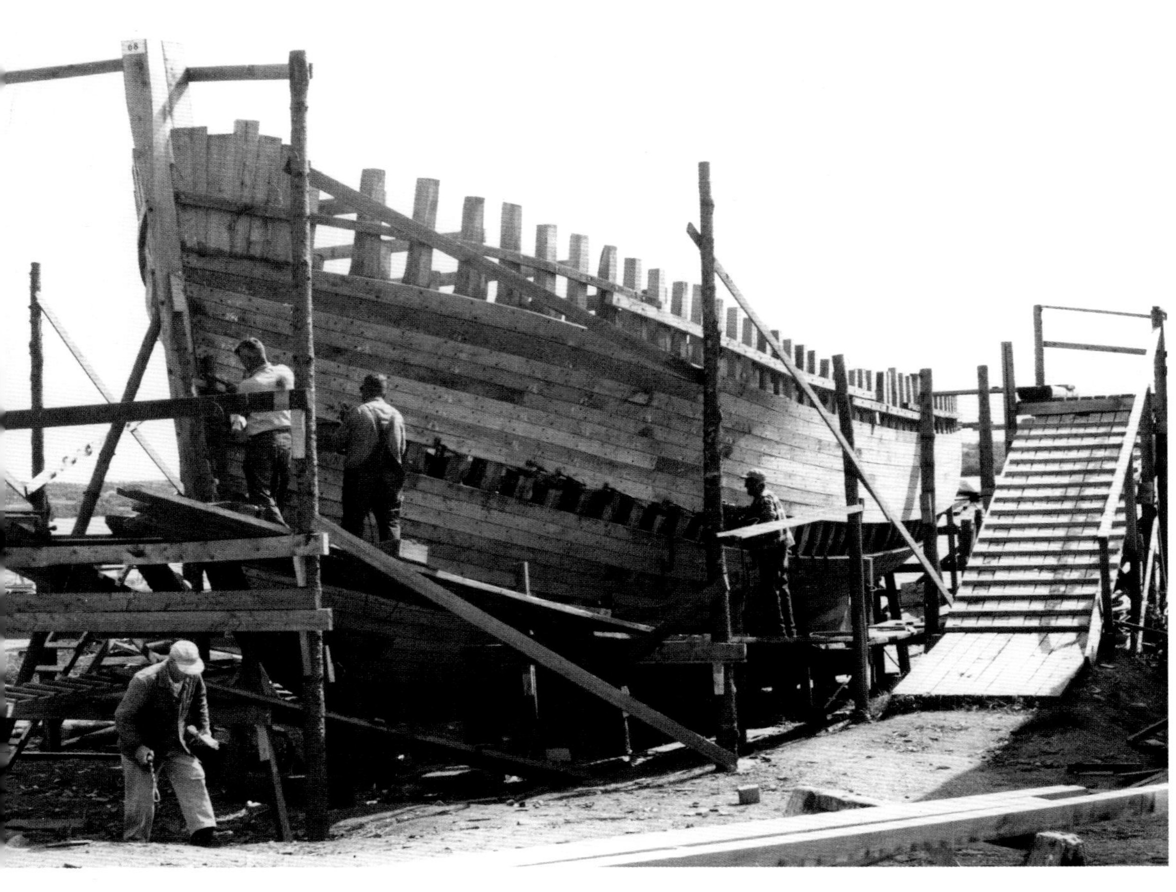

Wooden Dragger

In Thomaston, Maine, it's a clear, sunny day at the end of the 1963 summer, something the crew at the Newbert & Wallace Shipyard is taking full advantage of as they strive to complete this 65-foot wooden dragger hull before Maine's cold weather sets in.

They appear close to installing the "shutter" plank, the final plank that "shuts in" the hull. Before installing the two-inch-thick oak plank, workers made sure it was well steamed and flexible for fitting against the oak framing. Galvanized hatch nails fastened the planking to the frames. The dragger was built for a New Bedford fisherman and was a duplicate of the *Pauline*, another dragger launched by Newbert & Wallace the previous June.

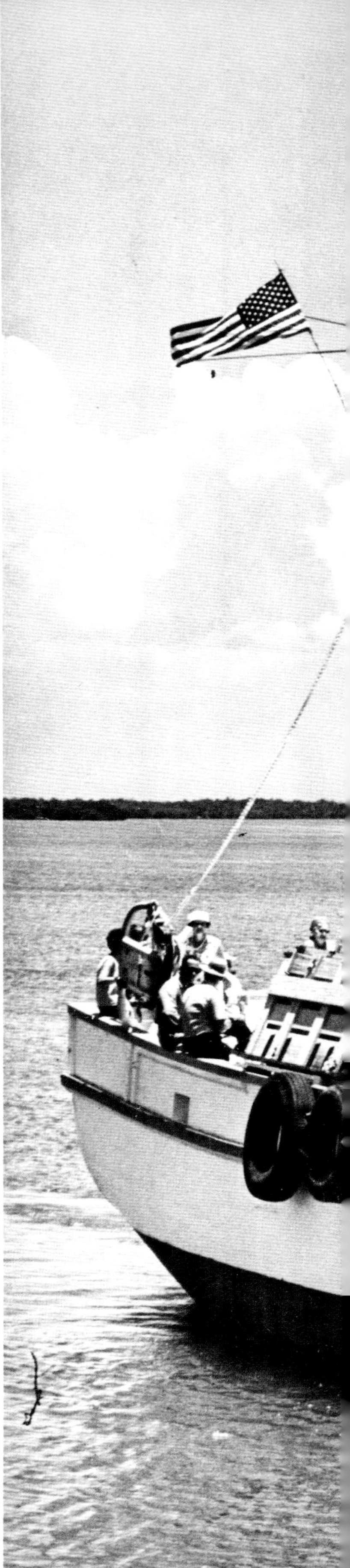

Southern Shrimpers

The 76-foot *Chris-Corey*, fully rigged to go shrimping, is shown just after its May 1968 launch. An attractive raised sheer line sweeps up to the stem, and the deckhouse is different from the standard southern shrimper.

In the late 1960s, it wasn't easy finding experienced crewmen willing to work Florida shrimp boats and spend the summer fishing off the Texas coast. But Chris Olsen, the skipper and owner of the *Chris-Corey*, figured he had the answer—more comfort. Shrimp boats, he argued, needed to have better living conditions if their owners expected to keep crews aboard for months. He must have had a point—when the *Chris-Corey* launched, forty to fifty boats remained tied up at the docks in Fort Myers Beach, Florida, because their owners couldn't convince crews to spend the summer shrimping in Texas. Some boat owners were even willing to bail men out of jail to get a crew.

Meanwhile the *Chris-Corey*, which cost $77,000 and was built by P.K. Trawlers, Inc. in St. Augustine, offered uncommon amenities including hot and cold running water for showers, a refrigerator and freezer in the galley, and comfortable bunks.

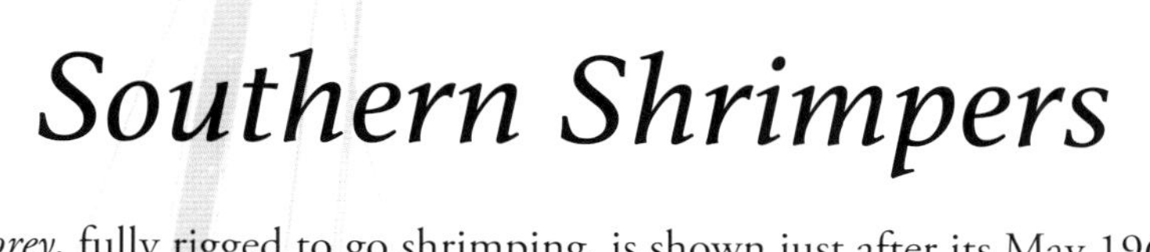

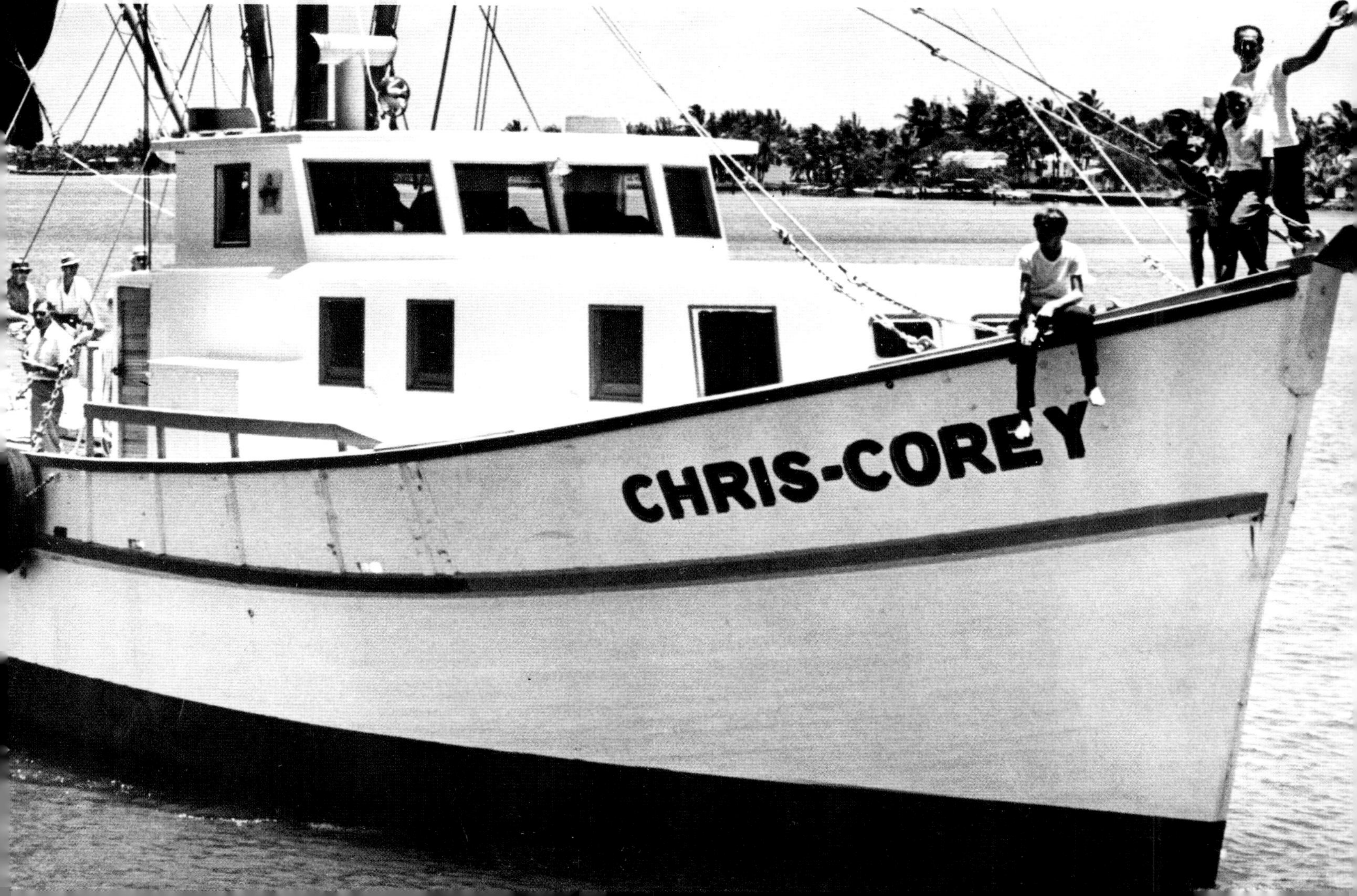

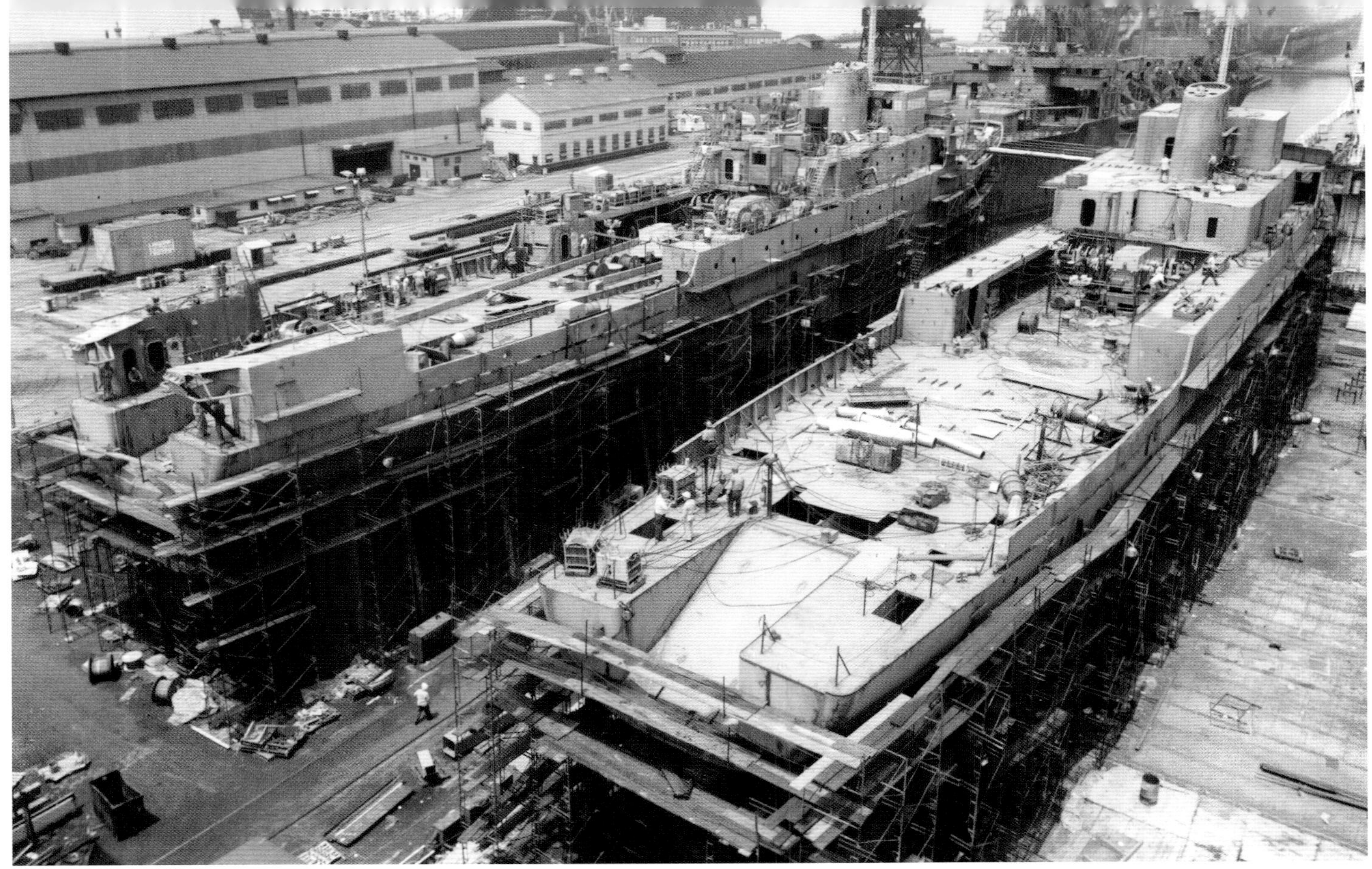

Factory Trawlers

At the end of the 1960s, about half the fish consumed in the United States came from Russian and Japanese fishing boats. America simply did not have a significant offshore fishing fleet, and many people felt American boats couldn't compete with foreign vessels.

The response to that challenge was two-fold—the 294-foot sister ships *Seafreeze Atlantic* and *Seafreeze Pacific*, shown here being built at Maryland Shipbuilding and Drydock in Baltimore. Billed as the country's first factory trawlers, the vessels were designed to stay at sea for weeks at a time to catch, clean, and blast-freeze fish. They could land 60 tons in a single haul, and could catch and process 400 tons a day.

Seafreeze Atlantic and *Seafreeze Pacific* were the first of their kind to be built in America, and were said to be the most sophisticated vessels ever seen by American fishermen.

Learning to fish them would be a bit of a process, as much of the machinery was built in other countries and American fishermen hadn't worked on this type of vessel before. "We will have to learn our way with this equipment," said the *Seafreeze Atlantic*'s skipper.

Each vessel cost about $5.2 million to build, with the U.S. government subsidizing about half the cost.

The *Seafreeze Atlantic* was christened September 21, 1968, after which she worked the northwest Atlantic out of Gloucester. The vessel would later be renamed *Arctic Trawler* (1980), *Polyarniy* (1985), and *Seafreeze Alaska* (1995).

The *Seafreeze Pacific* was christened the following December and fished the Pacific. Its name changes included the *Royal Sea* (1973) and *Katie Ann* (1996).

Tuna Superseiner

At its launch, the 216-by-42-foot *Conquistador* was said to be the largest tuna purse seiner ever built in San Diego. That probably explains why more than five hundred people turned out to witness the December 12, 1970 launch at Campbell Industries. The $2.5 million vessel could pack 1,500 tons of frozen tuna, and its launch was noteworthy enough that it pulled in some significant speakers, including August Felando, general manager of the American Tuna Boat Association. "The superseiner *Conquistador*," he said, "exemplifies today's trend toward bigger, faster and more powerful vessels for the American tuna fleet."

Congressman Lionel Van Derrlin of San Diego followed up by emphasizing that, "The American tuna fleet is growing in importance as a factor in worldwide fisheries markets." The building of the *Conquistador* (whose name was later changed to *Daniela*) and the purse seiner *Ocean Queen* a year earlier marked the start of a major boatbuilding boom at the San Diego shipyard. Over the next five years, Campbell Industries built twenty-five tuna purse seiners, ending with the *Zapata Discoverer* in 1976.

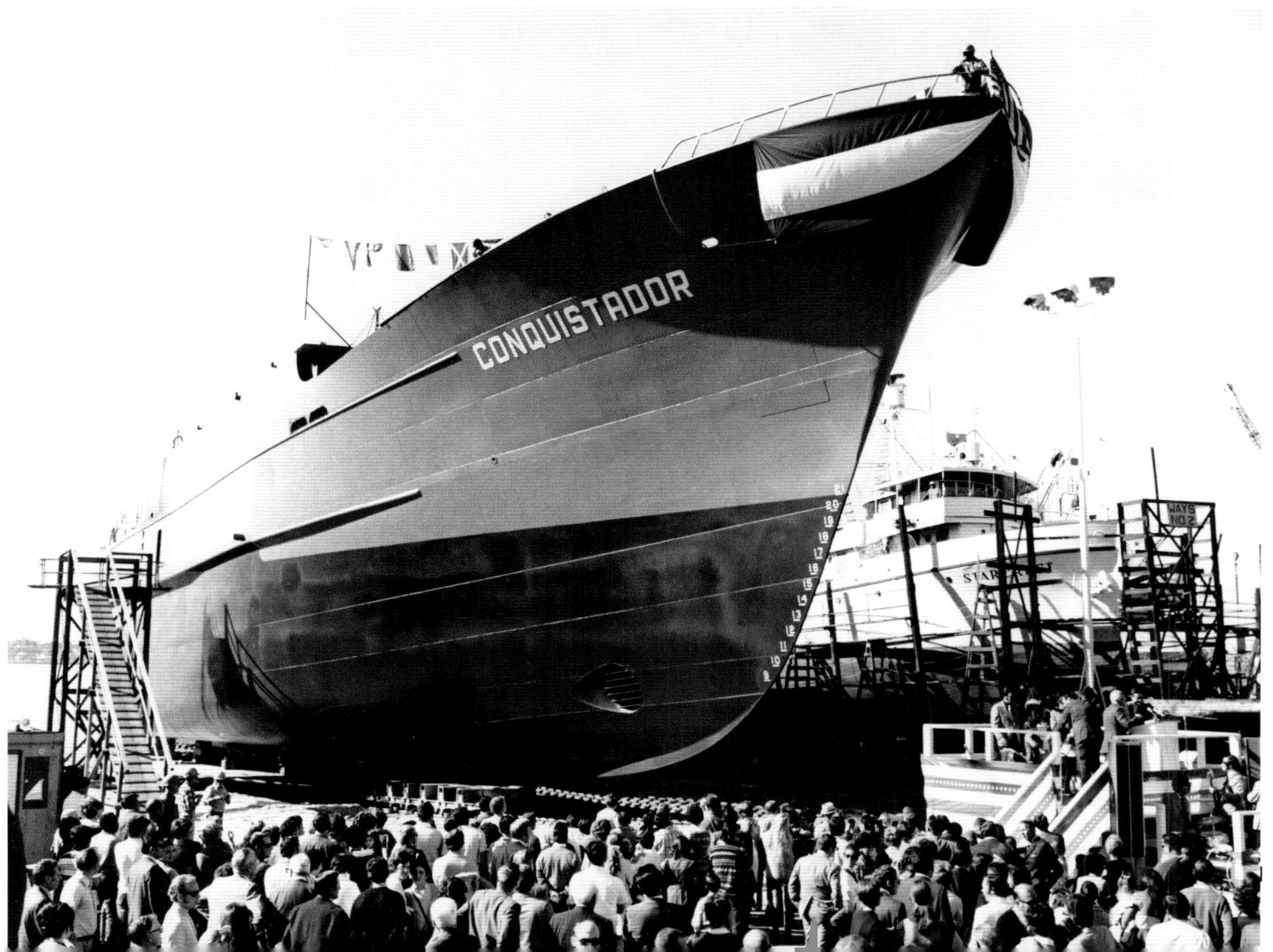

Steel Salmon & Tuna Boat

Not all new fishing boats slide out of a boat shop's doors and down greased ways to settle into a calm harbor. Certainly not the *North Star*, a 56-foot steel salmon and tuna boat that is waiting for an incoming full tide to lift it out of its cradle at Port Hudson Beach at Port Townsend, Washington, on July 24, 1971. Charles Poe built the *North Star* over four years of off-season fishing work to replace his boat of the same name.

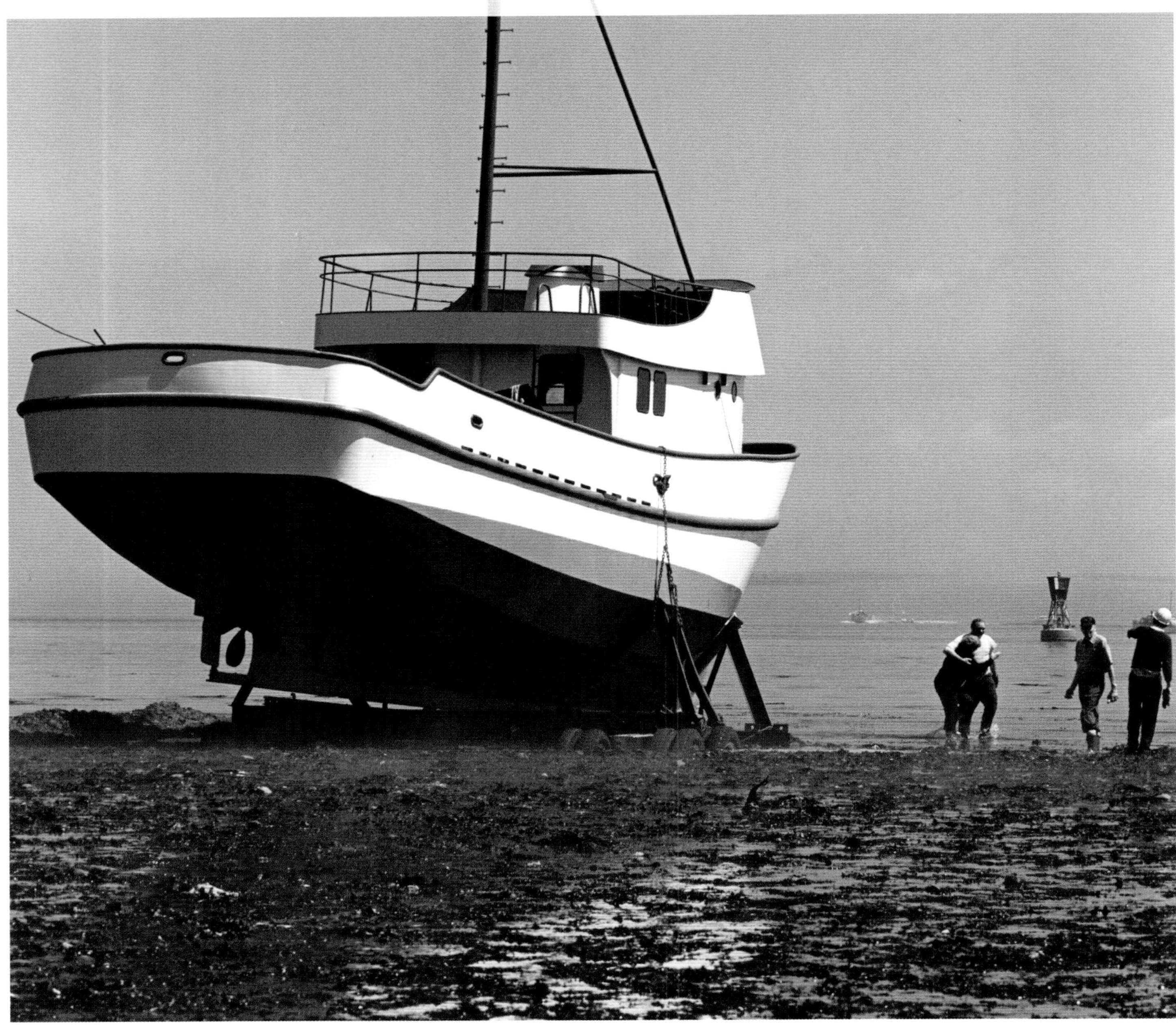

A Boatyard Milestone

There are many milestones in the life of a boatyard. Completing the one hundredth hull is definitely one of them. It obviously was that way for Frank Johnson and J.L. Howard, the owners of Quality Marine in Bayou La Batre, Alabama. When it came time to launch the *C & S Smile* in 1979, they made it known to all around this was their one hundredth vessel by decorating it with a very large "100" and a multitude of colorful pennants streaming from raised outriggers. The *C & S Smile* was a 97-foot scalloper operating out of Hampton, Virginia, and named after the Citizens and Southern National Bank of Georgia. The name was later changed to *Andrea Jean*.

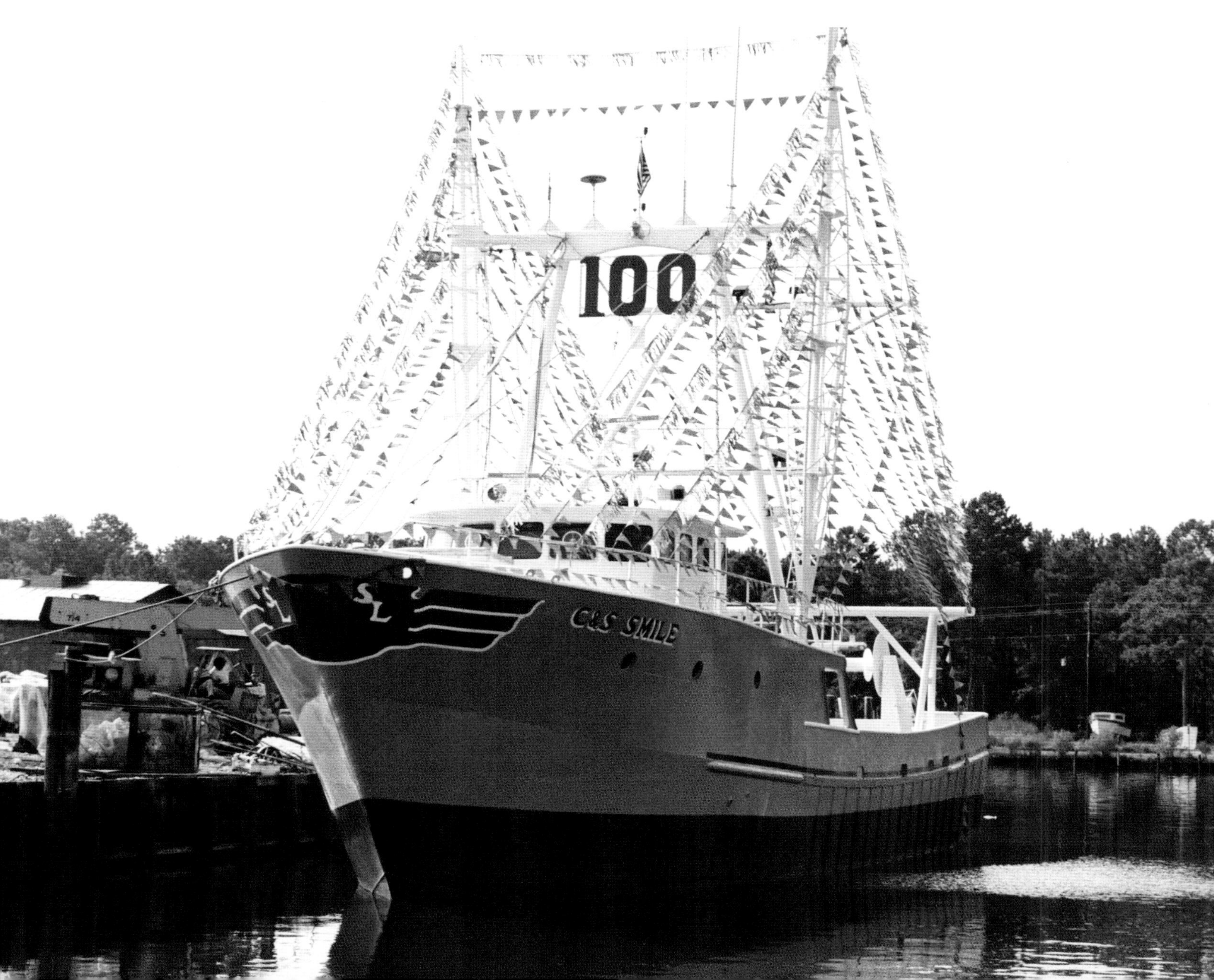

Steel Stern Trawler

The *Act I*, a 60-foot steel stern trawler, slides down the ways at the Harvey F. Gamage Shipyard in South Bristol, Maine, on February 18, 1974. Before building its first steel boat, the fishing vessel *Elizabeth* in 1970, the Harvey F. Gamage Shipyard was well-known for its wooden vessels, be they lobster boats or offshore vessels for fishing fleets in Gloucester and New Bedford, Massachusetts. The *Act I* was the fifth steel boat and the 256th hull built at the Gamage yard since 1925. She would fish out of New Bedford with a crew of four.

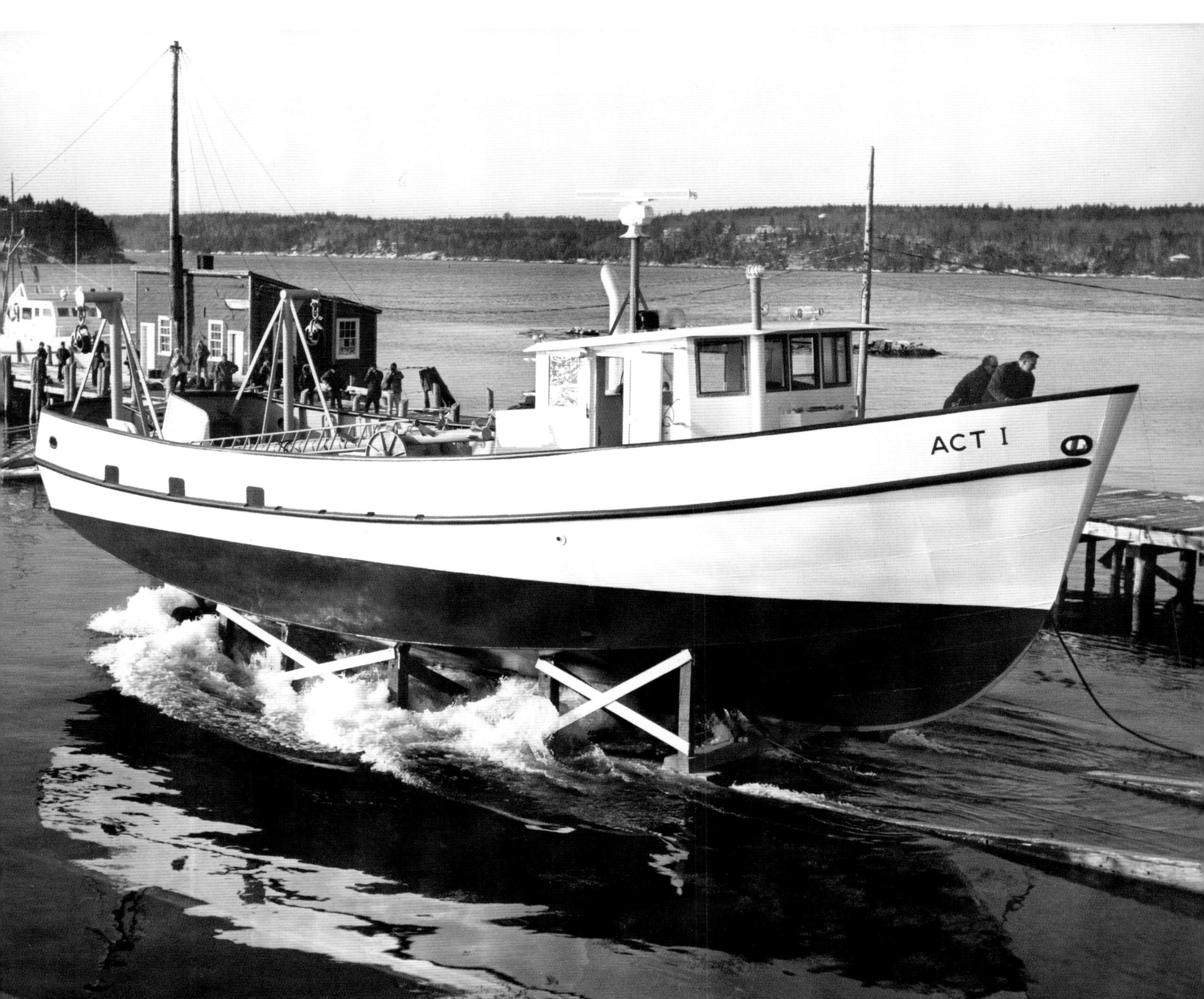

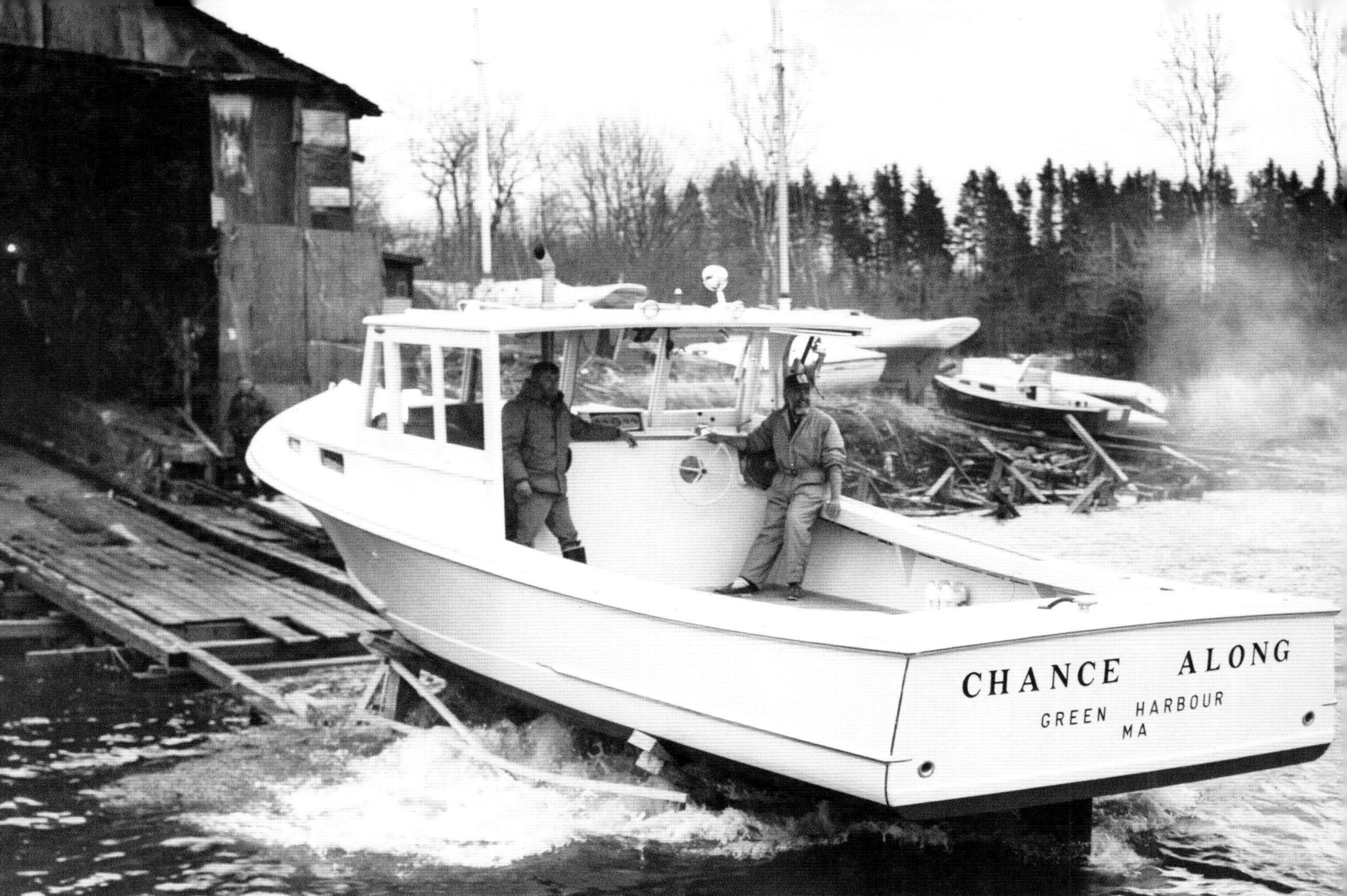

The Lobster Boat

The 35-foot *Chance Along* is about to float free of its cradle on launch day in the summer of 1977 at Lash Brothers Boatyard in Friendship, Maine. The boat's owner, Robert Wheeler, is taking it all in, while leaning against the bulkhead at the hauling station. Wheeler, who at one time commanded the Navy destroyer *Purdy*, had previously lobstered in *Sea Probe*, a 25-foot fiberglass boat that he built himself. In the off-season he built fiberglass dinghies.

The *Chance Along*, with mahogany planking over oak frames, was a major departure from the smaller *Sea Probe*. Wheeler wanted to contribute to his new boat, so he built a fiberglass rudder and covered iron fuel tanks with fiberglass. He did wonder, however, "what fishing a wooden boat will do to my image as a builder of fiberglass craft."

Coastal Schooner

At high noon on August 8, 1979, a gloriously sunny day perfect for making a statement—the coastal schooner *John F. Leavitt* slid down the ways at the Newbert & Wallace Shipyard in Thomaston, Maine, and into the St. George River. Hundreds of onlookers stood on the shore and on nearby schooners to see the first sailing cargo ship built in more than forty years.

The *John F. Leavitt*'s owner, Ned Ackerman, dreamed that wind-powered cargo could still play a role in shipping and that he would revive the tradition. He named the boat after the late John F. Leavitt, a well-known boatbuilder and author of maritime books, and it was designed by R.D. "Pete" Culler along the lines of cargo-carrying schooners common to the East Coast until the mid-1930s.

The 97-foot *John F. Leavitt* was framed with white oak and yellow pine and planked with yellow pine. It had 6,000-cubic feet of cargo space below deck, which Ackerman said was equivalent to five tractor-trailer trucks. True to form for a sail-powered cargo vessel, there was no engine. It would rely on a 15.5-foot yawl with an 85-horsepower diesel engine for harbor maneuvering.

Ackerman's dream, however, was short-lived. The *John F. Leavitt*'s maiden voyage was in November to Quincy, Massachusetts, to pick up a cargo for Haiti. But she ran into a heavy three-day winter gale off Delaware and sank on December 29, 1979. National Guard helicopters rescued the crew.

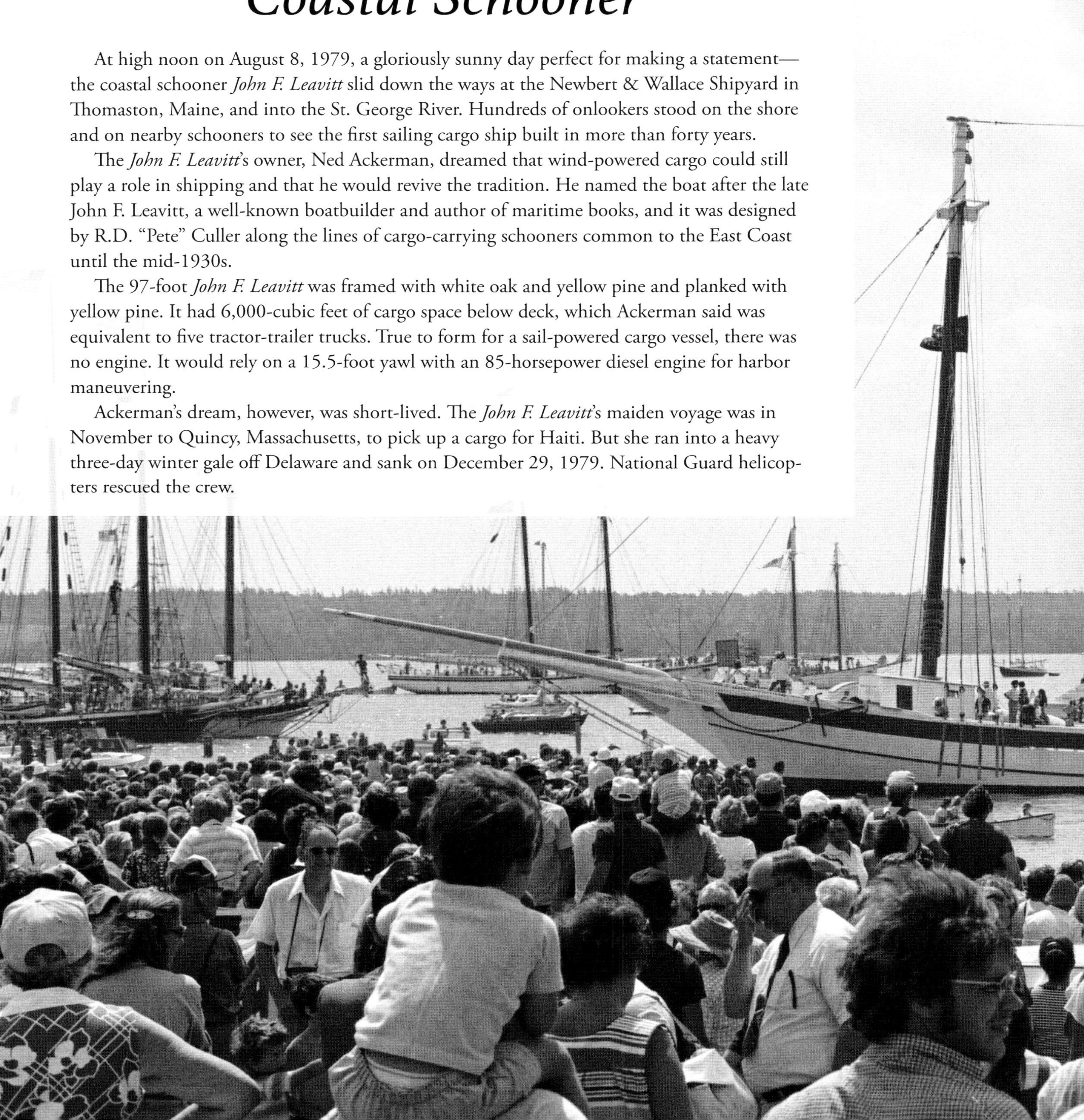

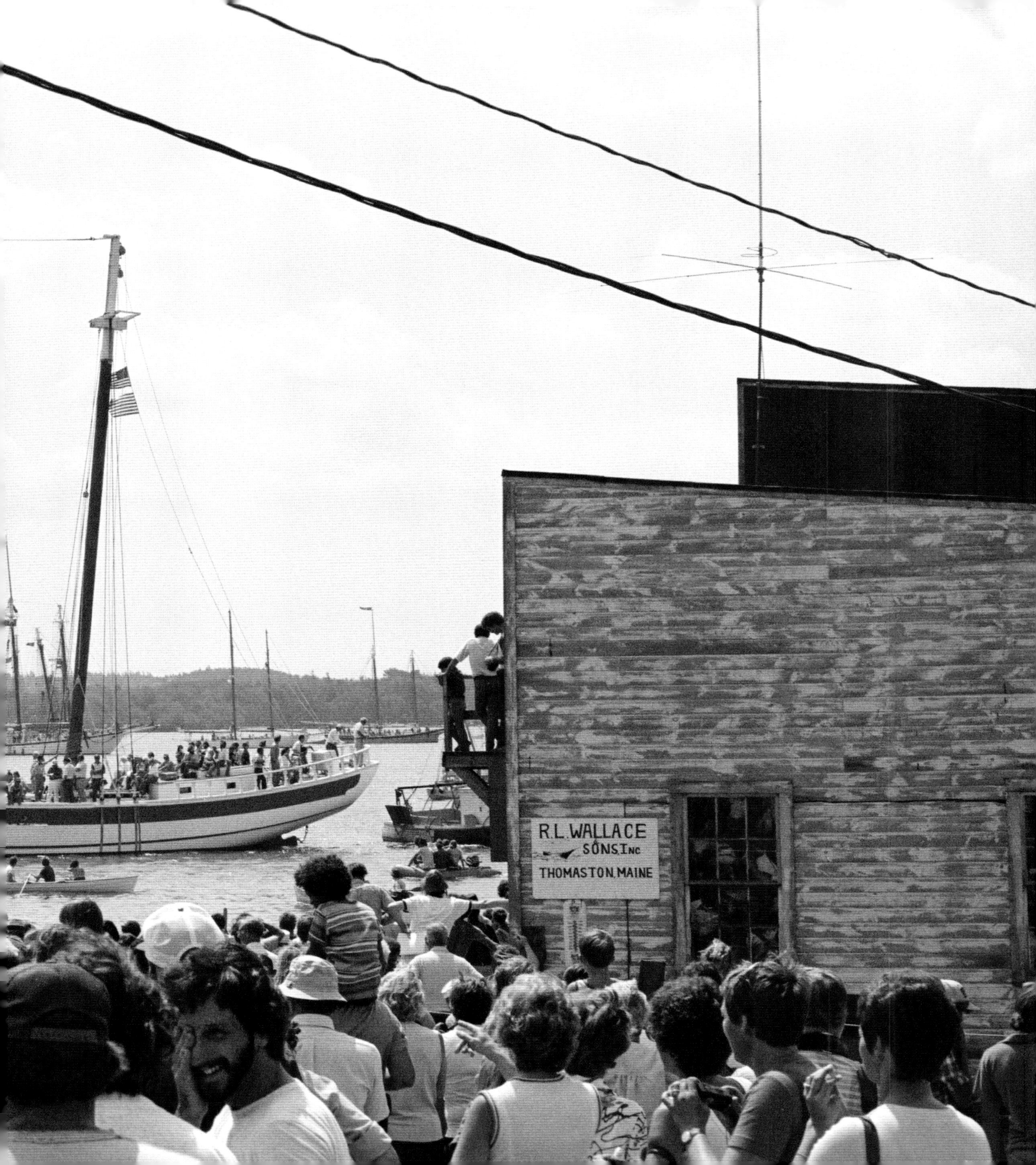

R.L. WALLACE
SONS Inc
THOMASTON, MAINE

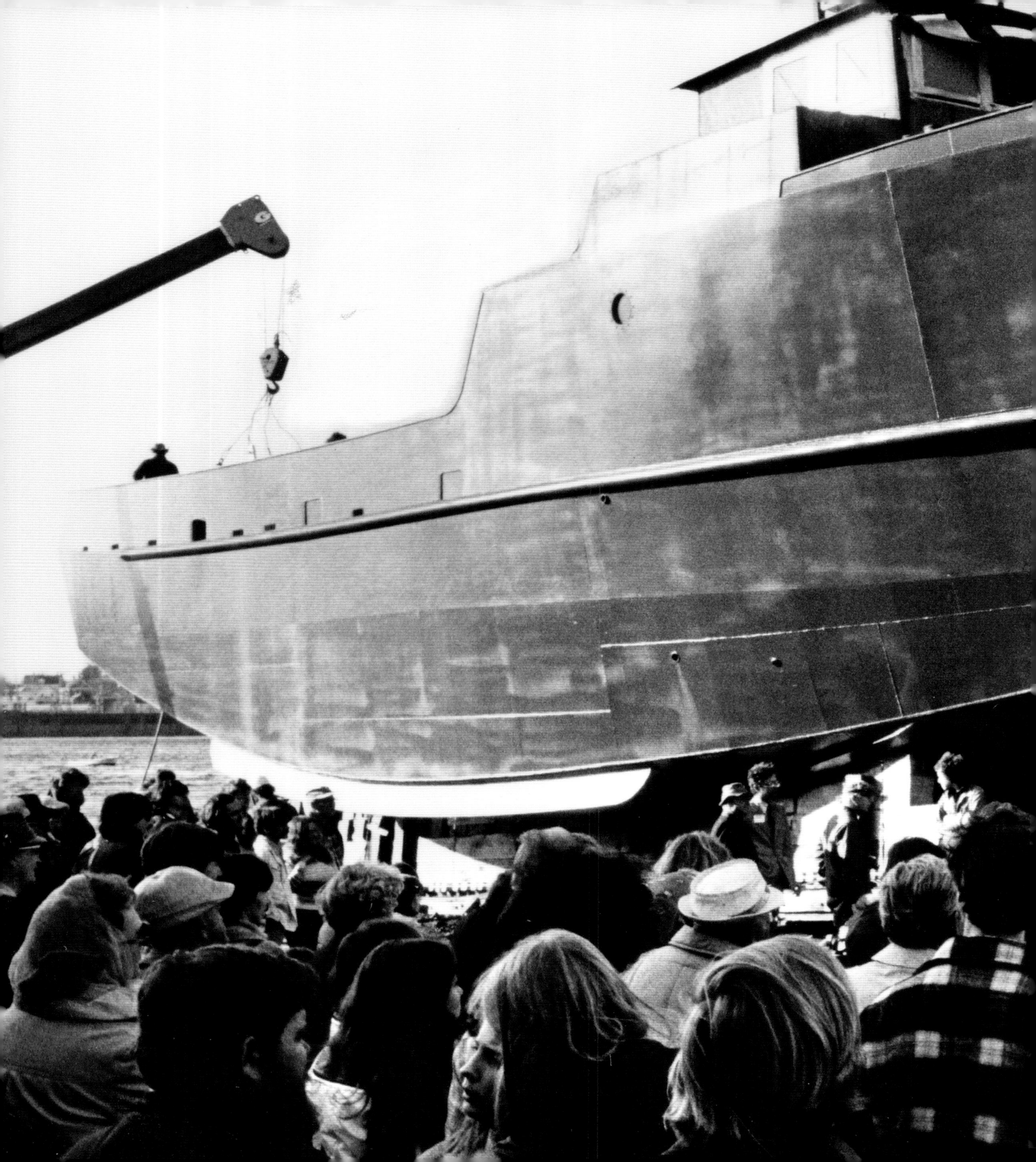

Washburn & Doughty

The shipyard Washburn & Doughty Associates in East Boothbay, Maine, has built more than 120 boats since its founding in 1979. Like many new businesses, Washburn & Doughty had difficulty finding that first customer because it hadn't built a boat to demonstrate the quality of its work. "Without a demonstrator it would be impossible to get off the ground," said Bruce Doughty.

So Bruce Washburn designed a 70-foot steel dragger and, working with three other men, he and Doughty began building the dragger that would become the *Brenda Louise*. They paid for materials by taking money from the salaries of their regular day jobs at Bath Iron Works. They could work on the vessel only at night and on weekends.

The shipyard's first customer turned out to be Rhode Islander Richard Goodwin, who traveled to Washburn & Doughty to check out the operation. He liked the workmanship he saw, but the *Brenda Louise* was too small for what he wanted. He ordered an 86-foot dragger and offshore lobster boat, the *Provider*, which was delivered in 1979.

Goodwin followed that with the 86-foot *Huntress*, which was completed just a few months later. The *Brenda Louise*, the trawler that allowed Washburn & Doughty to be more than a dream in the minds of two men, was completed two months later and delivered to a buyer in New Bedford, Massachusetts.

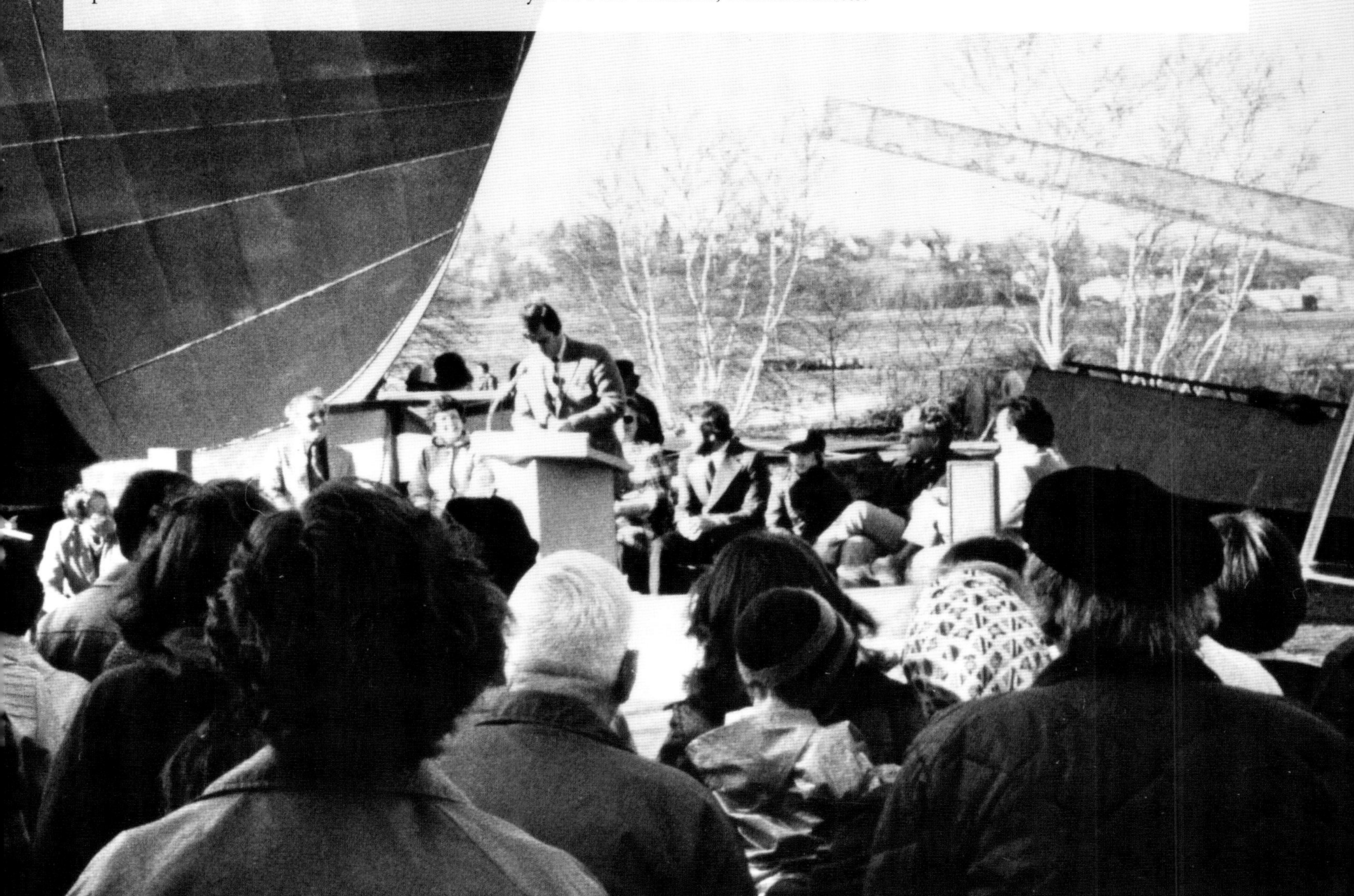

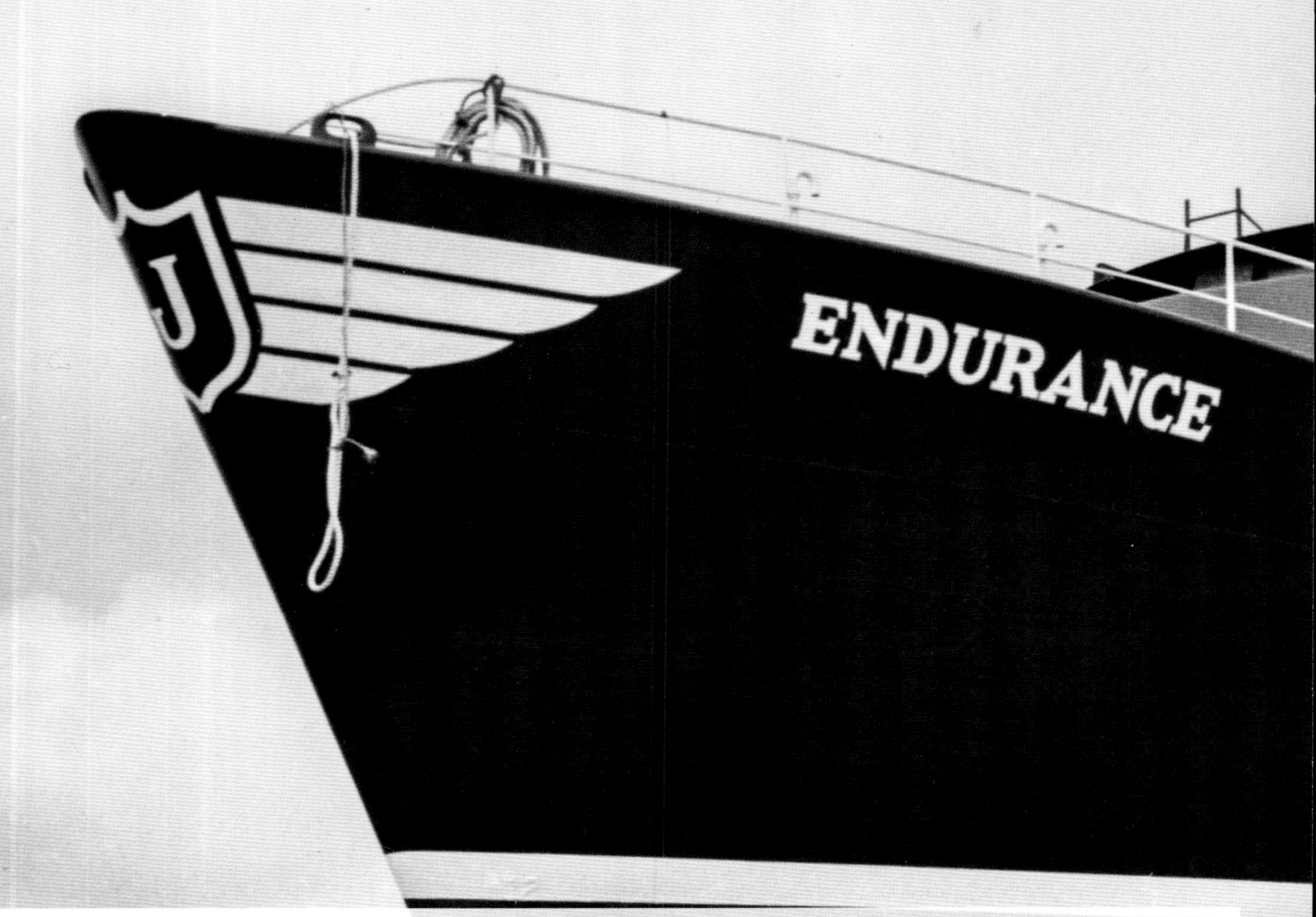

The Endurance

By the 1980s, southern boatyards had sent enough poorly designed and ill-constructed offshore steel vessels to New England and Pacific Northwest waters that those boatyards were gaining a dubious reputation. The 119-foot dragger *Endurance*, constructed by Duckworth Steel Boats in Tarpon Springs, Florida, and launched in 1983, was built to show that a southern boatyard could deliver an offshore vessel able to compete with northern-built boats even in the worst kinds of weather.

"Northern builders won't have anything on this boat," said the boatyard's owner, Junior Duckworth. Besides Duckworth Steel Boats' workmanship, the *Endurance* had the advantage that it was a ten-year-old design from John Gilbert & Associates of Boston that had proven itself in New England waters, and was was built for Leif Jacobsen, a New Bedford, Massachusetts, fisherman who had owned several offshore trawlers. The success of the *Endurance* allowed Duckworth Steel Boats to compete with northern boatyards for a share of the New England market for new trawlers.

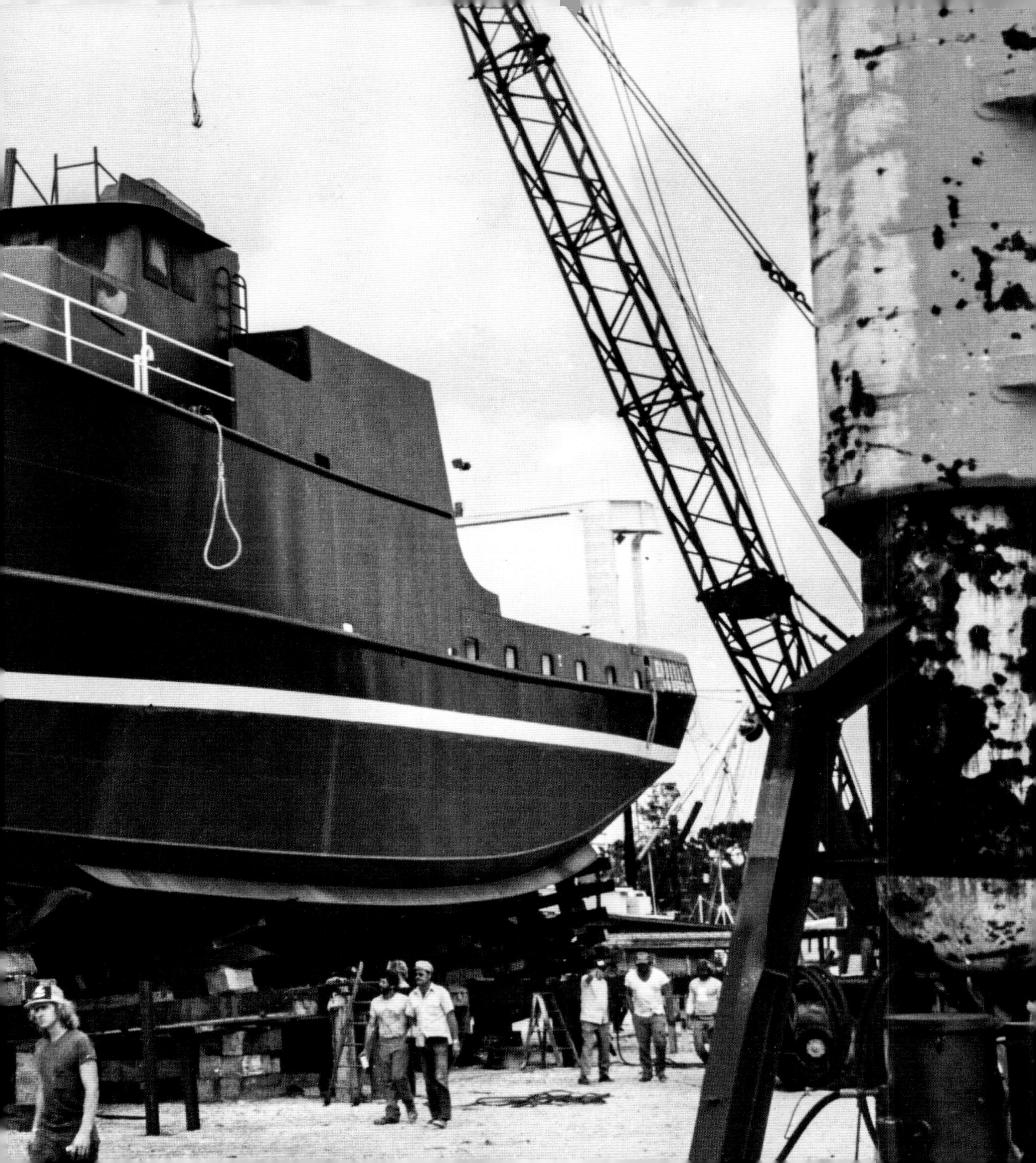

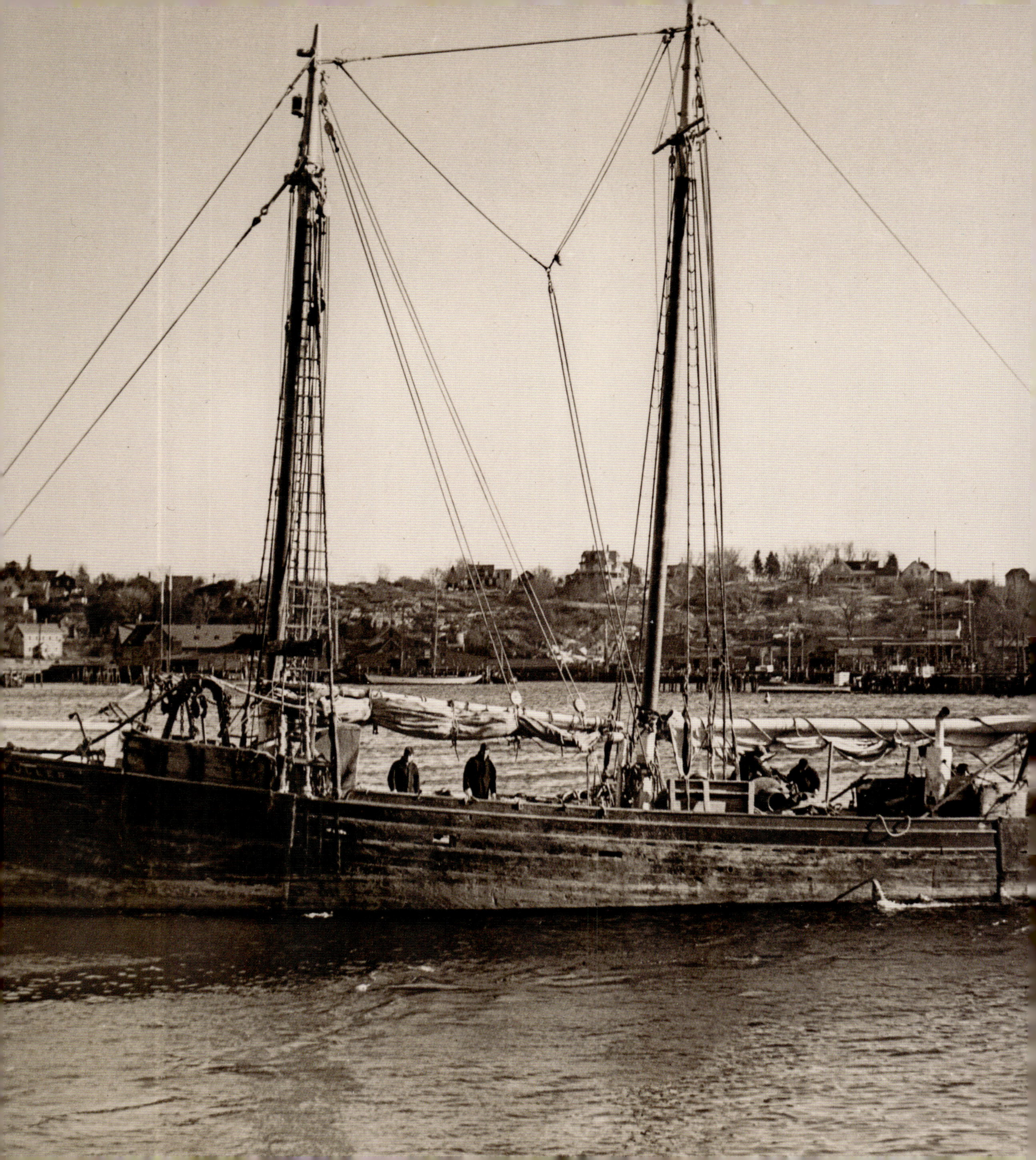

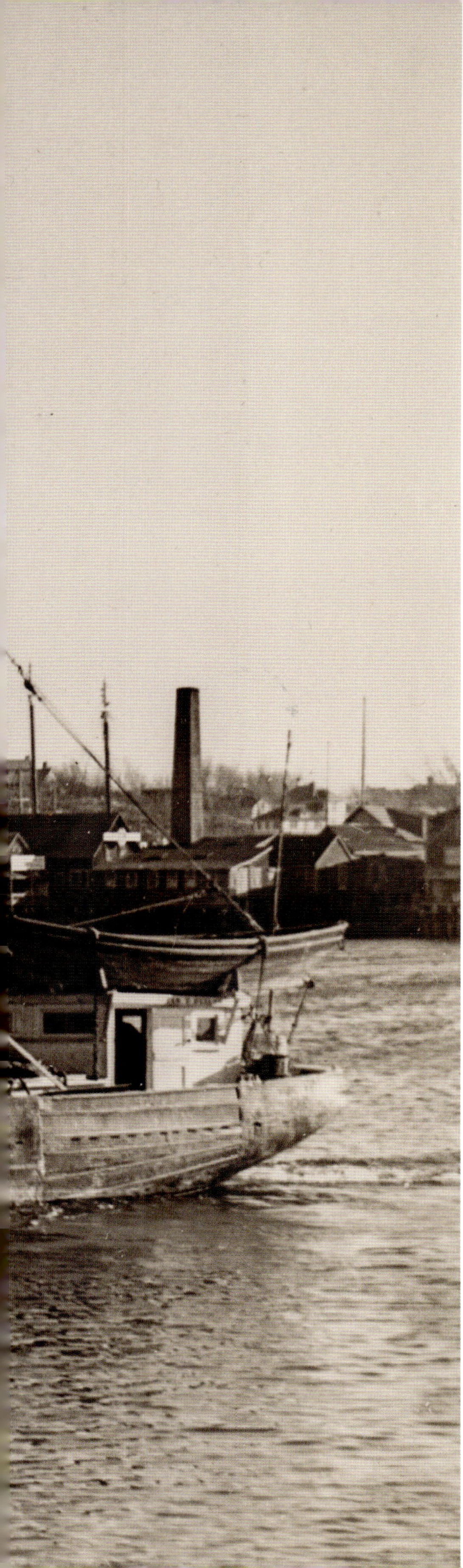

At Sea

Going to sea wasn't as simple as getting in a car, turning a key, and driving off. When heading to sea, boat owners and captains needed to consider things like gear, supplies, crew, and the seaworthiness of their vessels. Not to mention the weather forecast, rocky shores, hidden craggy ledges, tides, and other navigational hazards.

Ships and boats have gone from manpower to wind power to steam power through the centuries, while improved designs have made for better boats. Fishing boats use a variety of gear to harvest their catch, from nets, hooks, and traps to dredges, harpoons, and funny-looking long-handled tongs that scoop up shellfish from the ocean floor. Boats might go out for days, weeks, months, or even years on end, as some vessels did while sailing the globe on the hunt for whales in the days of yore.

Columbia River Gillnetter

Not many early West Coast small boat designs have the name recognition of the East Coast's pinky or Friendship sloop. But one boat that still draws an inquisitive response is the Columbia River gillnetter.

First built in San Francisco in 1868, the double-ended gillnetter was taken to the lower Columbia River where it was quickly adopted as the boat of choice by fishermen and several boatyards. Salmon were being harvested on the lower Columbia at a staggering rate, and it wasn't long before double-ended boats were tied up to most docks and used across the bays. In time, they were used from San Francisco to the Bering Sea. At the peak of the Alaska salmon season there might be up to four thousand Columbia River gillnetters on the coast, most owned by canneries.

Sizes varied over time, but by 1890 most new double-enders were 24 feet long with washboards, a three-foot foredeck, and a two-foot afterdeck. There was not a wheelhouse, but that wasn't a problem. In inclement weather or when they needed to sleep during the day, the two-man crew just used the sail as a tent over the forward part of the boat, with the sprit serving as the ridgepole.

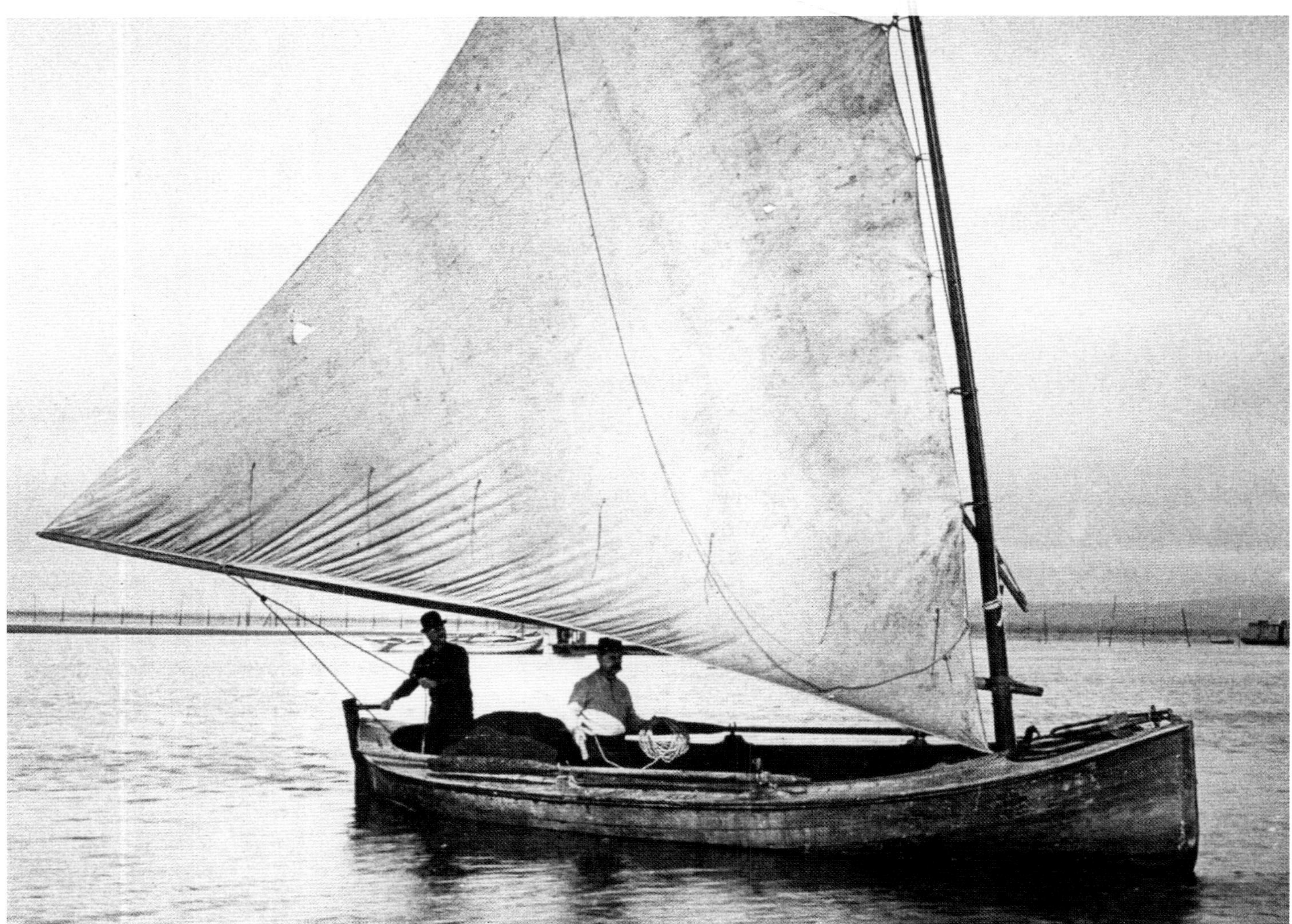

By Sail and Steam

The past and future are shown together in this photo, taken in the early 1900s, with two radically different technologies sitting side by side at a dock in Gloucester, Massachusetts. The two boats represent the fishing industry's shift from wind to steam power.

The *Spray*, an English-designed and English-crewed steam trawler—although built at the Fore River Shipyard in Quincy, Massachusetts—is tied up next to the *Kernwood*, a pure sailing machine with a gaff-rigged main and foresail and jibs forward. On the grounds, men rowed away from the *Kernwood* in dories to hand-line for cod.

Beginning in 1885, a few steam-powered boats were fishing in local waters for mackerel. But it was not until Boston bankers and fish buyers sent to England for a set of design plans for a steam powered fishing vessel that New England got an offshore steam trawler and this country's first side trawler. Perhaps that's not surprising, since it was the English who developed the otter trawl, the net used to catch the fish.

The steel-hulled 136-foot *Spray* was powered by Scotch boilers and a triple expansion steam engine of 450 horsepower at 110 revolutions. She cost $60,000, almost three times the price of a wooden sailing schooner. By 1913, the *Spray*'s owner, Bay State Fishing Company, had about six steam trawlers that delivered 16 percent of Boston's fish. By 1920, fifty-five steam trawlers were operating out of Boston. Still, sail power and dories would hang on—wooden boats were cheaper than steel boats and steam engines cost a lot more than sails—but the future was clear.

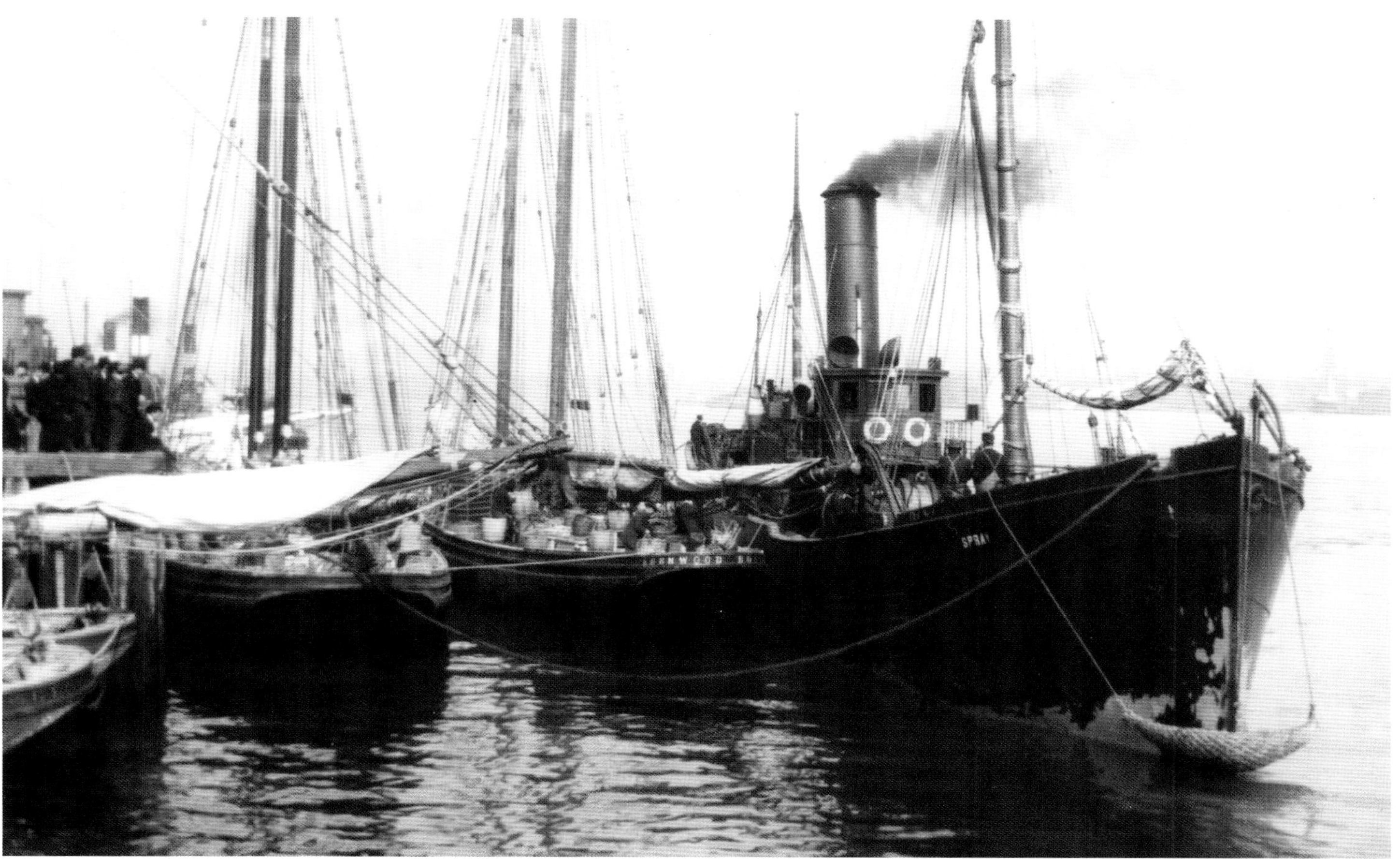

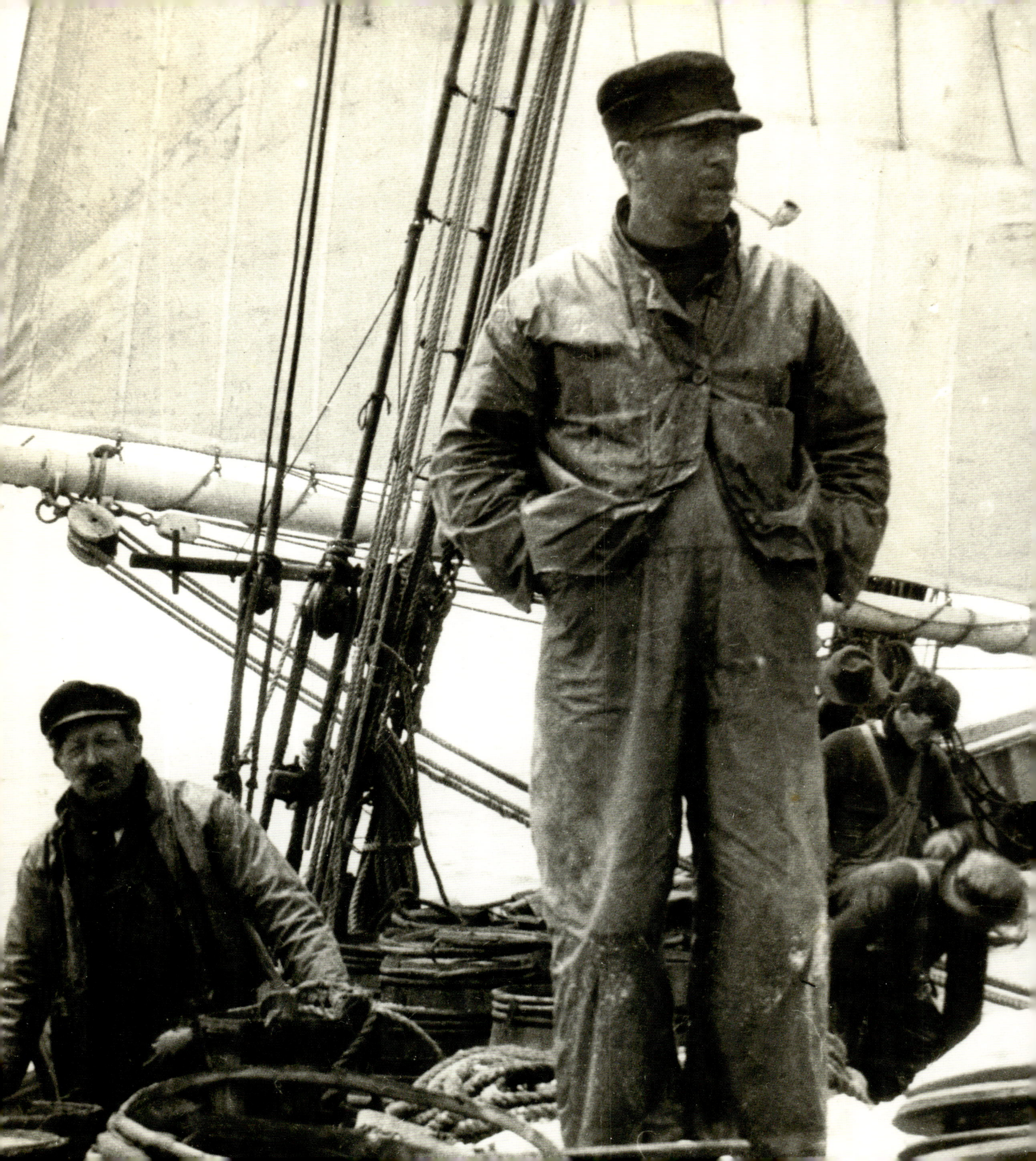

Mackerel, Oilskins, and Clay Pipes

Doug McLean, skipper of the 92-foot mackerel schooner *Pinta*, looks to be at ease, probably because the barrels of mackerel lined up between the deckhouse that he's standing on and the port railing are being headed as the *Pinta* runs back to its homeport of Gloucester, Massachusetts. Judging from the foresail that's hauled out to port, she's going wing-and-wing—or "wung out" as they would say—with the mainsail boom pulled out to starboard and the wind at their backs.

The photo was taken around 1906, thirteen years after the *Pinta* was built at the James & Tarr Shipyard in Essex, Massachusetts. The clay pipe McLean is pulling on was a favorite of working men at the time. They weren't hard to come by; some Gloucester smoke shops had them stacked a foot high across their front windows. Notice what McLean is wearing to protect him from the rain, spray, and boarding seas of the North Atlantic. Some fishermen today still call the jacket and pants they wear "oilskins" (even though they're usually made from PVC-based fabric or some other synthetic material), but McLean is wearing the real thing. The pants and jacket started out as unbleached cotton-cloth fabric stitched together and dipped in vats of yellow or black linseed oil mixed with turpentine and a drying agent.

After the fabric was run through wringers to remove surplus oil, it was hung up to dry. The pants and jacket were then coated by hand, dried, and coated once more. A final coating required the addition of varnish to the mixture, which helped seal the cloth and made the fabric shine. In 1880, Gloucester had six companies manufacturing oil clothing. In 1944, oil clothing was still being made at Gloucester's D.O. Frost & Co., which advertised its Frost Brand "superior" oiled clothing.

The *Pinta* was sold to a fisherman in Newfoundland, Canada, just before World War I and ended up as a floating yacht clubhouse in Chicago.

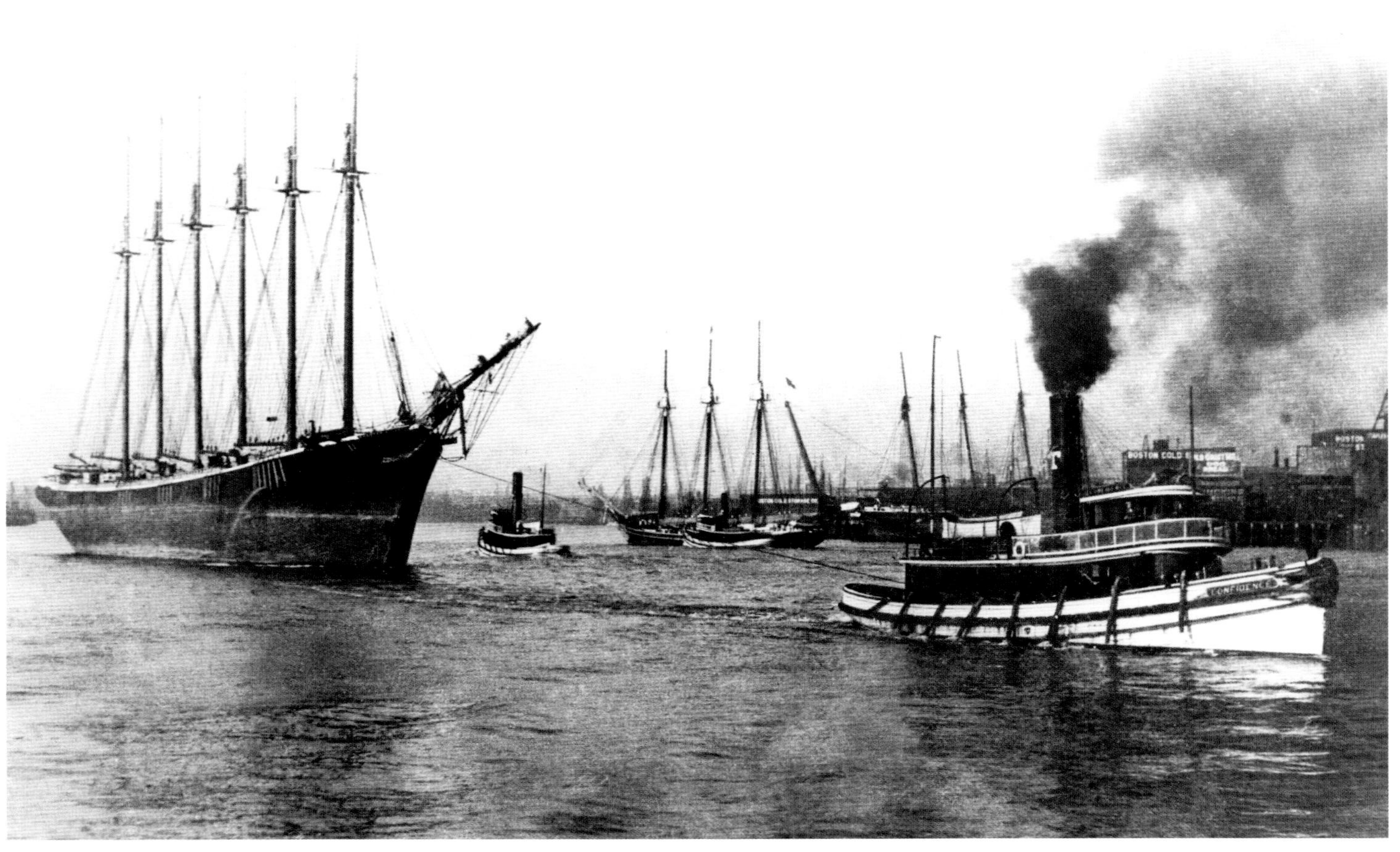

The Tugboat and The Cargo Carrier

The six-masted schooner *Eleanor A. Percy*'s cargo of coal has been unloaded and she is being towed across Boston Harbor and out to sea by the steam tug *Confidence* in 1906. Once clear of land, *Percy*'s crew will drop the towing hawser, hoist the sails—with the assist of a steam hoisting engine, which was needed because the lower sails were all 2/0 duck, the heaviest canvas in the world. She is probably headed south, possibly to Baltimore, to get another load of coal before returning to northern ports.

The 347-foot by 50-foot *Percy* was launched October 10, 1900, at the Percy & Small shipyard in Bath, Maine. When she was built, the *Percy* was the world's third-largest sailing vessel, able to pack just over 6,000 tons of coal. Even though the *Percy* is not hauling cargo in this photo, the amount of smoke coming from the stack of the 79-foot *Confidence* indicates it requires most of the power its 325-horsepower steam engine to tow the *Percy*.

The "T" on the tug's stack marks it as one of the Boston Tow Boat Company's tugs, as are the two white-hulled tugs astern of it, one of which is tied off to a three-masted schooner it is maneuvering to a dock.

Without steam tugs, the potential for sailing cargo carriers like the *Percy* would have been limited, because there wouldn't have been a way to maneuver schooners in small harbors and into docking spaces other than with pulling boats propelled by oars. A steam tug's ability to tow large sailing vessels into and out of harbors and assist in berthing them spurred the growth of coastal trade.

The *Eleanor A. Percy* was the flagship of the Percy & Small fleet until they sold her in December 1915 for $125,000 (she cost $157,576 to build in 1900). The buyer, Harby Steamship Company, soon sold her to a Norwegian outfit, which renamed her *Dusie*. In 1919, she was sold to an American buyer and took back her original name, but on Christmas morning that year the ship sunk while carrying grain from Rio de Janeiro to Denmark. Of the eighteen-man crew, only five were rescued.

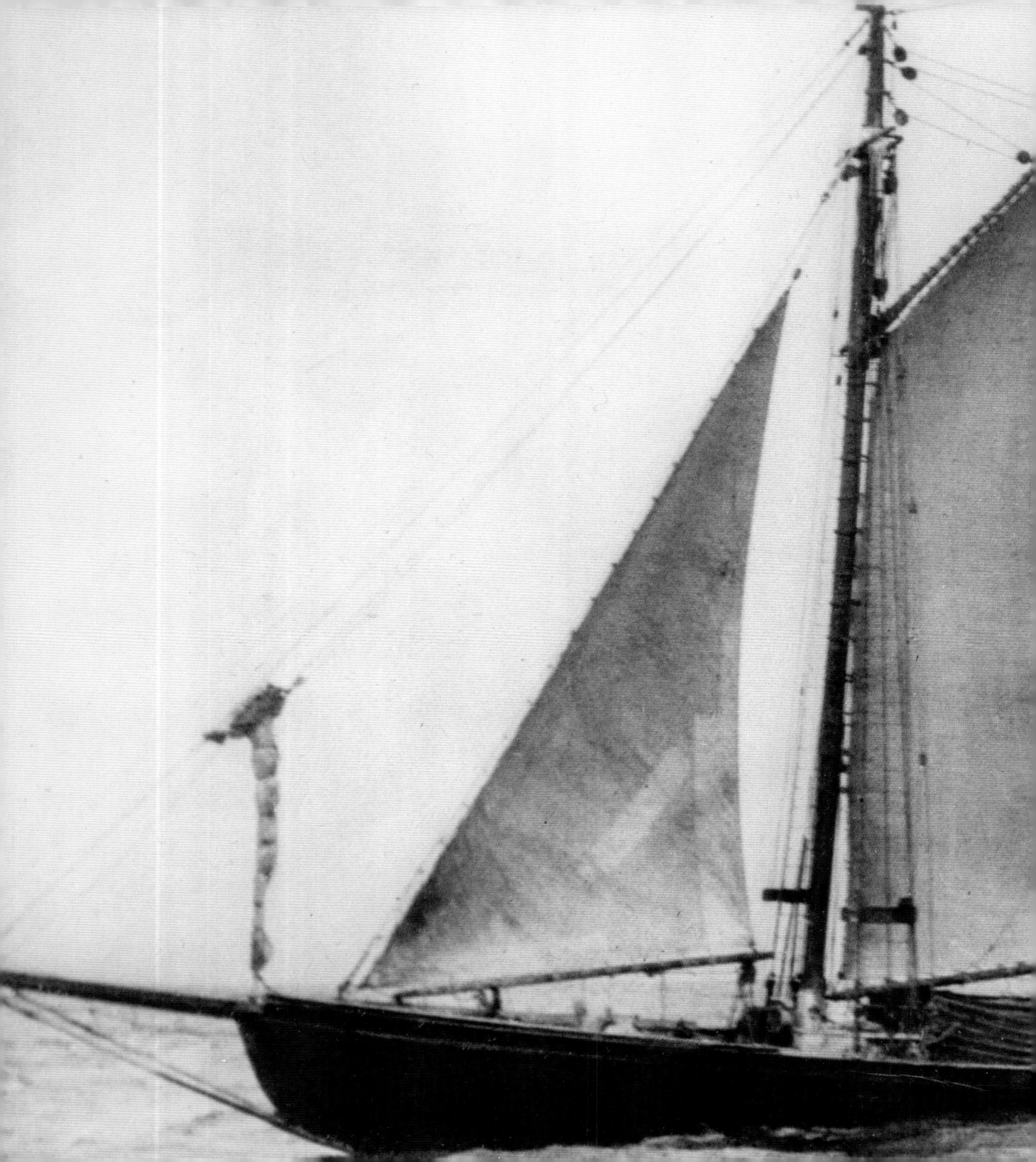

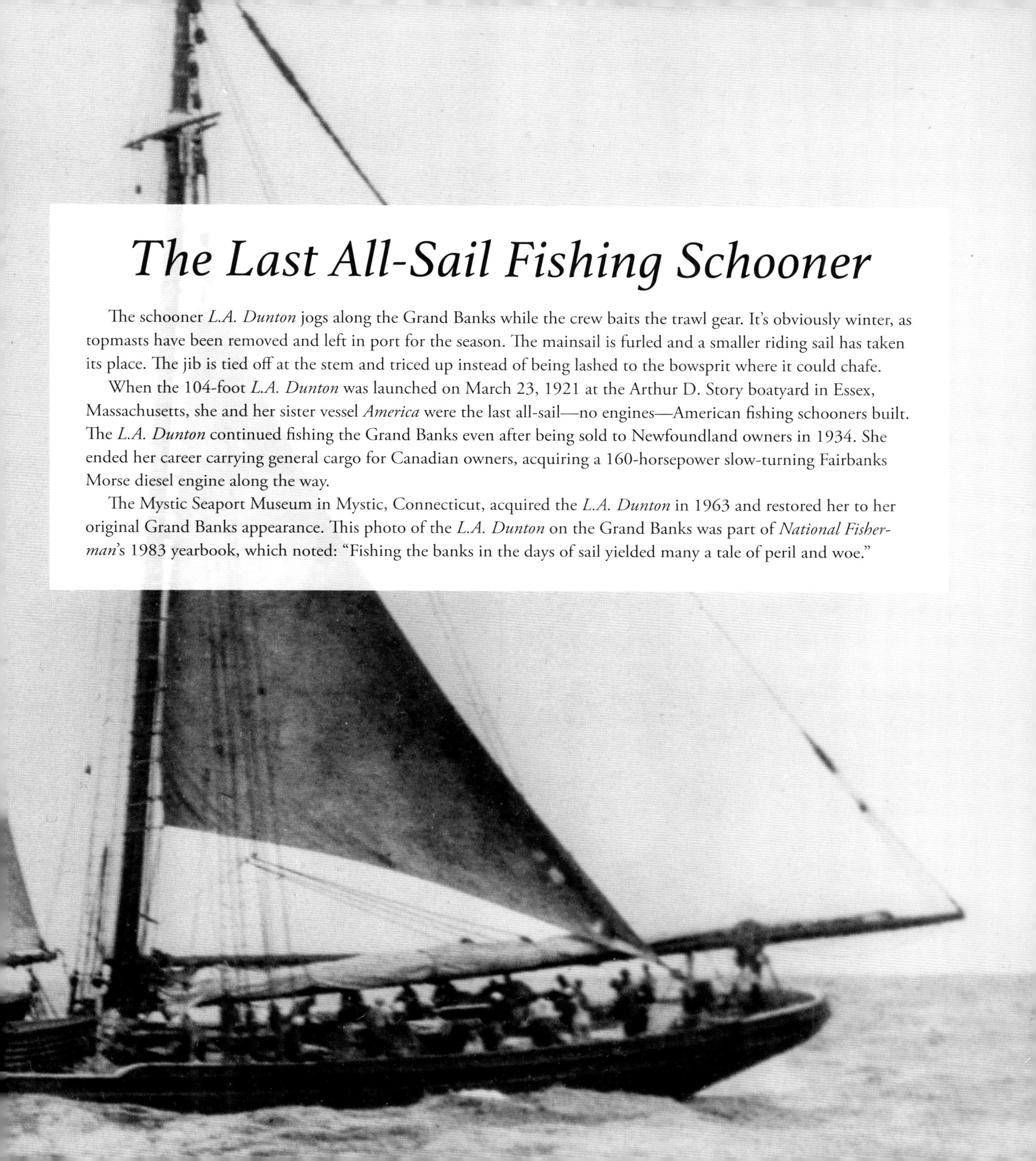

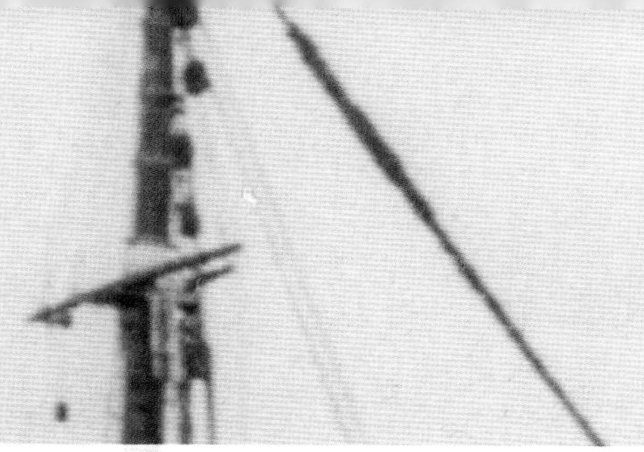

The Last All-Sail Fishing Schooner

The schooner *L.A. Dunton* jogs along the Grand Banks while the crew baits the trawl gear. It's obviously winter, as topmasts have been removed and left in port for the season. The mainsail is furled and a smaller riding sail has taken its place. The jib is tied off at the stem and triced up instead of being lashed to the bowsprit where it could chafe.

When the 104-foot *L.A. Dunton* was launched on March 23, 1921 at the Arthur D. Story boatyard in Essex, Massachusetts, she and her sister vessel *America* were the last all-sail—no engines—American fishing schooners built. The *L.A. Dunton* continued fishing the Grand Banks even after being sold to Newfoundland owners in 1934. She ended her career carrying general cargo for Canadian owners, acquiring a 160-horsepower slow-turning Fairbanks Morse diesel engine along the way.

The Mystic Seaport Museum in Mystic, Connecticut, acquired the *L.A. Dunton* in 1963 and restored her to her original Grand Banks appearance. This photo of the *L.A. Dunton* on the Grand Banks was part of *National Fisherman*'s 1983 yearbook, which noted: "Fishing the banks in the days of sail yielded many a tale of peril and woe."

North Pacific Halibut Schooner

The halibut schooner *Attu*, with her flag flying from the foremast, passes a backdrop of square riggers and schooners on what was probably her launch day in 1924. That might be her owner, Ralph Ekrom, standing next to the wheelhouse.

North Pacific halibut schooners like the 74-foot *Attu* were at the head of the sail-to-engine evolutionary curve. The *Attu* was launched with a 125-horsepower Atlas-Imperial diesel engine, but as the photo shows, she also had a schooner's two masts. She carried masts and sails because traditions die slowly and fishermen in the early 1900s had plenty of skepticism about internal combustion engines, especially when fishing out of sight of land.

The halibut schooner's plumb stem and long, straight keel were from a power-boat model, but the slender hull, counter stern and pleasing sheer allowed them to retain some of the graceful lines and seaworthiness of the sailing schooners.

The crew of a halibut schooner originally fished out of dories. But by the 1930s a power winch—the "gurdy"—was developed and dories were outlawed, mostly because dory fishing was too dangerous. The gurdy was mounted amidships, between the fish hold and the fo'c'sle, where it hauled in a line with a hook every few feet. Hooks today are spaced about 16 feet apart. Once a halibut was brought aboard, it was gutted then iced down in the fish hold. The *Attu* held ten tons of ice and 70,000 pounds of halibut.

A schooner's accommodations were sparse. Up forward, the *Attu's* fo'c'sle had bunks for eight, a cook stove, and folding table. Six more bunks were located in the stern and aft of the engine room, and the skipper slept in the wheelhouse. The *Attu*, which was built by Matt Anderson of Olalla, Washington, was constructed of virgin oak and fir with a ten- by twelve-inch keel and keelson, and sister keelsons that measured fourteen by eight inches.

While the last halibut schooner was built about 1930, from 1920 through the mid-1950s there were as many as 180 of them fishing the Gulf of Alaska and Bering Sea. Since then there's been a slow decline, with probably only nine still fishing for halibut in 2016, and another two or three chasing albacore. The *Attu* is not one of those—she struck a ledge and sank off Alaska's Kayak Island in March 1990.

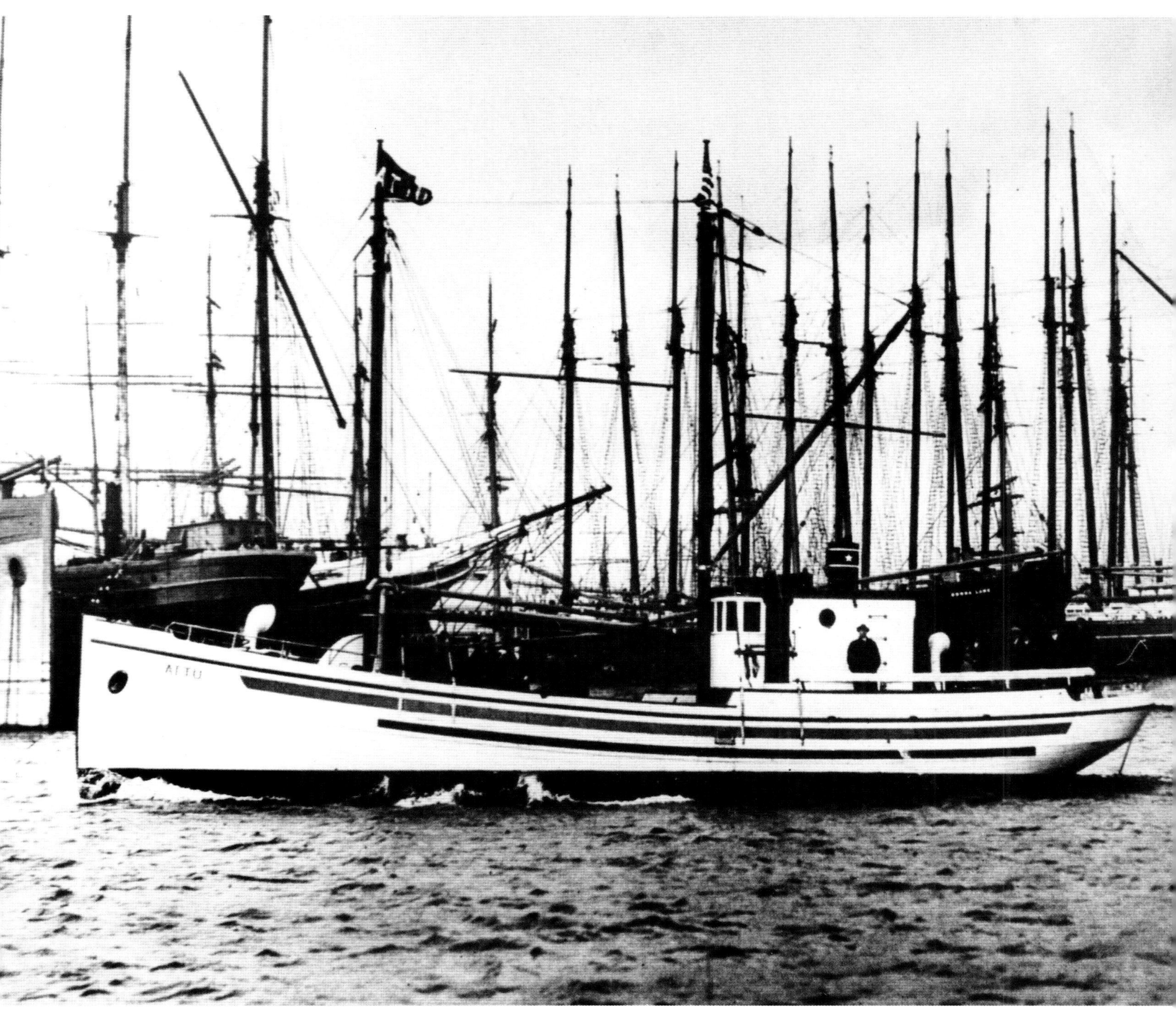

"Last of the Old Pinkies"

The pinky schooner *Maine* sails on an easy reach near Jonesport, Maine, in the late 1920s with a rig of gaff sails on the fore and main masts and a single jib. The pinky was different from other New England schooners because of her distinctive hull shape. Behind a relatively full bow and sharply steeved bowsprit, the hull tapered back to abruptly sweep up near the stern. Wide bulwarks followed those lines and came together past the sternpost in a pointed or "pinched" manner, at a transom that was cut out as a storage spot for the main boom and served as a drying rack for nets. The bulwarks provided some protection for the helmsman and the open, overhanging space between the bulwarks and behind the sternpost made a good lavatory.

The *Maine* was built in Essex, Massachusetts, in 1845 and was home-ported in Brooklin, Maine. When this photo was taken, the pinky schooner had long gone out of fashion—replaced by larger, faster offshore schooners. The *Maine* was reputed to be "the last of the old pinkies."

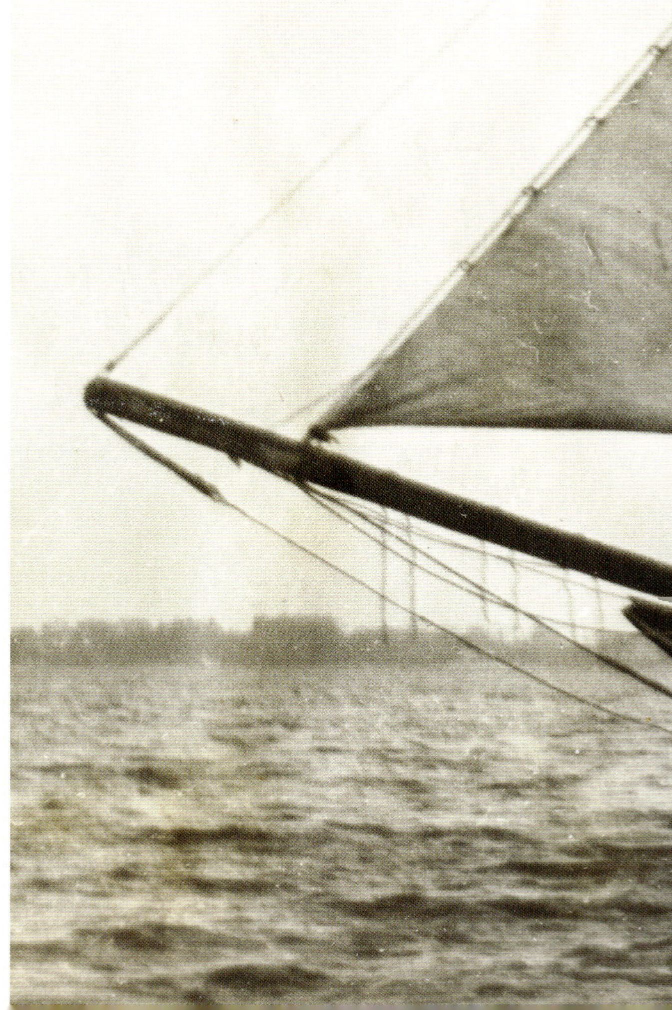

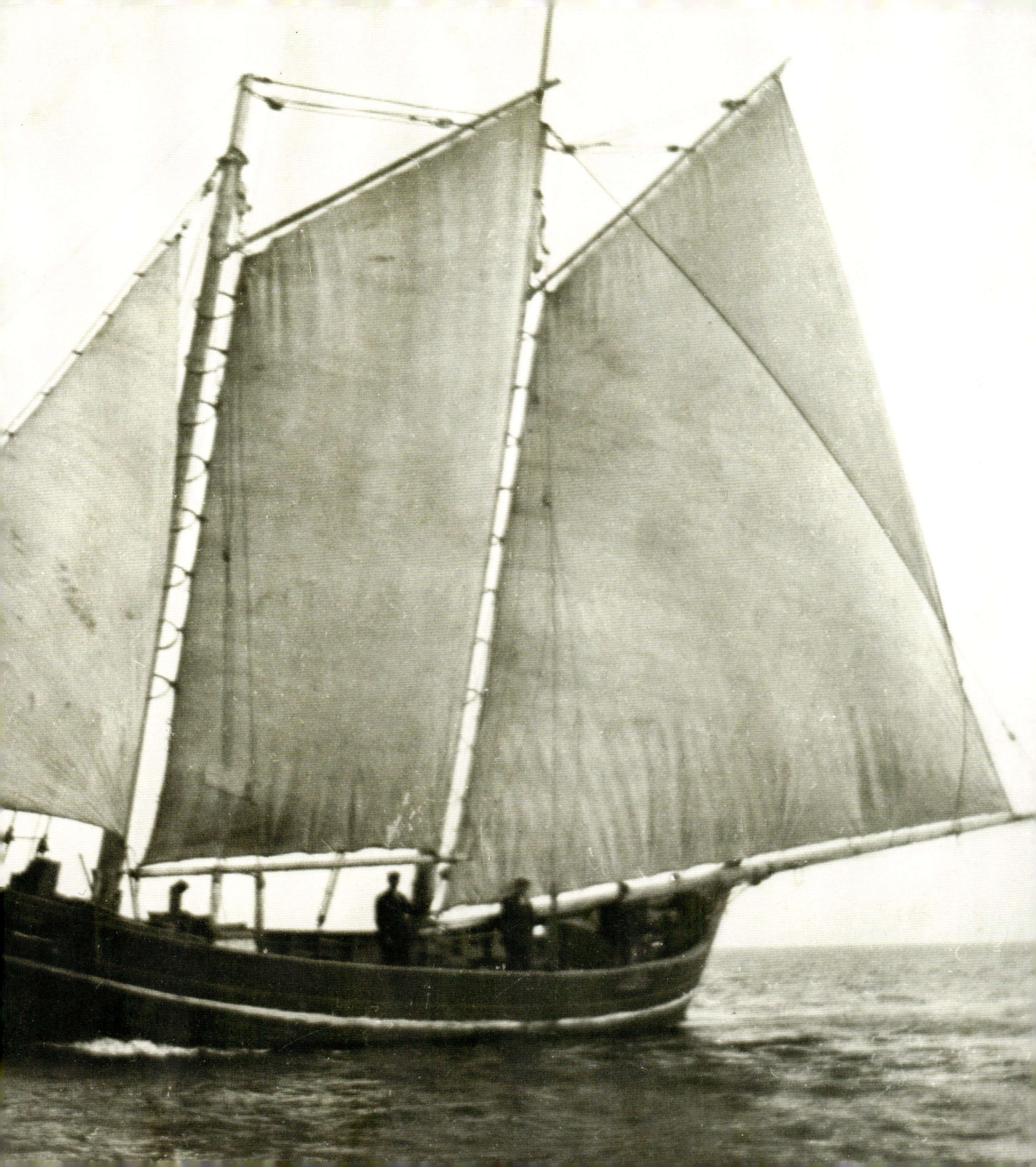

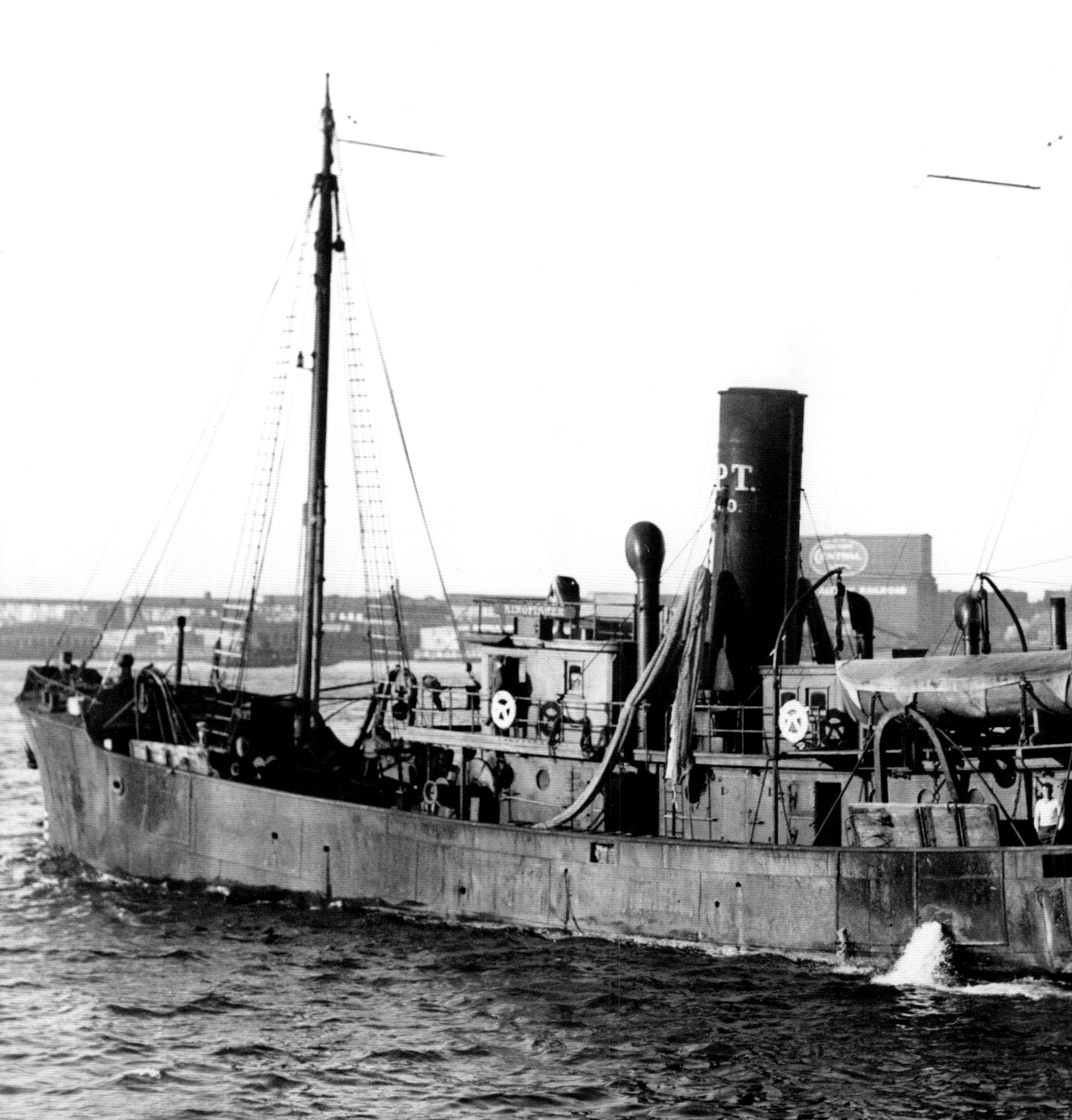

Minesweeper Turned Trawler

The *Kingfisher*, shown as a side trawler in this 1931 photo, was built to be a minesweeper for the French government. But after being launched in 1919 at the Foundation Company in Savannah, Georgia, the *Kingfisher* was purchased by the East Coast Fisheries Company and fished out of Rockland, Maine.

In 1926, the Portland Trawling Company bought the *Kingfisher* and had her reconditioned at Bethlehem Shipbuilding Corporation's Atlantic Works in East Boston. Once back in the water, the *Kingfisher* began landing fish in Boston, New York, and Groton, Connecticut. The *Kingfisher* was powered with a triple expansion steam engine that developed 500-horsepower at 125 revolutions per minute. A three-furnace single-end Scotch boiler developed steam pressure of 175 pounds per square inch.

The *Kingfisher*'s dual generators were a feature considered unusual for a trawler. One was a seven-and-a-half kilowatt Enberg reciprocating generator for night lighting and the other was a three kilowatt Moon turbine for daytime use. The cost of an additional generator quickly proved itself with reduced maintenance and ensured that the *Kingfisher* could always communicate with its Groton office.

The *Kingfisher* was also outfitted with a depth finder, which was relatively rare on fishing boats at the time, according to a 1929 *Atlantic Fisherman* article. The story projected that depth finders in time would be indispensable on fishing boats. "Particularly the trawler must know how deep the water is," the article reads. "For trawling on the edges of fishing grounds and over broken bottoms, a hand lead cannot compare with the fathometer."

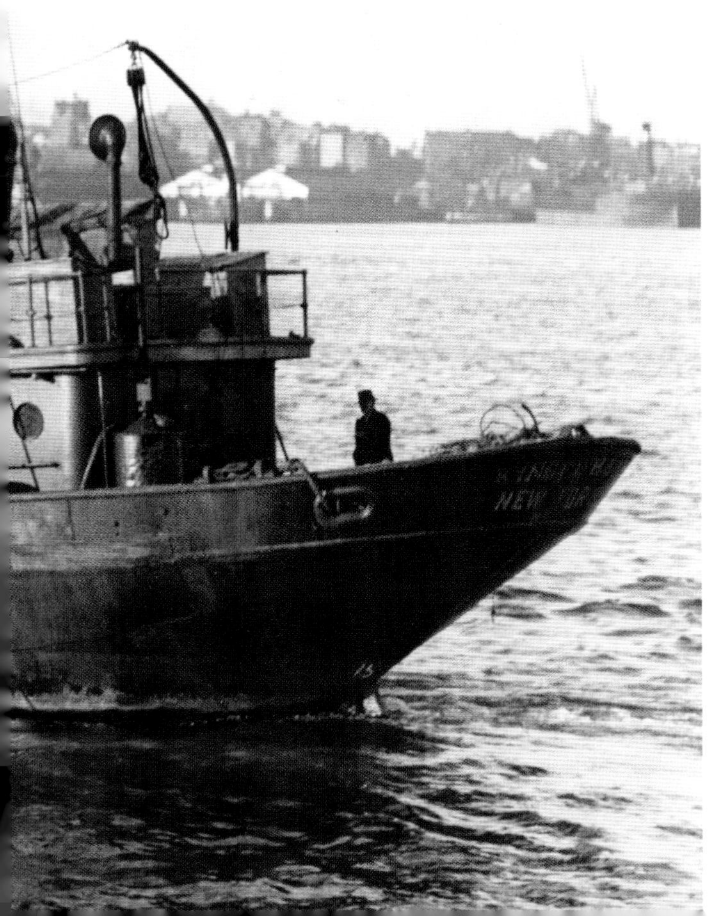

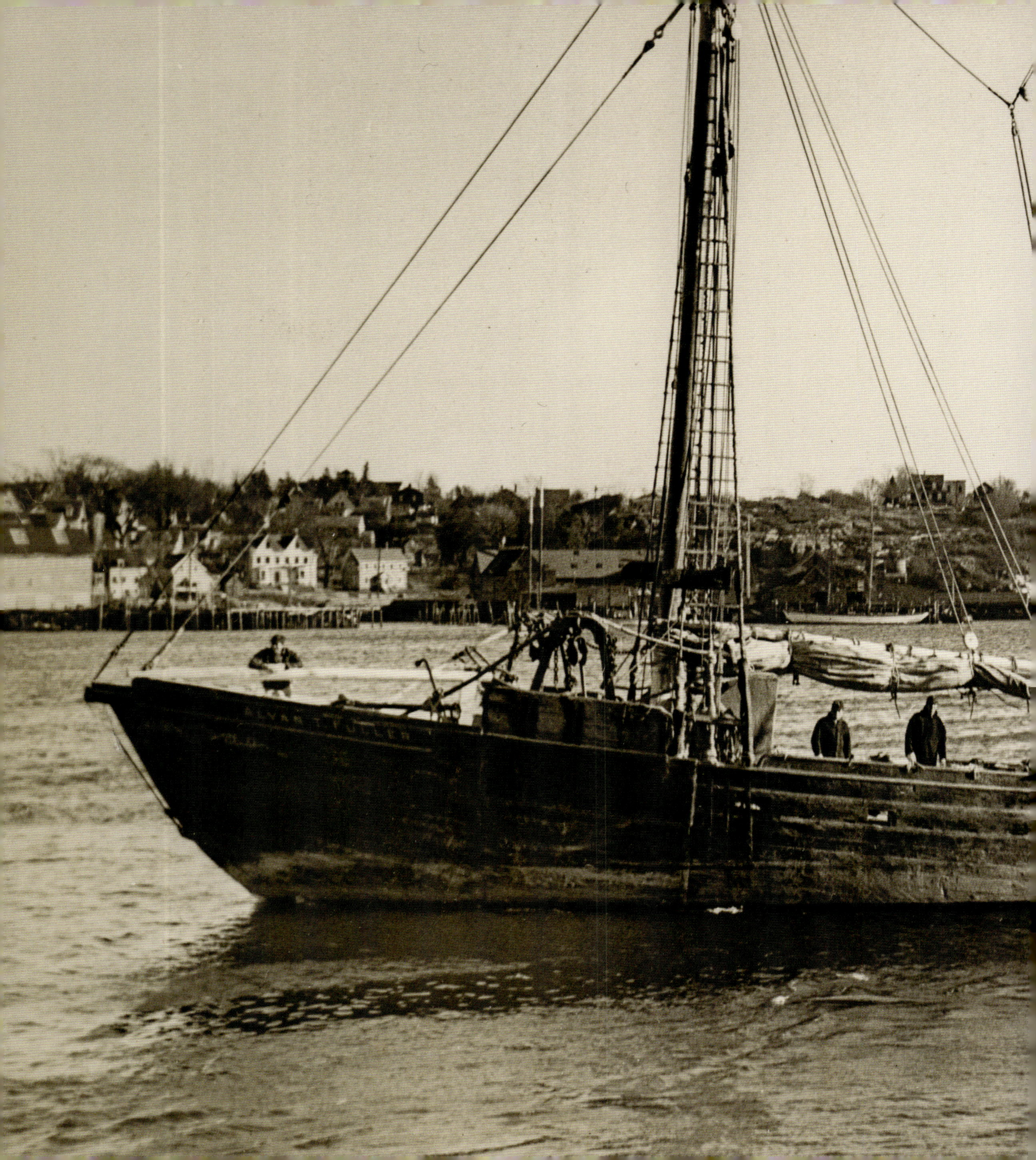

Adopting the New, Keeping the Old

Fishermen are sometimes slow to completely trust new innovations. Witness the *Alvin T. Fuller*, an 89-foot diesel-powered dragger built in 1931 at the Arthur D. Story Shipyard in Essex, Massachusetts. That's thirteen years after the launch of the *Lucia*, a mackerel seiner that was the first diesel-powered American fishing vessel, and two years after the *Rush*, the first diesel-powered otter trawler.

While the *Alvin T. Fuller* was powered by a 275-horsepower Atlas diesel engine, this 1942 photo shows that its fishermen owners, like others, were not all that comfortable with the internal combustion engine. That explains why they felt the need to retain a schooner's main and foresails for auxiliary power and stick with the schooner's easily driven hull.

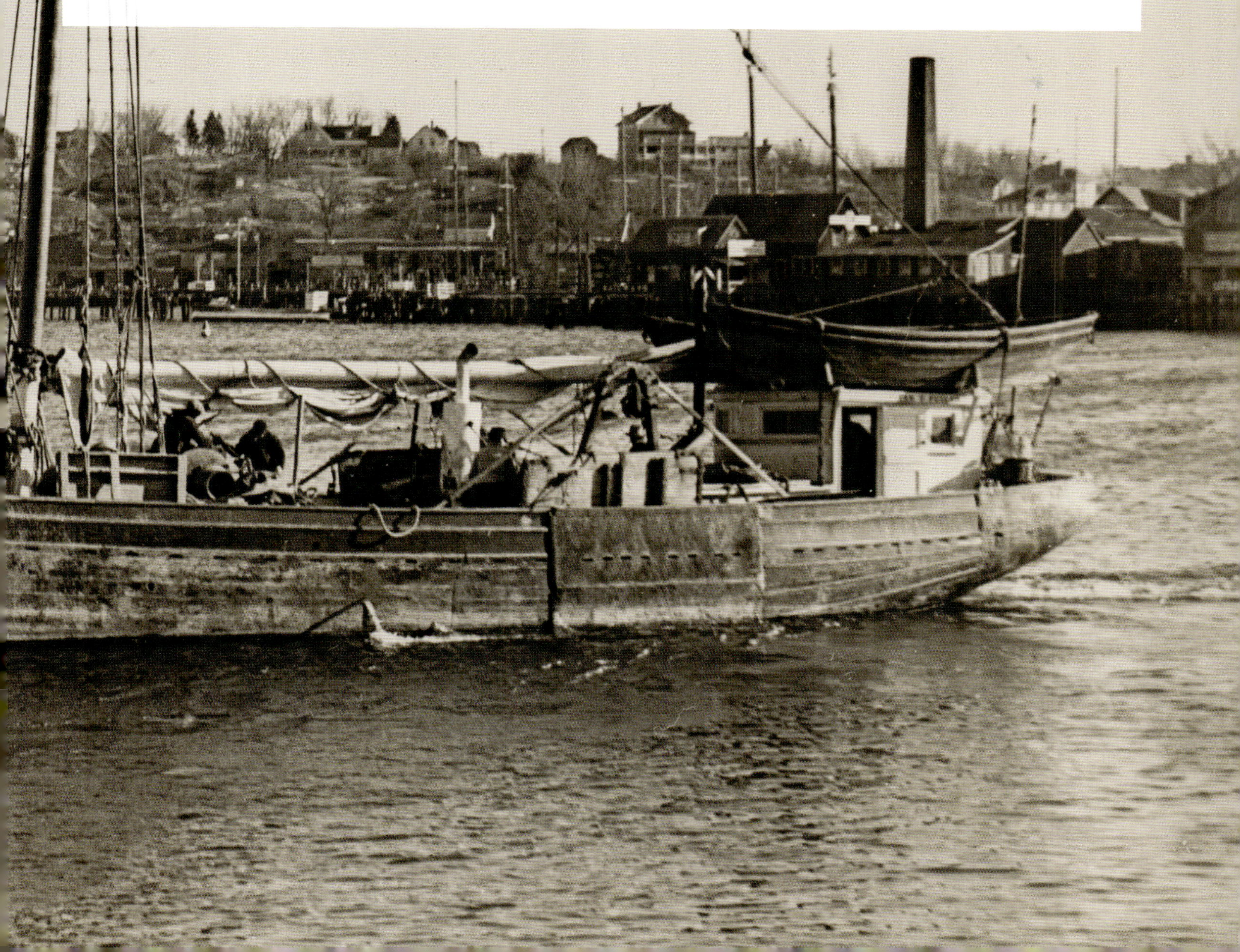

The Viking

In its profile view, the *Viking* resembles many offshore fishing vessels of the late 1920s and early 1930s that were converting from sail power to the internal combustion engine. In the case of the *Viking*, it was a 150-horsepower Wolverine diesel. The 82-foot *Viking,* launched in April 1931, still carried sails, but only for steadying the boat in adverse wind conditions and to get home if the diesel engine shut down. Though the hull bears some semblance to an offshore sailing schooner, the *Viking* has given up the schooner's mast arrangement for a ketch rig.

Of more interest, however, is how she is outfitted for fishing, which was unusual. The *Viking* was a halibut long-liner. The common practice at the time was to set and haul the trawl line from dories, but the *Viking* would be the first to keep the crew aboard, having them set and haul the line from the deck.

What made that possible was the deck-mounted Rowe halibut gurdy, a revolving drum that would haul in the fishing line. The *Viking* was one of the first, if not the first, New England boats to be outfitted with a gurdy. That's probably why it was said the *Viking* "will be watched with great interest by the local fishermen." After all, who wouldn't want to work from the deck of an 82-foot boat, as opposed to being tossed about in a small dory out on the open Atlantic Ocean. The *Viking* was built at the Charles A. Morse & Son yard in Thomaston, Maine, and operated out of New Bedford, Massachusetts.

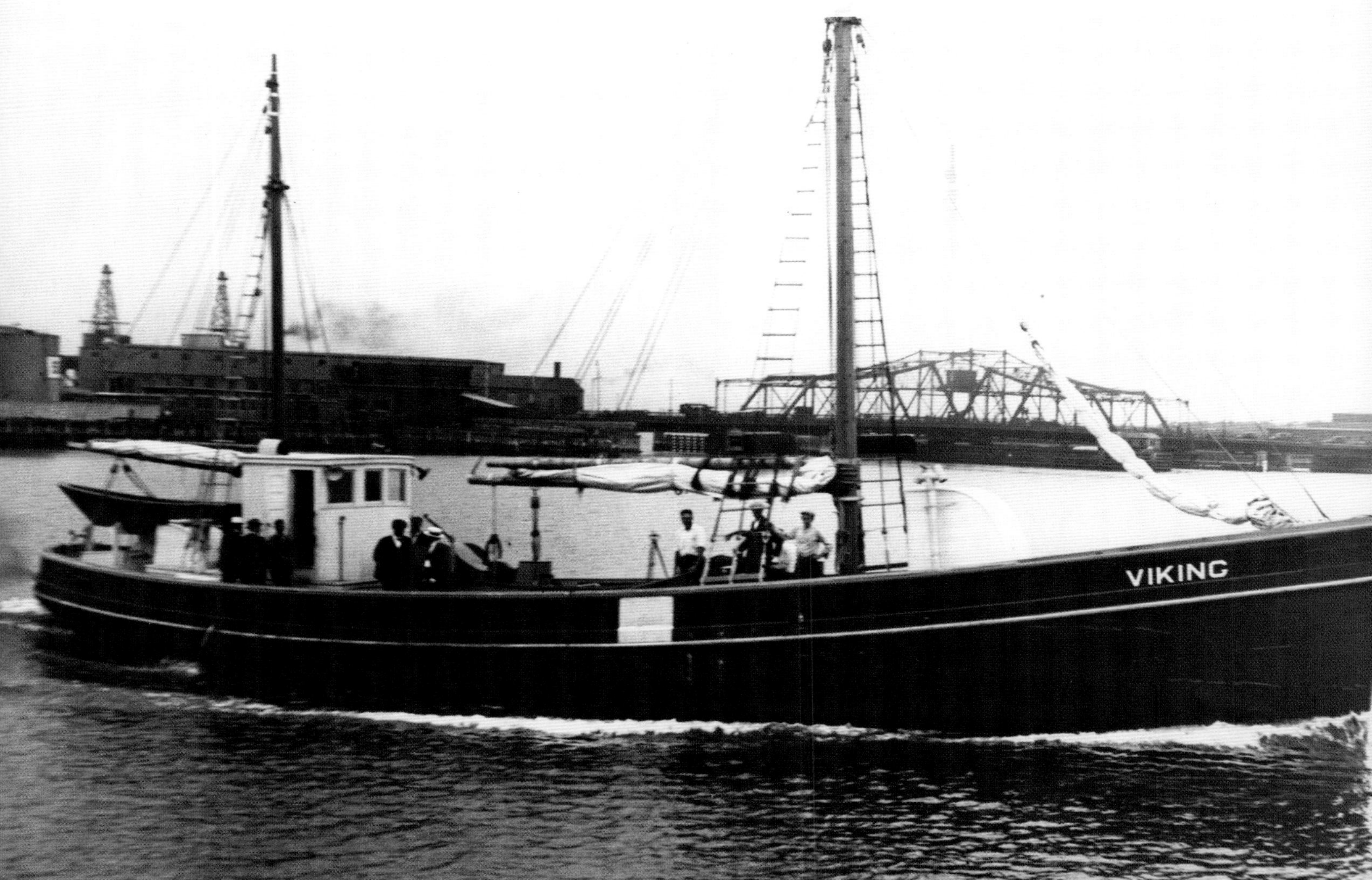

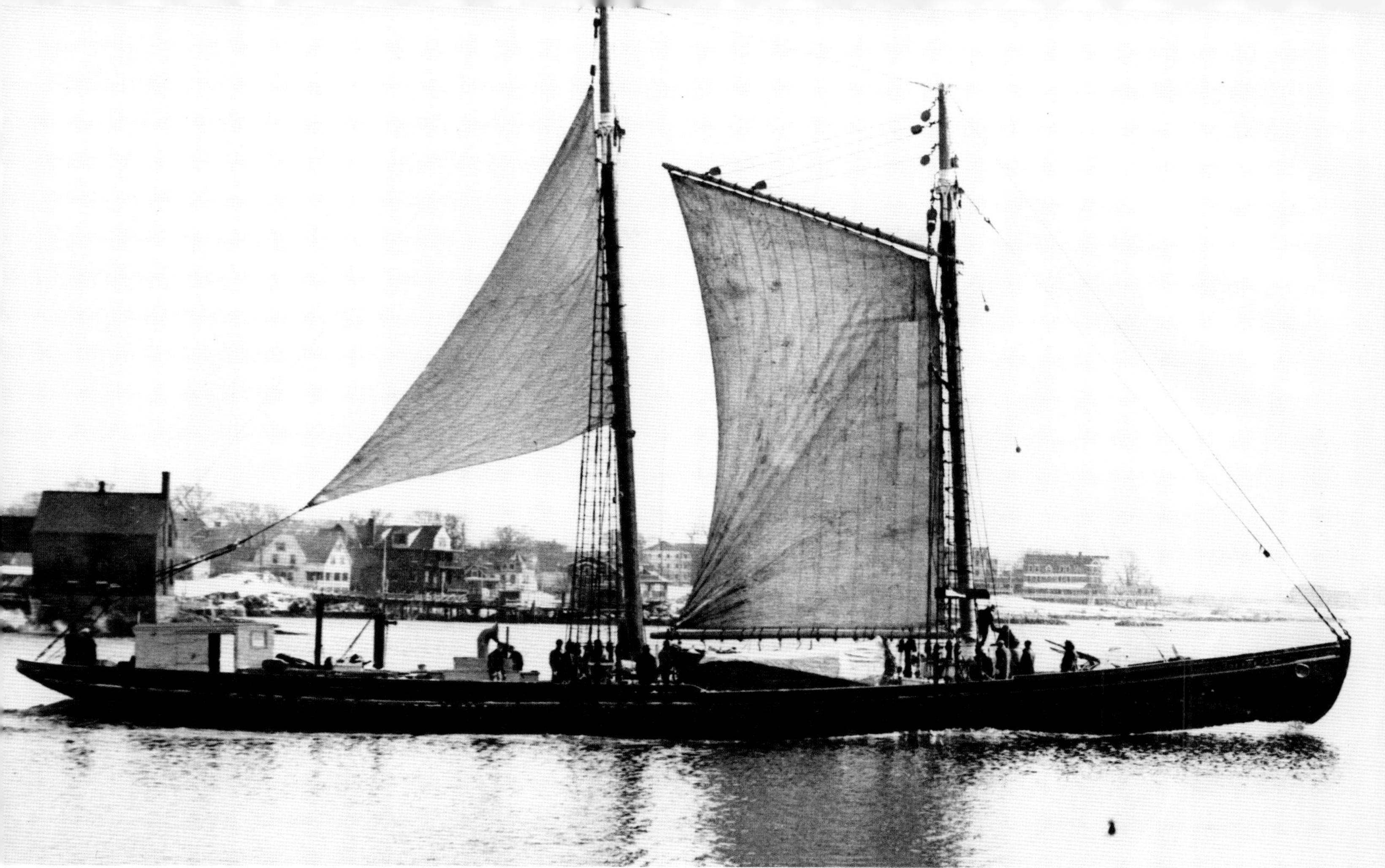

The Joffre

The 105-foot schooner *Joffre* is sliding through calm waters powered by its 200-horsepower diesel engine, but with its foresail up and a steadying sail stretching out from the main mast. The *Joffre*'s skipper must be anticipating more turbulent conditions outside the harbor. The *Joffre*, shown in early 1932, was designed by prominent naval architect Thomas F. McManus and launched from the Arthur D. Story Shipyard in Essex, Massachusetts, on April 16, 1918, for O'Hara Vessels. McManus's design is credited with providing safer and more comfortable conditions for fishermen, while allowing for greater speed to reach fishing grounds faster.

The *Joffre* was originally a mackerel seiner and would also send dories after haddock and halibut. In the late 1930s, she was converted to an eastern-rigged dragger, with the nets pulled in over her sides. On August 9, 1947, while returning to Gloucester from a fishing trip off Nova Scotia, the *Joffre*'s engine caught fire, forcing the ten-man crew to abandon ship before she sank the following morning. Today, the remains of the lower hull structure rest 300 feet down on the Stellwagen Bank National Marine Sanctuary off Massachusetts. The ship was listed on the National Register of Historic Places in 2009.

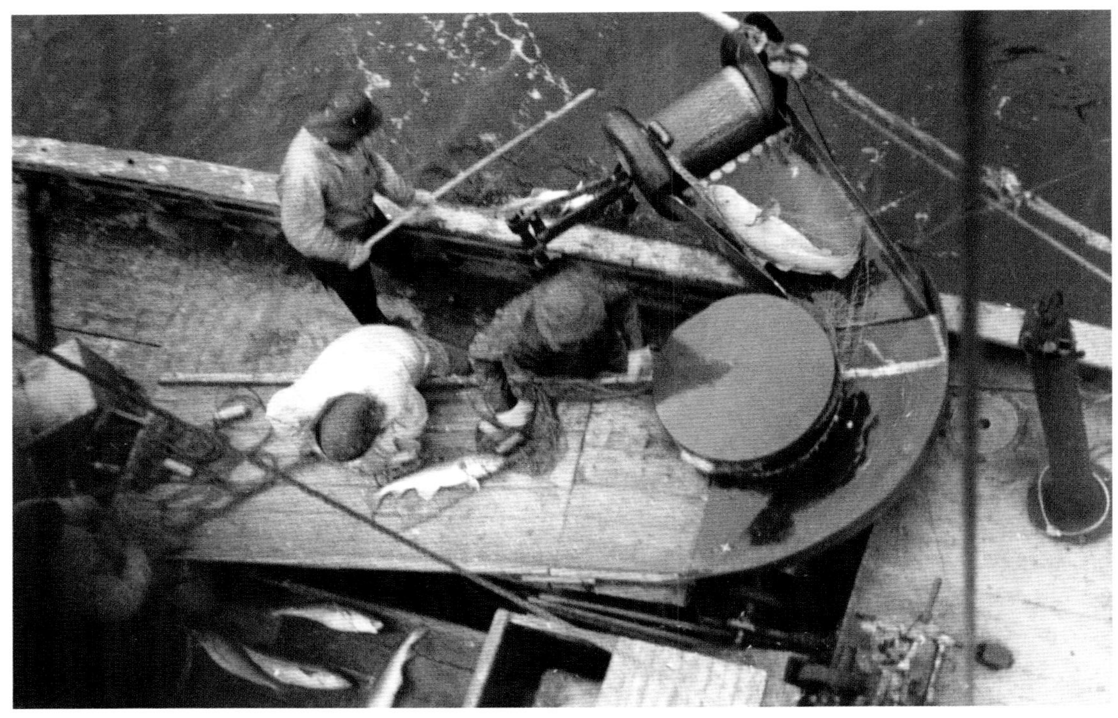

Gillnet Hauling

This photo showing cod, haddock, and pollock being hauled aboard the gillnetter *Naomi Bruce III* dates from the summer of 1934. The 75-foot boat is hauling back fifty-four gillnets that were set the previous day on Jeffries Bank, about thirty-five miles from Gloucester, Massachusetts. The set was one long continuous three-mile line of gillnets, each about 450 feet long and eight feet high with four-inch square mesh, all held to the bottom with small weights and kept upright with aluminum floats.

The gillnets and fish are coming in over a horizontal roller just outside the boat's railing at a speed of about one mile an hour. As a fish emerges from the water, a crewman stands by the railing with a gaff, making sure the fish doesn't fall out of the net back into the ocean. If it does, he'll gaff it and bring it aboard.

A capstan powered by a steam-powered winch known as a donkey engine is pulling the gillnet and fish over the roller and around the capstan. That's where the fish are untangled from the gillnet and then pushed off the table and into the fish hold. Once all the gillnets are hauled back, it's time to set out the dry gillnets that have been stored on the stern in wooden net boxes, three nets to a box, which will be fished the following day. After the new gillnets are positioned, the boat will head back to East Gloucester, where the fish will be unloaded. The wet nets that were hauled will go on reels on the dock to be dried out, and dry gillnets will go on the *Naomi Bruce III*, to be set the following day.

Post-Depression Rebound

Coming out of the Great Depression, the commercial fishing industry began rebounding in the mid-1930s at the New England ports of Boston, Gloucester, and Portland. The following year, orders were placed for nine East Coast steel trawlers, which were valued at about $1.5 million and had many new design features.

New England operators of wooden vessels placed orders for eleven large wooden draggers, seiners, and gillnetters. In the Gulf of Mexico, boatyards reported that they were booked to capacity. This oyster dredge, the *Chesapeake*, was launched in 1936 and is a Chesapeake Bay example of a vessel that was built to take advantage of the changing economic times.

The 100-foot *Chesapeake,* with two dredges on each side, was "the last word in an oyster dredge," according to her captain Rufus Miles. She was built at Johnson & Cochrane in Crittenden, Virginia, with long leaf pine-heart planks, oak frames, and a 60-foot Oregon pine mast.

The *Chesapeake* was powered with a 210-horsepower Fairbanks-Morse diesel engine and had a Fairbanks-Morse 32-volt light plant. A deck hoist used power from the main engine to handle the aft dredges, and power from an independent engine for the forward dredges. The pilothouse was a little fancier than usual, with its interior finished off with California redwood and Gulf cypress. That was exceptional for an oyster dredge.

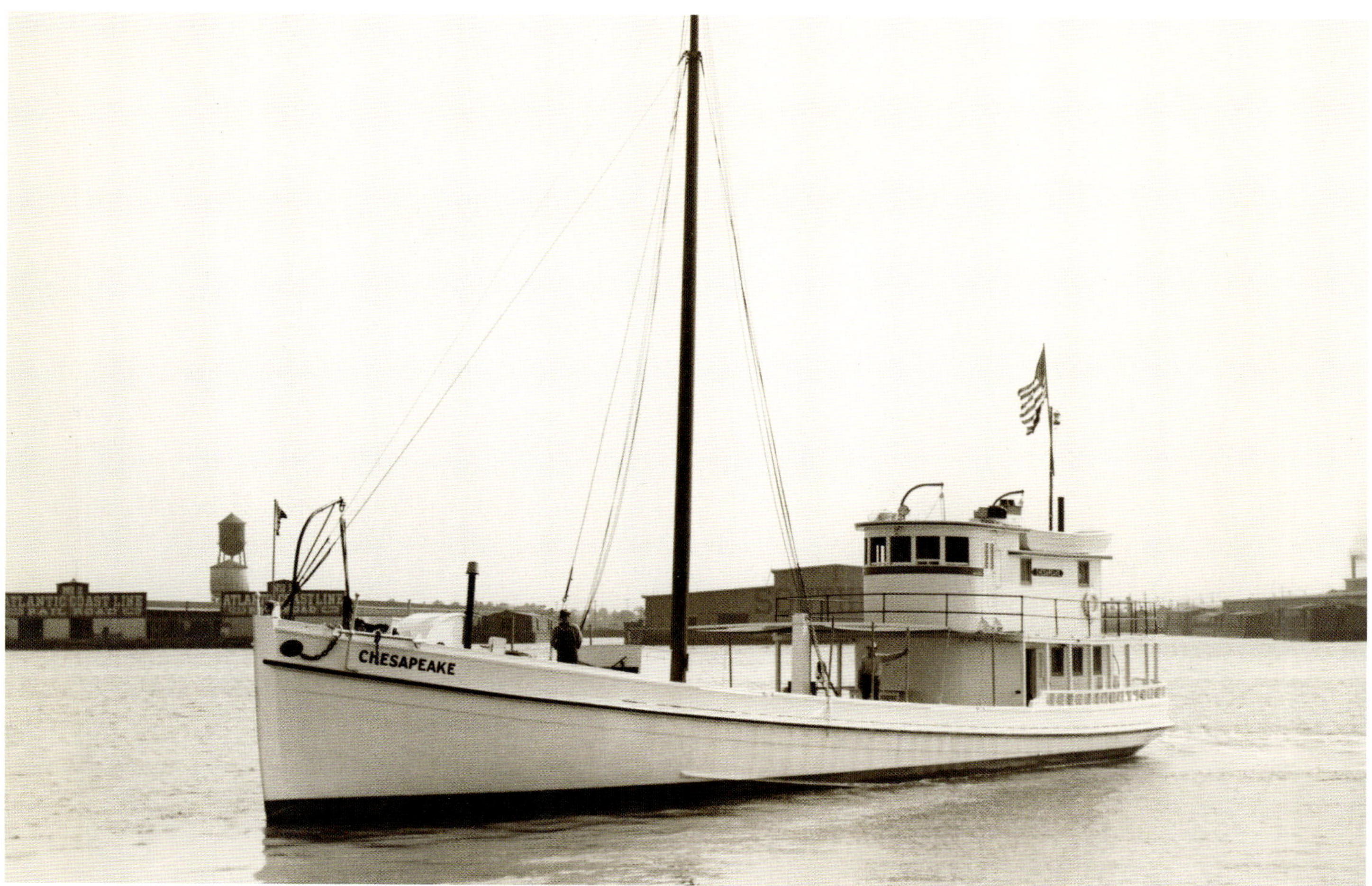

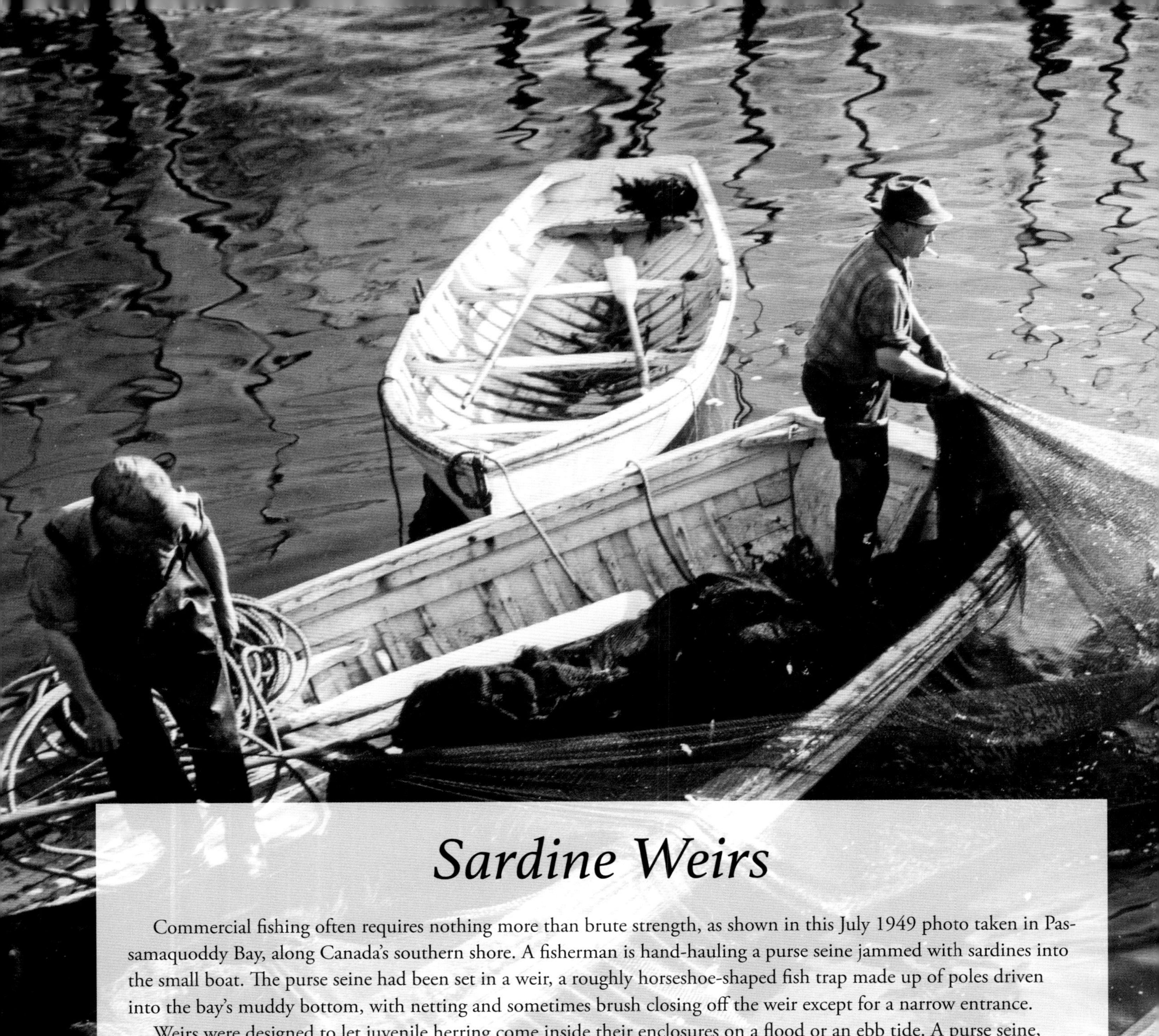

Sardine Weirs

Commercial fishing often requires nothing more than brute strength, as shown in this July 1949 photo taken in Passamaquoddy Bay, along Canada's southern shore. A fisherman is hand-hauling a purse seine jammed with sardines into the small boat. The purse seine had been set in a weir, a roughly horseshoe-shaped fish trap made up of poles driven into the bay's muddy bottom, with netting and sometimes brush closing off the weir except for a narrow entrance.

Weirs were designed to let juvenile herring come inside their enclosures on a flood or an ebb tide. A purse seine, with weights on the bottom and floats at the top, was then dropped in the weir and encircled the herring. After bagging up the fish, fishermen would pull their catch into a small boat before using a dip net to scoop the catch into a sardine carrier. These herring were taken to the Connor Bros. processing plant in Black's Harbor, New Brunswick, where the fish were packed and sold as sardines. At the end of the 1940s, Connors Bros. bought sardines from more than two hundred weirs, mostly owned by fishermen, and produced over five hundred thousand cases of sardines annually.

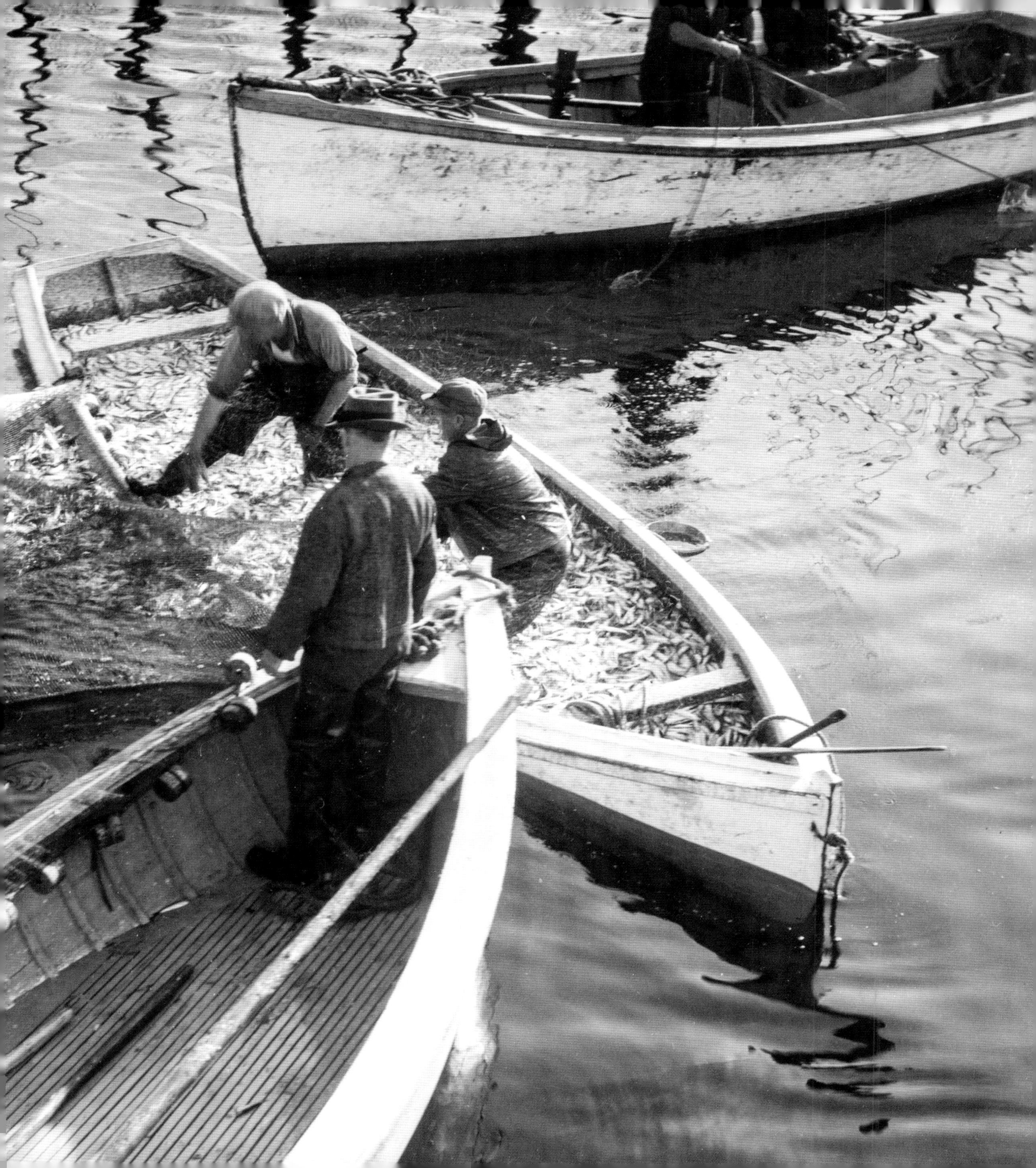

Tonging for Clams

In the Great South Bay along the southern coast of Long Island, New York, clams were never dredged. Rather, the gear of choice for most clammers was tongs, like this fisherman is holding in 1940. Operating out of a small anchored boat, clammers worked the two long wooden handles with a scissor-style motion, allowing the basket-like jaws at the end of the tongs to dig up clams that were two to six inches into the bottom. Then the jaws were closed, retaining the clams and allowing them to be brought to the surface.

Each clammer typically had three or four sets of tongs, each a little different, to be used according to the water depth and type of bottom. A clammer's average daily catch was six bushels, for which he received $1 per bushel. There were over three thousand clammers working the waters of the Great South Bay, producing about five hundred thousand bushels of clams annually.

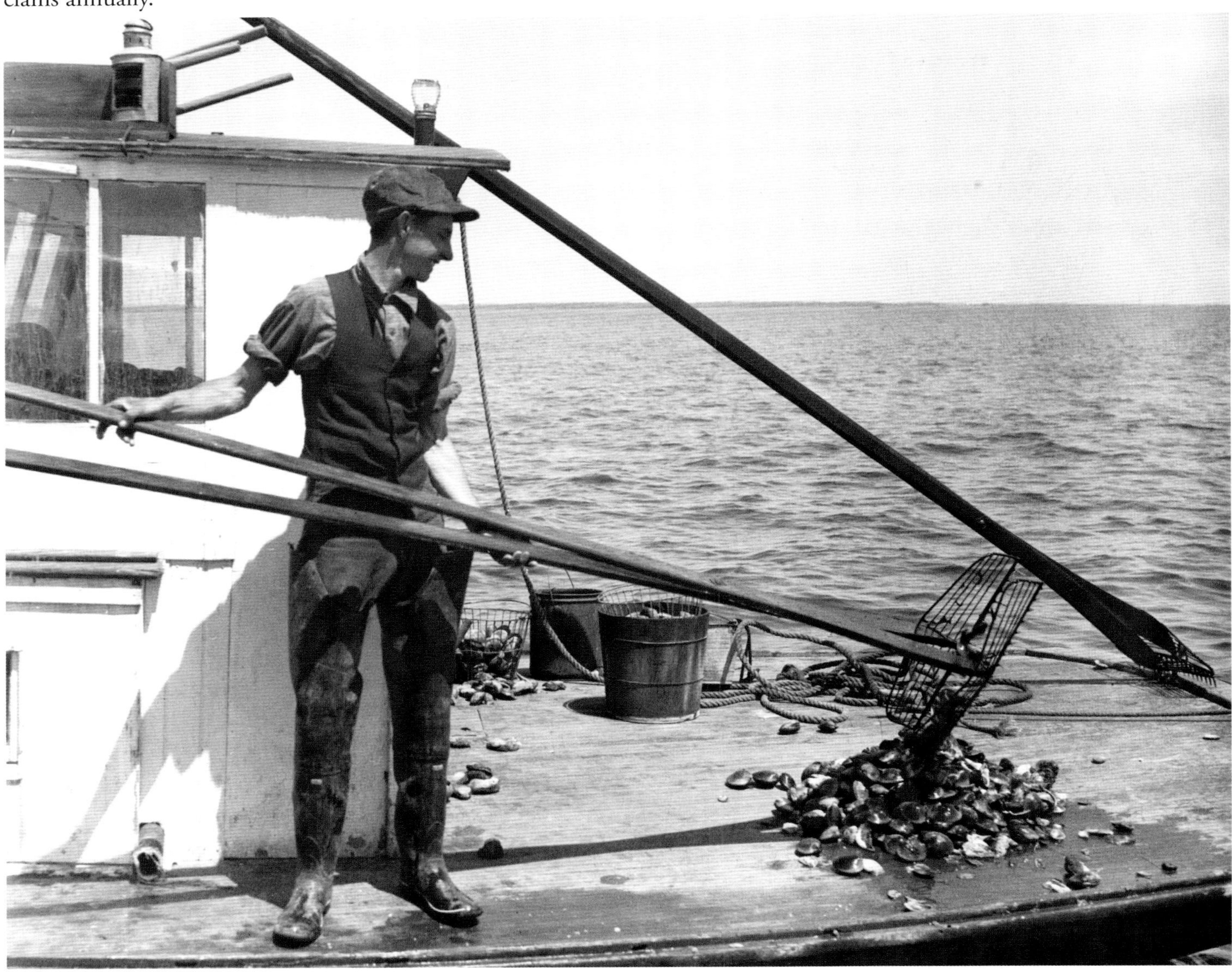

Shark Liver Frenzy

The liver inside the blue shark that is being handed across the deck on the *Elsie A.* out of Eureka, California, is the reason a lot of fishermen in California, Florida, and British Columbia started seeing sharks as lucrative targets rather than nuisances in early 1941. Shark liver oil was the driving force after it was determined to be a rich source of vitamin A, which was in high demand due to a reduction in vitamin A imports during World War II. From San Francisco to northern Oregon, tons of blue, soupfin, and cow sharks were landed only for their livers, which were worth $1 a pound. The cow shark, the largest of the three species, yielded a liver between 14 and 18 pounds.

Sharks that previously would have been thrown away after being caught became the targeted species, with salmon, rock cod, and flounder an afterthought. A fisherman could make several thousand dollars on a single fishing trip.

In San Francisco, fish dealers were offering $250 a ton for sharks, a 500 percent jump. The shark liver frenzy even pulled in everyday people who had no connection to commercial fishing, but who jumped in and became fishermen because of the potential financial bonanza. Across the country, the booming demand also reeled in Florida, with the industry jumping from $5,000 to $100,000 a year.

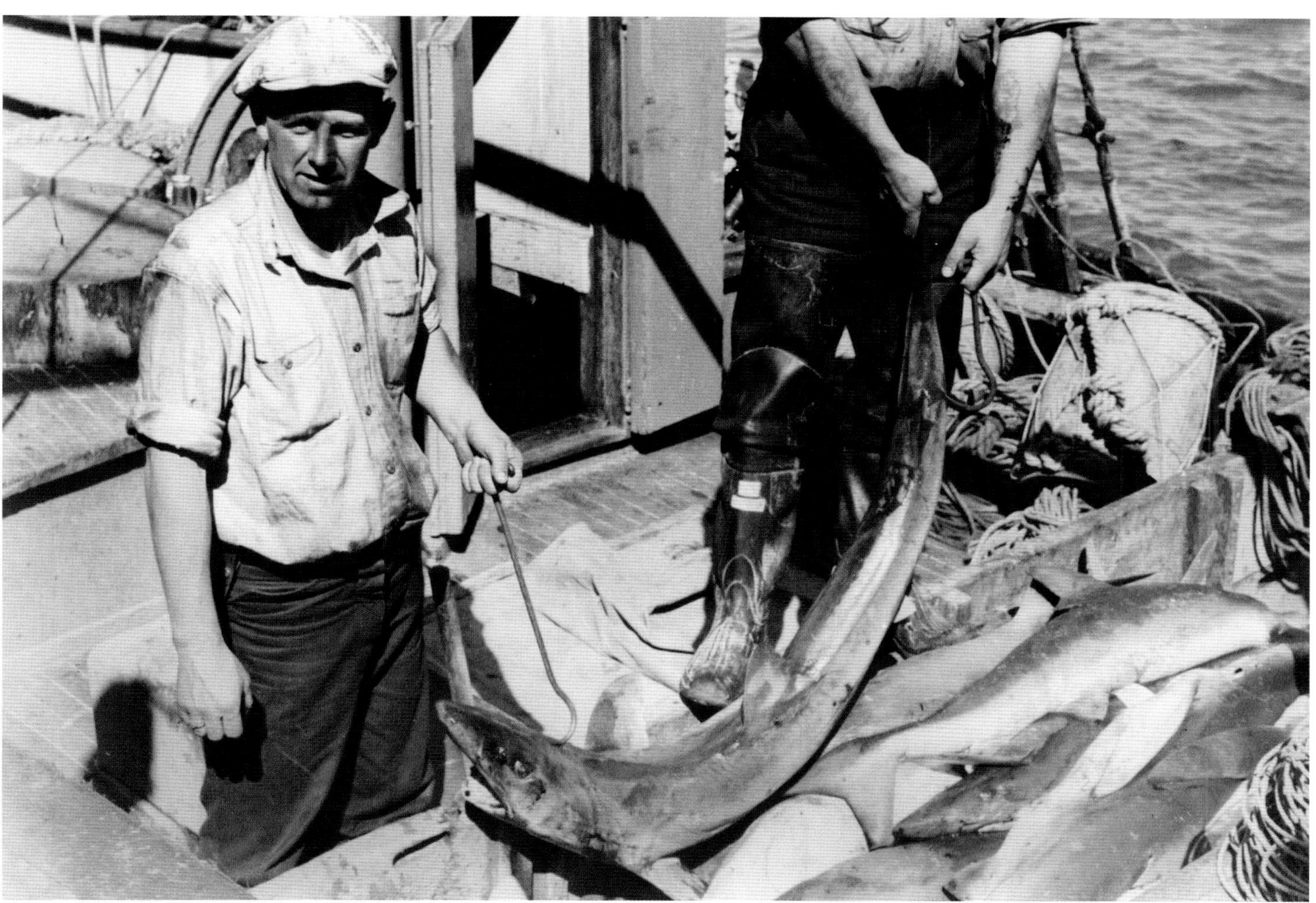

"Proud Sailors"

Maine lobster boats like *The Swan*, shown here on Moosabec Reach between Beals Island and the mainland town of Jonesport, were known as "proud sailors" because they were pleasing to look at and moved quickly and easily through the water. Being long for their beam, they were also known as "razor cases" or "sharpshooters."

Beals Island boatbuilder Vinal Beal and his son, Osmond, built *The Swan* in 1954. Her generous sheer and diamond-shaped windows are characteristic of lobster boats of the 1950s and 1960s. At that time, Beals Island and Jonesport were the epicenter of Maine's wooden lobster boat-building industry.

The Swan was Osmond's first boat and was initially named the *Barbara J.* Shortly after she was completed, however, he sold the boat to his cousin, Archie Alley Jr., who renamed her *The Swan*. At 33 feet, *The Swan* wasn't an unusual size for that era. With a Buick gasoline engine somewhere in the range of 200 horsepower, *The Swan* had a top speed between 28 and 30 miles per hour.

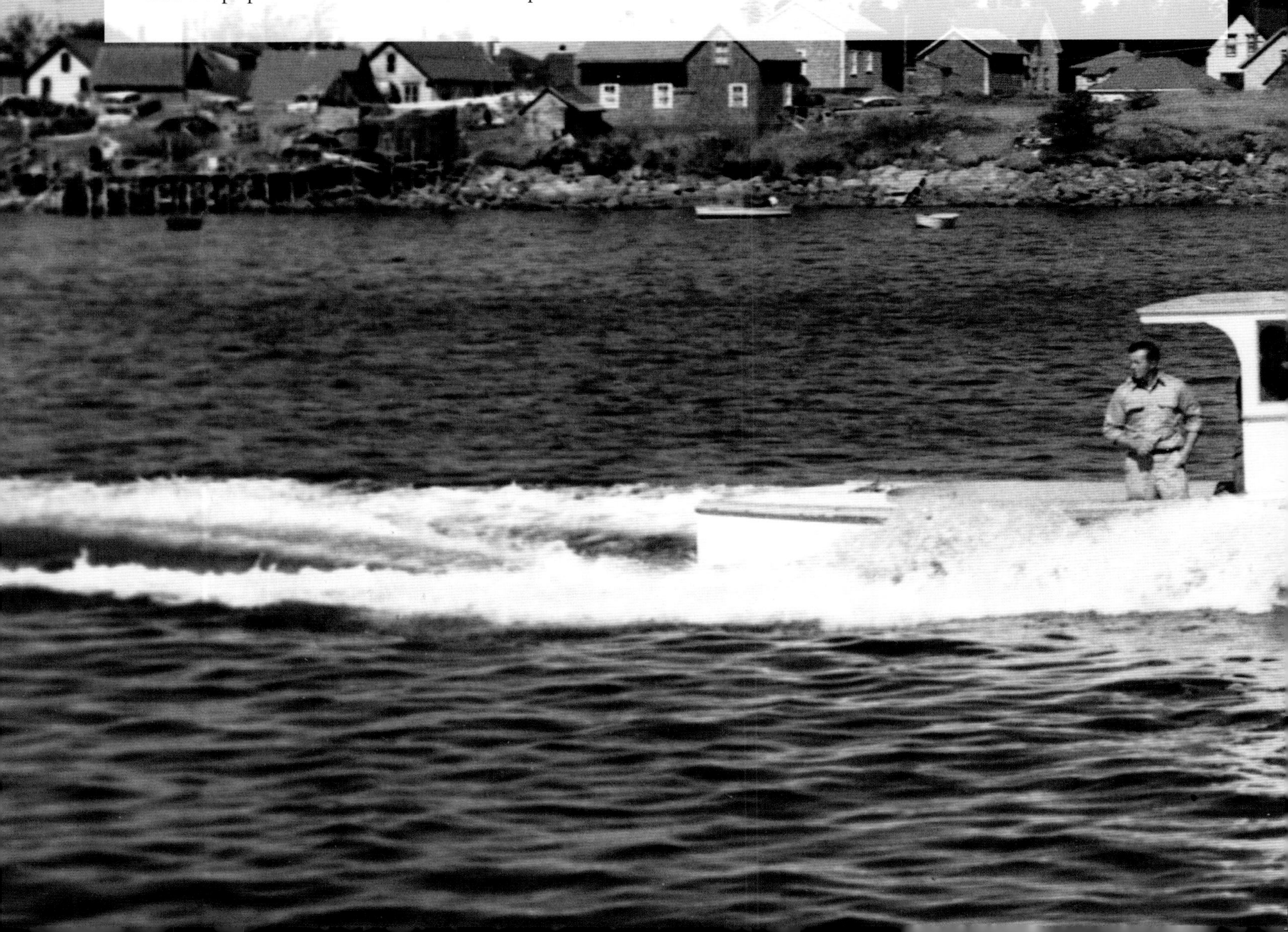

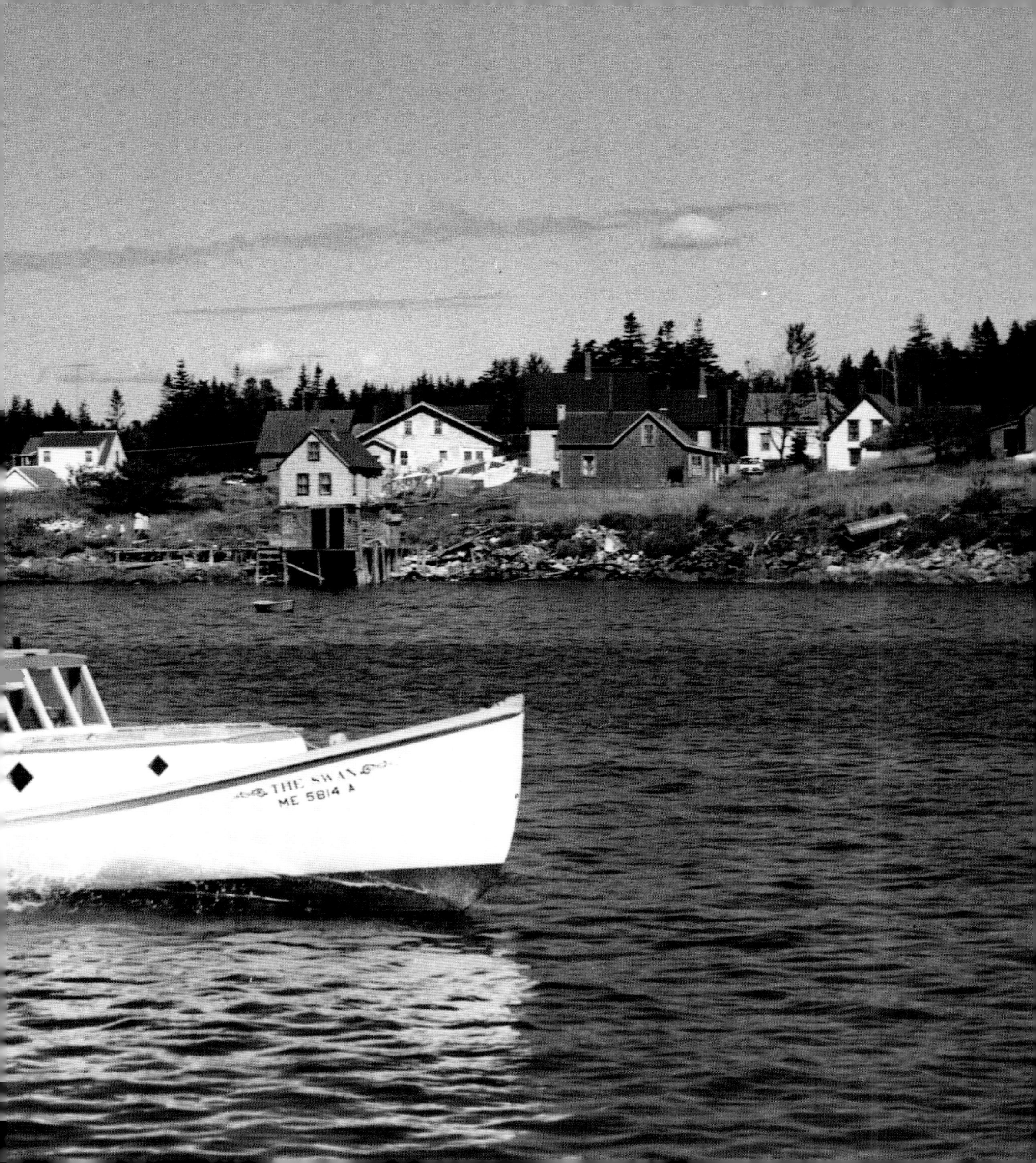

THE SWAN
ME 5814 A

Lobster Boat Races

Maine lobstermen didn't live for work alone. When they weren't hauling their lobster traps during the summer and fall harvest seasons, many of them raced for bragging rights and prizes in ports all along Maine's coast. At first, racing among lobstermen was an informal affair that began more than a century ago when lobstermen were hauling traps by hand from small rowing and sailing boats. If two lobstermen were going out to haul traps in the same area it might be: "You goin' haul? Well, I can beat you," and off the two boats would go, with nothing more on the line than the bragging rights.

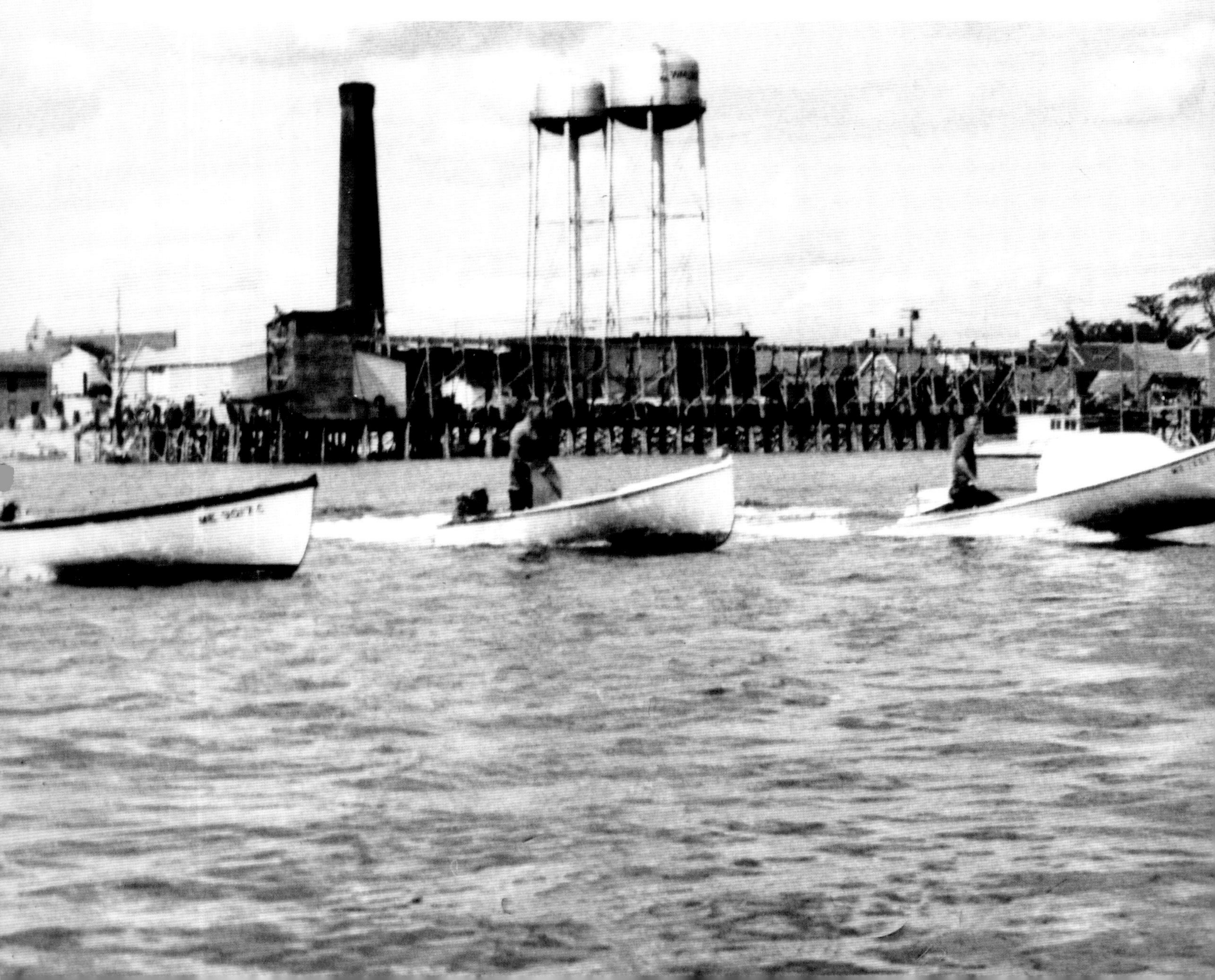

Things grew more intense and noisier when internal combustion engines replaced sails and oars. In the 1960s, races started to be officially organized in several harbors, with classes based on a boat's length, horsepower, and whether it was gas or diesel powered.

The races shown in these two photos were part of the 1964 Labor Day Races held at Moosabec Reach, which cuts between Jonesport and Beals Island. In the background photo, five outboard skiffs (which had classes of their own) look to be pretty close together at the start of their race. In the photo below, Archie Alley Jr.'s 33-foot *The Swan* with an eight-cylinder Buick gas engine has a winning lead over Alfred Beal. *The Swan* was probably hitting 30 miles per hour. In the background photo the skiffs were going even faster.

Through the years, the races have turned into action-packed contests where boats with souped-up engines scream and roar at speeds of 60 miles per hour and more, leaving roostertails and rolling swells in their wakes as spectators line the shores and watch from boats that crowd the race courses. Boats that race in the World's Fastest Recreational Lobster Boat class might have 1,000- and 2,500-horsepower engines that can hit more than 60 miles per hour—with a record speed of 72.8 miles per hour.

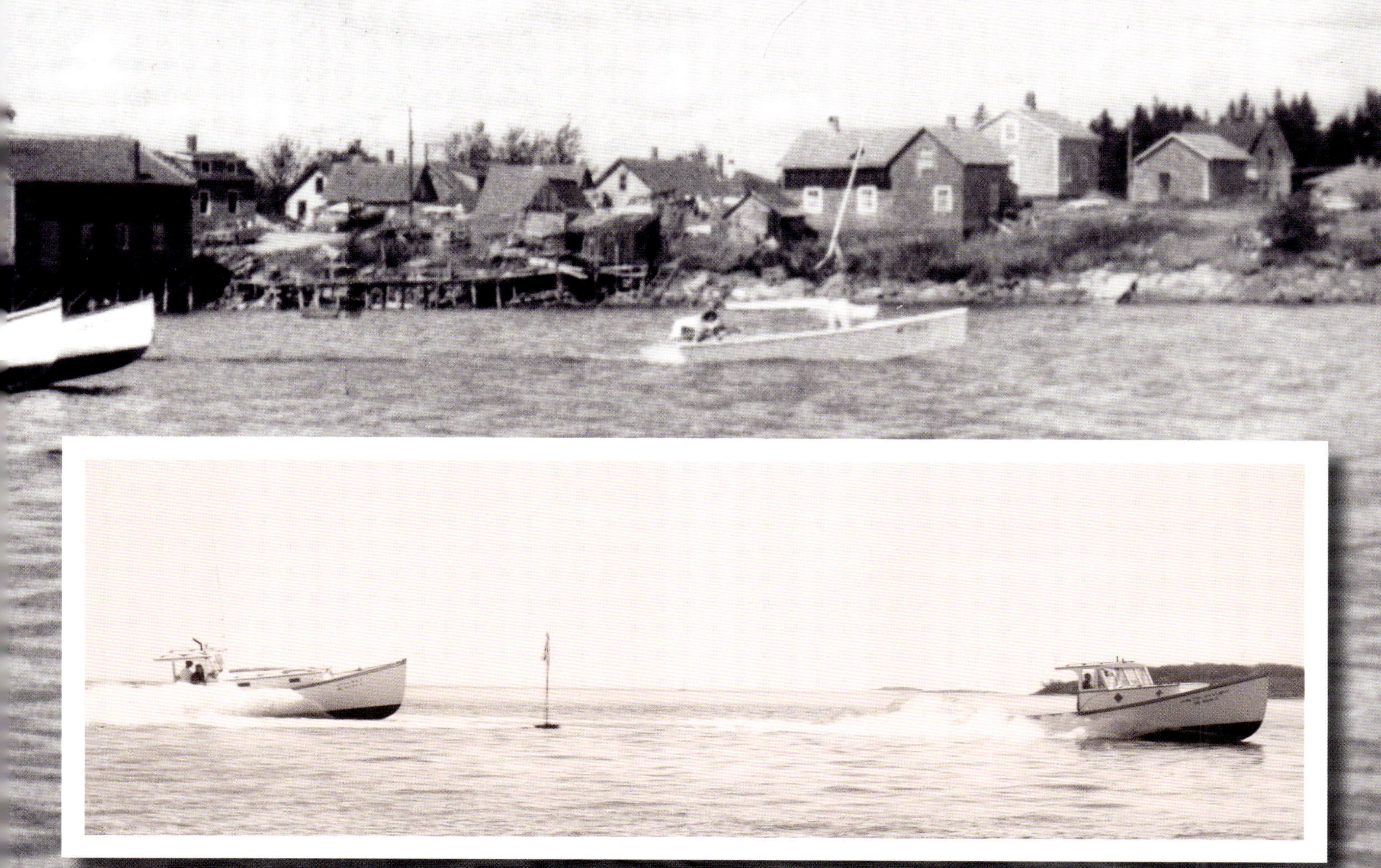

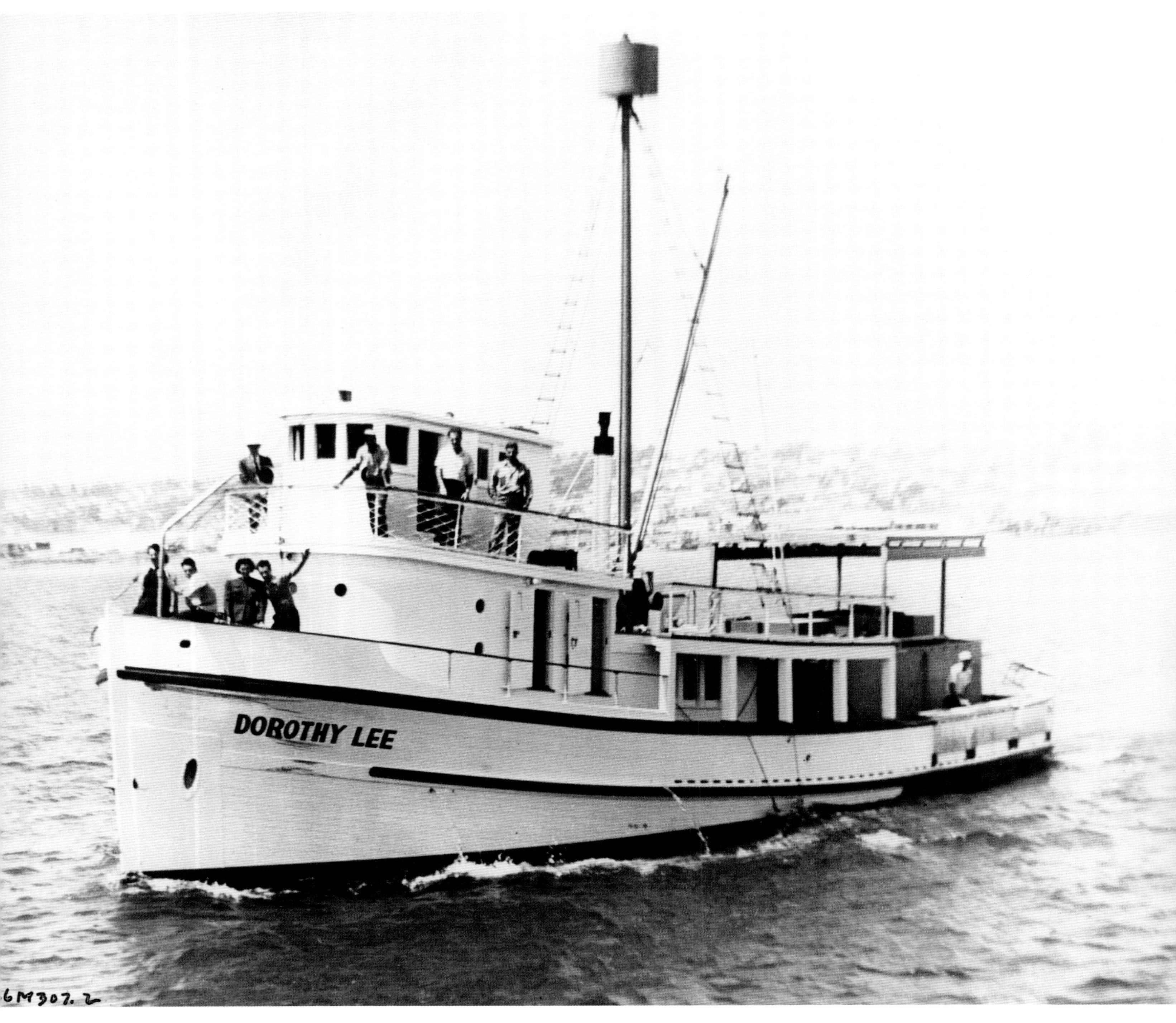
DOROTHY LEE

The Dorothy Lee

Throughout most of the 1900s, San Diego dominated the tuna industry. By 1927, the Southern California port was billed as the "tuna capital of the Pacific," with thousands employed in catching, canning, and marketing tuna. So it's not surprising that a new design for a tuna boat would make its introduction in the San Diego tuna fleet. The *Dorothy Lee* (probably named after the 1930s actress of the same name) was built in 1941. At 78 feet, she was said to be the largest tuna boat in the San Diego fleet. Besides her size, what set her off from other tuna boats was the fully raised deck that extended back to the bait boxes.

This was a pole fishing tuna boat, on which fishermen used eight- to nine-foot bamboo poles with handholds fashioned into the poles. There would be a heavy cotton line about six feet long with a leader and hook. The chum, or bait, kept in the bait boxes would be distributed over the stern to lure the tuna close to the boat.

The *Dorothy Lee* was built to carry 85 to 90 tons of tuna, which was frozen by ammonia coils and crushed ice. The refrigeration system was pulsed by a five-by-five-foot ice machine, driven by a 15-horsepower motor that would frost several thousand feet of ammonia coils in the main hold and deck tank. In the mid-1940s fishermen got $200 to $800 a ton for yellowfin tuna.

The *Dorothy Lee* had a five-thousand-mile cruising range with six thousand gallons of diesel fuel that allowed her to spend a couple of months at sea at a time. She was powered by a 200-horsepower, five-cylinder diesel engine that, when fully loaded, gave her a top speed of just under nine knots.

Great Lakes Fisherwoman

Most fishermen working the waters of Michigan's Saginaw Bay in 1965, when this photo was taken, knew Irene Litner as "Catfish Kate." Litner had gained the nickname over her previous twenty-eight years fishing for catfish, although she preferred "Irene," the name stenciled on her hat.

Litner started fishing because she liked the lifestyle and freedom of fishing on Lake Huron. At the time she was featured in *National Fisherman*, she was believed to be the only woman fishing commercially in Michigan. She ran her catfish lines with fifteen hundred to two thousand hooks out of a 16-foot, open aluminum boat powered with a 40-horsepower outboard.

In good times, Irene landed 400 pounds of catfish per day, but by the mid-1960s it was likely less than 100 pounds. Despite the decreased revenue, Catfish Kate wasn't ready to give it up: "I've been at it so long I hate to quit."

While the domestic commercial fishing industry is best known for fisheries in the Atlantic, the Gulf of Mexico, and the Pacific, fish such as trout, perch, and whitefish are among the many species that have been harvested commercially in the Great Lakes going back hundreds of years.

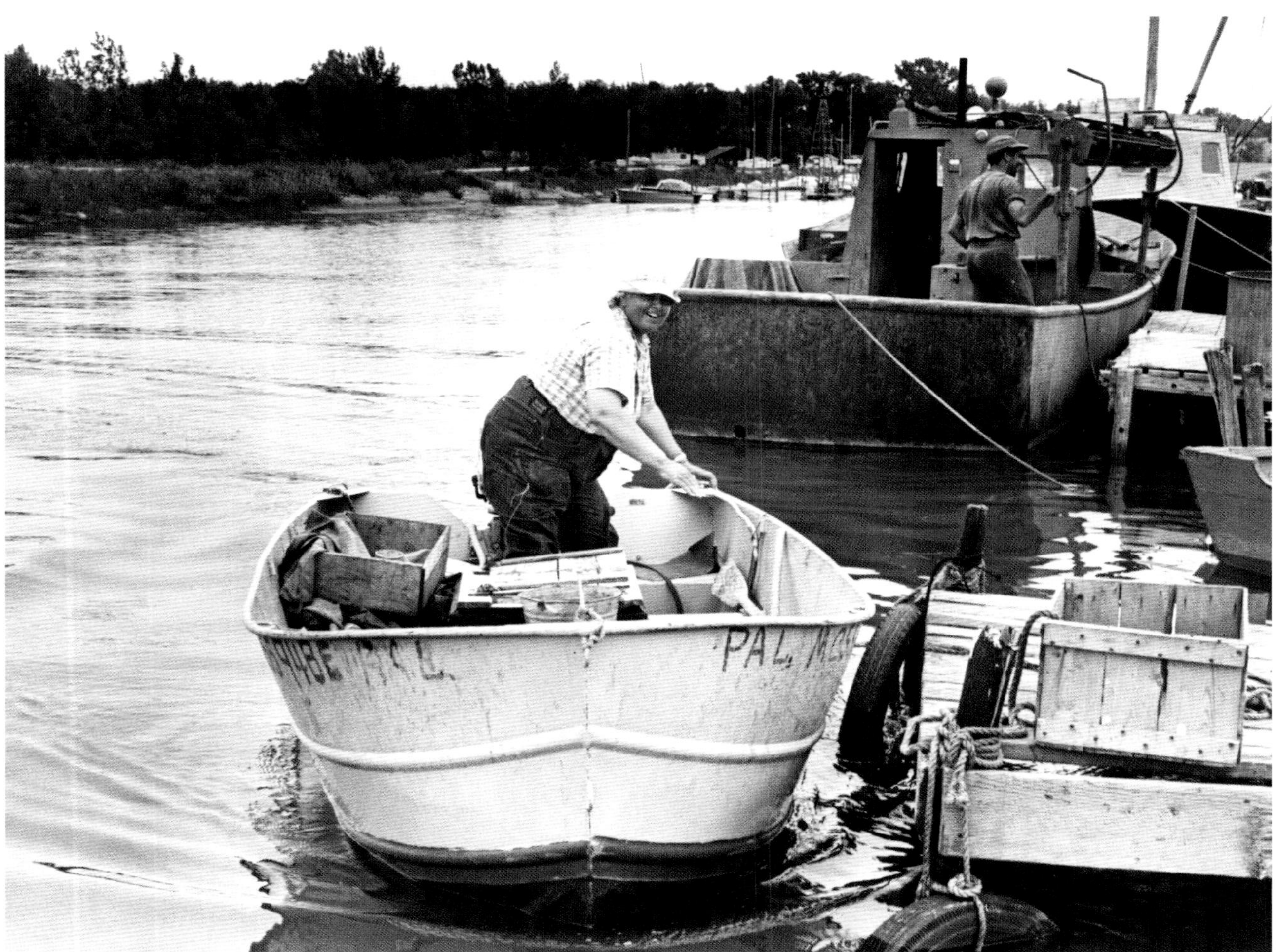

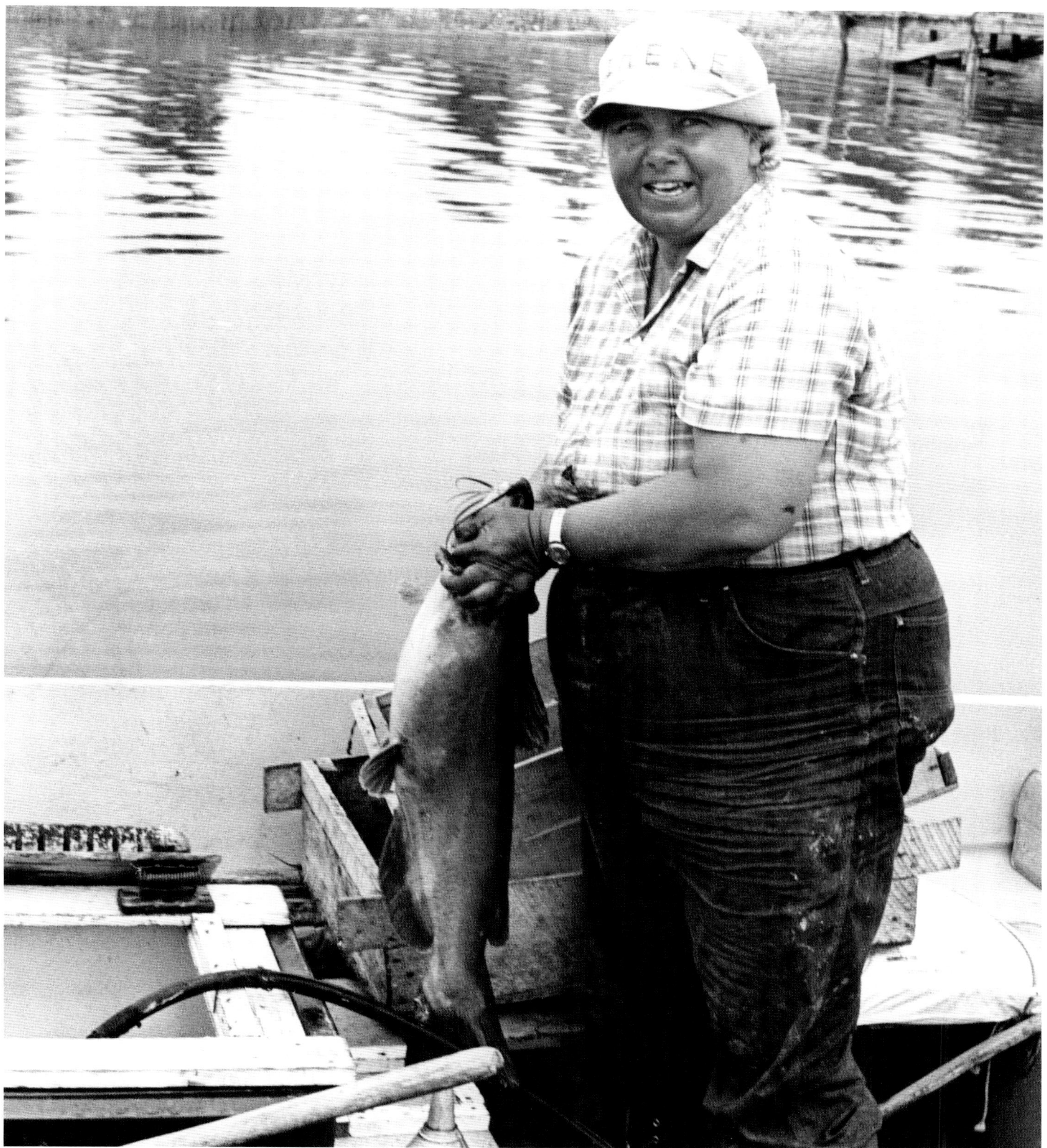

Scallop Bonanza

A crewman on the Canadian scalloper *Pat and Judy II* looks bemused as he stares aft, perhaps trying to figure out how to maneuver through the huge pile of scallops before him. There doesn't appear to be solid deck planking to walk on, only scallops, although you can bet he's not complaining.

During the summer of 1965 after working a stretch of the ocean floor that was one mile long and three quarters of a mile wide along the Middle Ground Bank, also known as the Stellwagen Bank, which seperates Massachusetts Bay from the Gulf of Maine, the *Pat and Judy II* pulled into the docks in Lunenberg, Nova Scotia, with 1,056 bags of scallops weighing 42,000 pounds.

It was the second largest catch ever landed at Lunenburg, behind only the 49,000 pounds that were offloaded two years before. It was also the largest haul of scallops ever taken from the Middle Ground Bank. Previous trips had been in the range of 20,000 pounds.

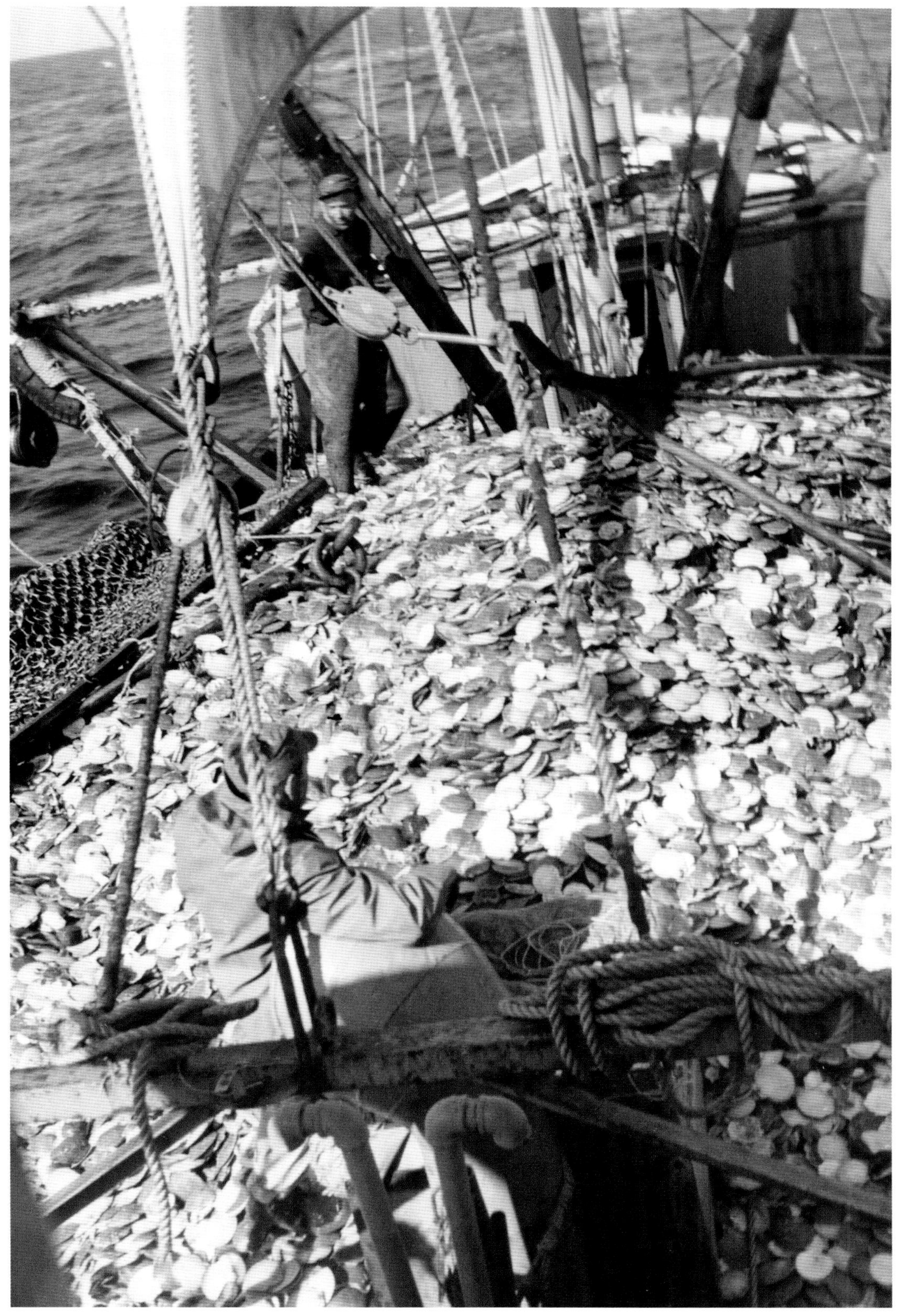

Oregon Surf Dories

The salmon trollers of the late 1960s in Oregon didn't fit into the historical meaning of the word "dory"—a double-ended boat powered by oars. Nonetheless, at one time it did describe the Oregon surf dory that became popular along a stretch of the Oregon coast. Once fishermen deemed outboards reliable, the transom or "square-stern dory" outfitted with a large outboard or opulent sterndrive became the boat of choice. Trolling poles and power gurdies to haul in the fish that were hooked created an efficient salmon-fishing machine that fishermen could tow behind a pickup truck.

The favored launching site for dory trollers in Oregon was near Pacific City. The writer of a dory trolling story in *National Fisherman*'s October 1968 issue counted 238 empty trailers on the beach. To launch their boats, fishermen would back their trucks with dory-loaded trailers into the water around four in the morning and slam on the brakes, causing the boats to slide off and into the water. They then headed out to sea without spotlights to see the oncoming waves.

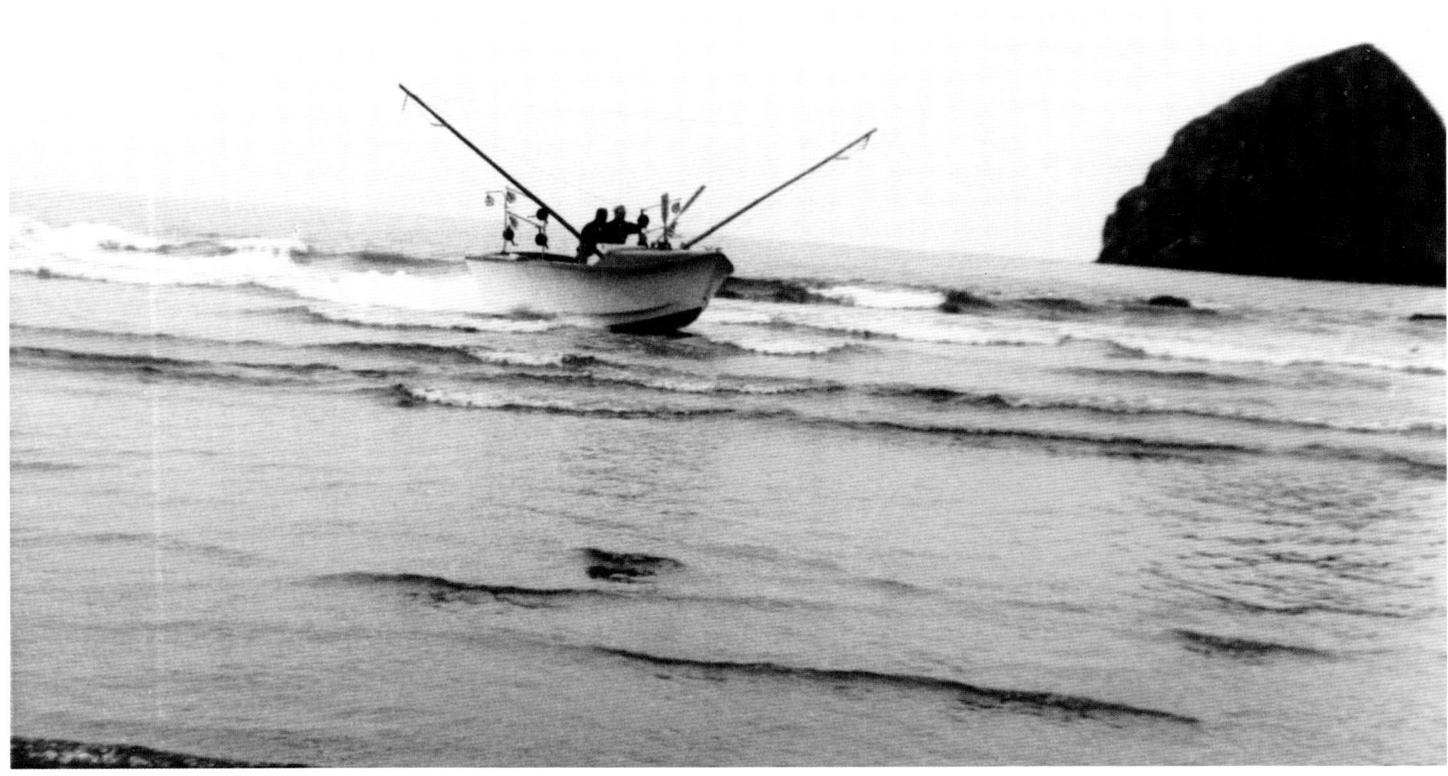

Blessing of the Fleet

Bayou La Batre, Alabama's Blessing of the Fleet, originated in 1945, and judging how the shrimp trawler *Catherine Suzanne* is decked out with hundreds of colorful flags, it was still going strong when this photo was taken in July 1972. The *Catherine Suzanne* won the title for the best decorated double-rigged boat. Nearly one hundred gaily decorated boats attended the event, parading down and up the bayou before being blessed by the local Catholic bishop. During the blessing, a cross and anchor-shaped flower arrangement was dedicated to those who had been lost at sea. About twenty thousand people attended the event in 1972, despite intermittent rain squalls.

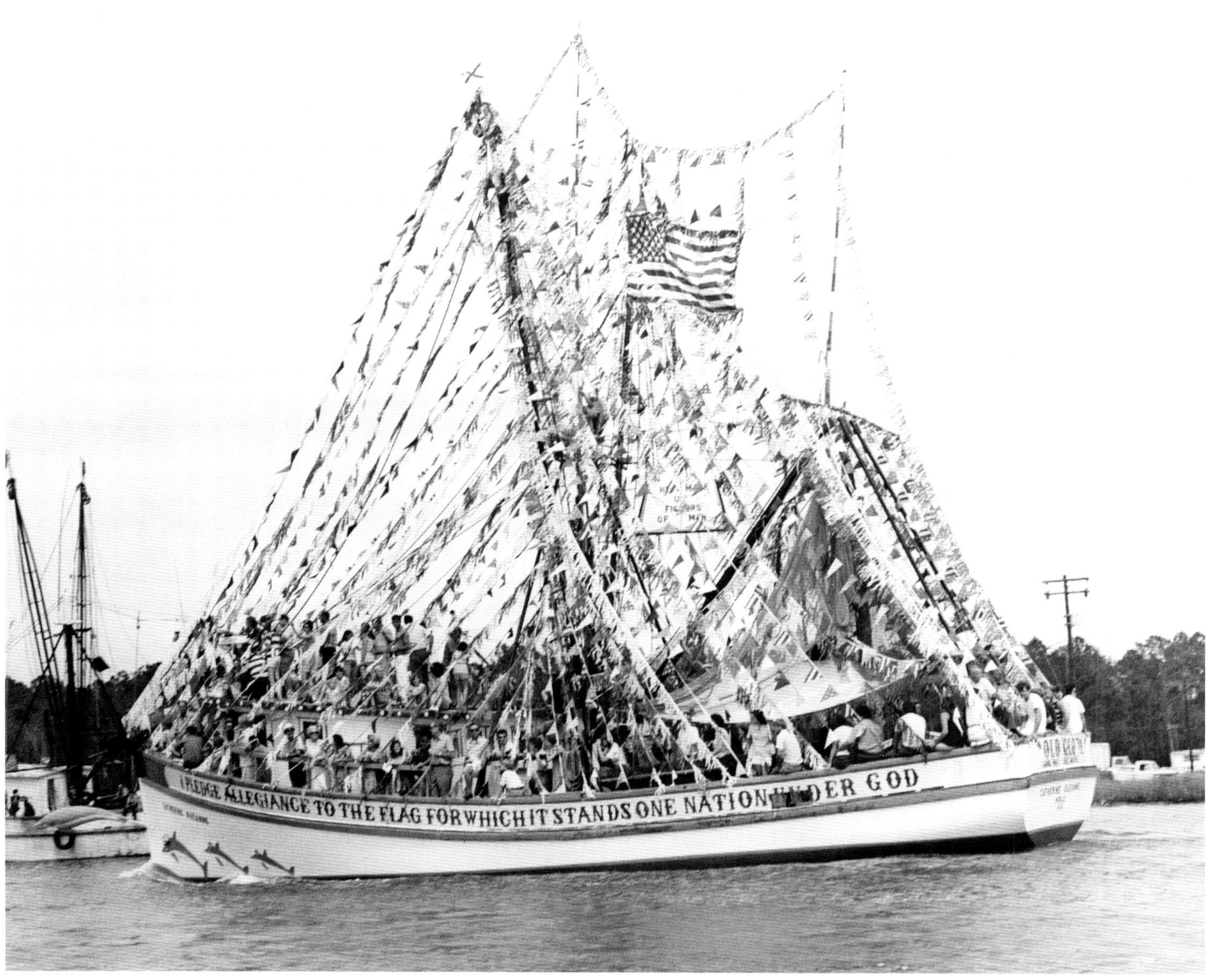

King Crabs

It's the 1978 Bering Sea king crab season, and two crewmen on the 110-foot crabber *American Star* open a just-hauled king crab pot, letting the crabs slide out to be sorted—legal-size males retained and small male and female crabs returned to the sea.

Each pot is hauled from the bottom after its pot warp, whose position is marked with a buoy on the ocean's surface, is brought aboard and placed between the two sheaves on the Marco hydraulic pot hauler on the left. As soon as the pot breaks the surface, a winch cable with a hook lifts the pot aboard and sets it on the pot ramp, where the deck hands let the king crabs slide out.

If crabbing is good, the pot is baited with herring, bottom fish, or skate; returned to the sea; and allowed to soak for a day or several days. If fishing isn't good, the pots are stacked on deck, and moved to a more favorable location.

The *American Star*'s crab pots, made of steel reinforcing rod, measured seven feet by seven feet by three feet, weighed 650 pounds and were fished at depths of 180 to 360 feet. The vessel landed over one million pounds in the 1978 season.

King crabbing has been called America's most dangerous fishing industry. Haul aboard a 650-pound pot with a lot of king crabs in it—say a thousand pounds—in rolling seas and high winds, while trying to stay upright on a pitching, rolling deck, and it's clear to see how easy it is to be severely injured.

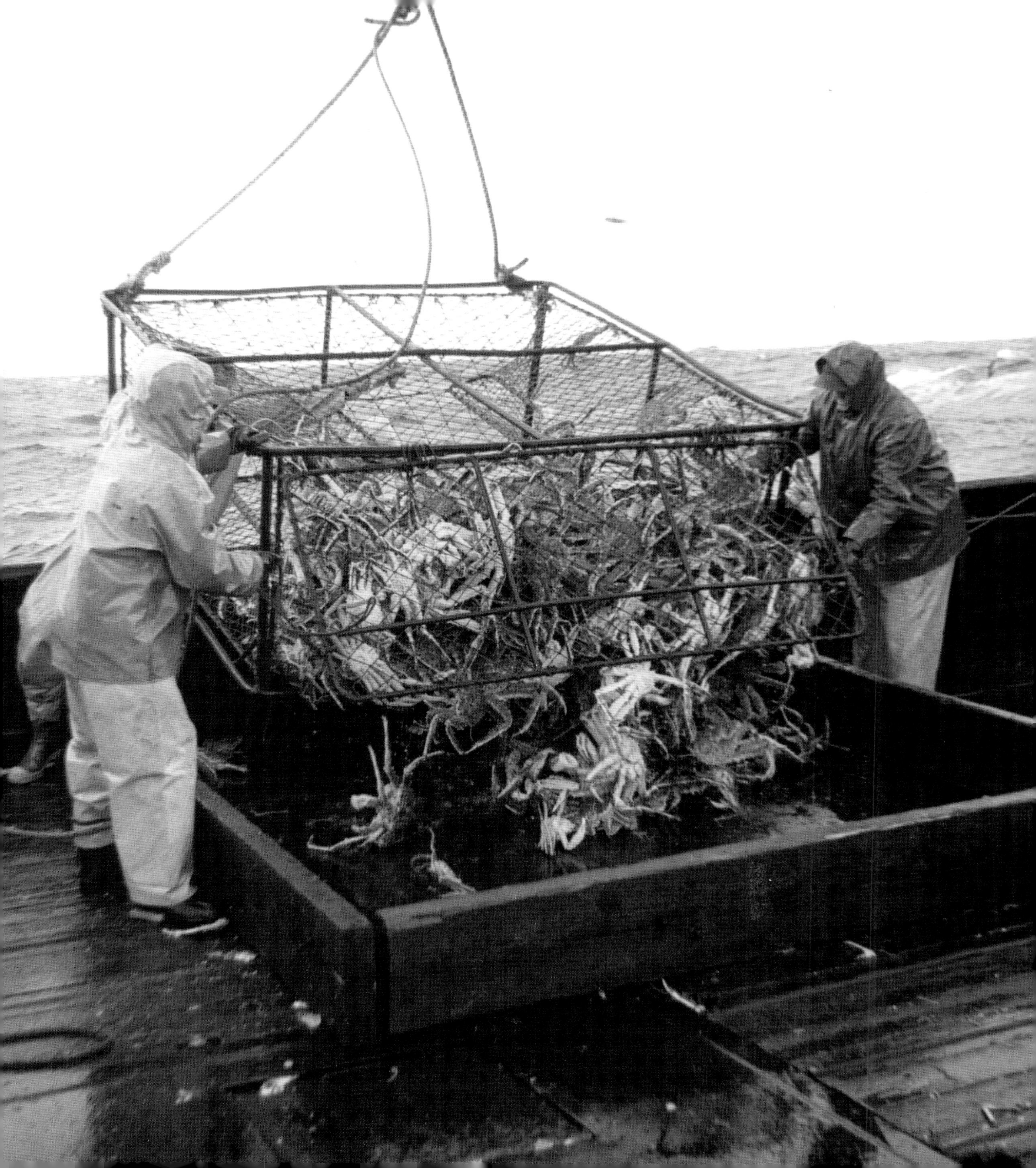

Japanese Trawler

Say you are caught fishing where you aren't supposed to be and the authorities find 30 pounds of illegally landed seafood in your possession. What do you think would be a reasonable fine, one that would keep you from doing the same thing again but not send you to debtor's prison?

How about $700,000? That's what the Japanese trawler *Kohoko Maru* No. 12 was fined in federal court after being seized by the Coast Guard cutter *Jarvis* off the western Aleutian Islands in 1976. Upon boarding the *Kohoko Maru* No. 12, Coast Guard officials and a National Marine Fisheries Service agent found thirty pounds of illicitly processed king crabmeat in her freezer and seven live crabs on deck.

That comes out to a fine of $14,000 per pound (30 pounds of crabmeat plus the estimated amount of meat from the live crabs) or $700,000 total. Obviously, the *Kohoko Maru* No. 12 was in the wrong place at the wrong time—in this case, the outer continental shelf that was under U.S. jurisdiction.

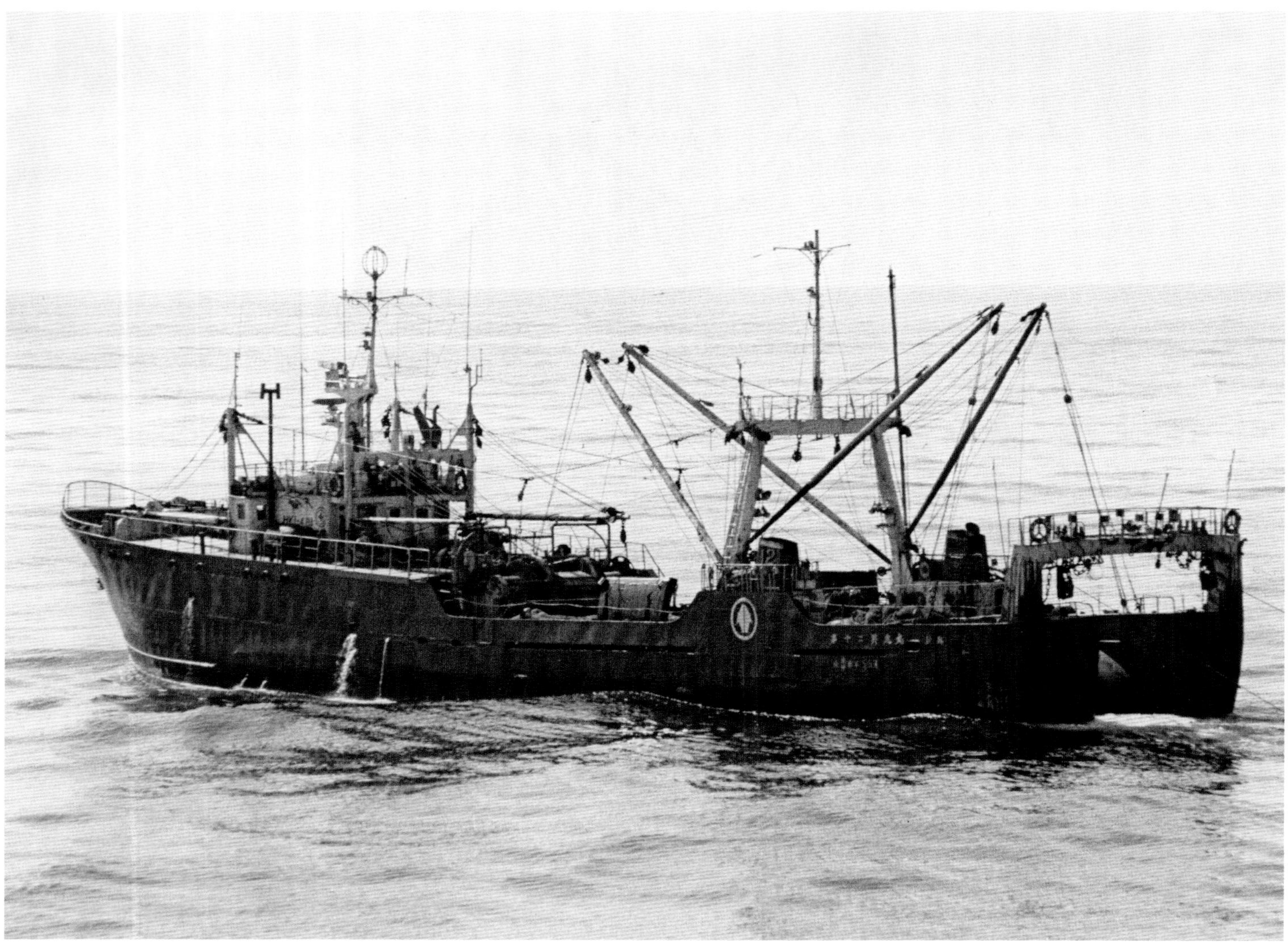

The Louise Ockers

It doesn't appear there's much more room for oysters on the deck of the *Louise Ockers*, but judging from the chain going out over the roller on the boat's railing, its eight-man crew is still dredging for seed oysters in May 1973. The *Louise Ockers* was one of several boats dredging New Jersey's Upper Delaware Bay, the state's most productive oyster bottom. The dredged-up seed oysters were then transplanted in the Lower Bay, known as the Maurice River Cove beds, where better growing conditions allowed fishermen to harvest the oysters in two or three years. The 1973 transplanting season lasted only a few weeks, but the goal was to move between 150,000 and 200,000 bushels of seed oysters.

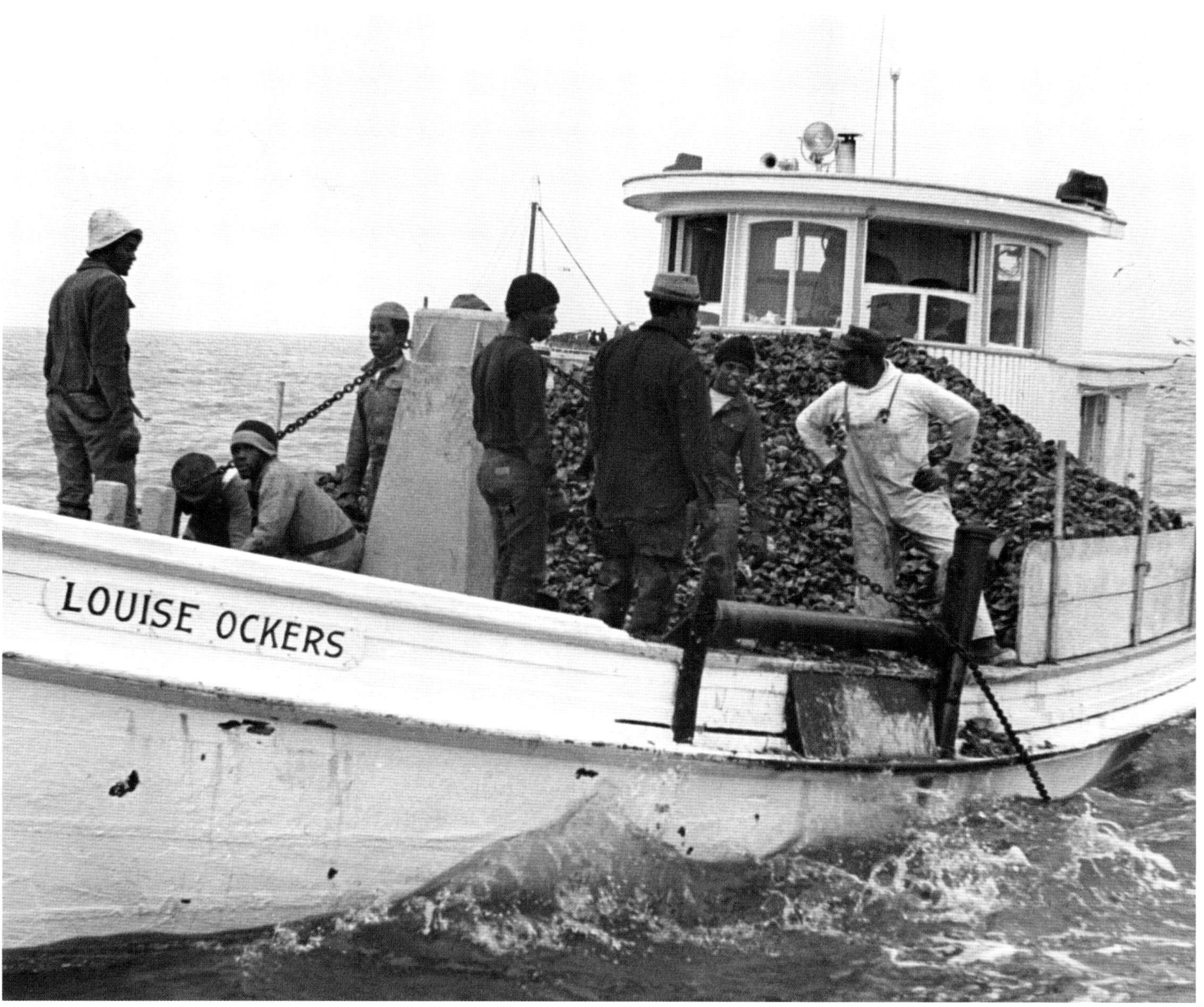

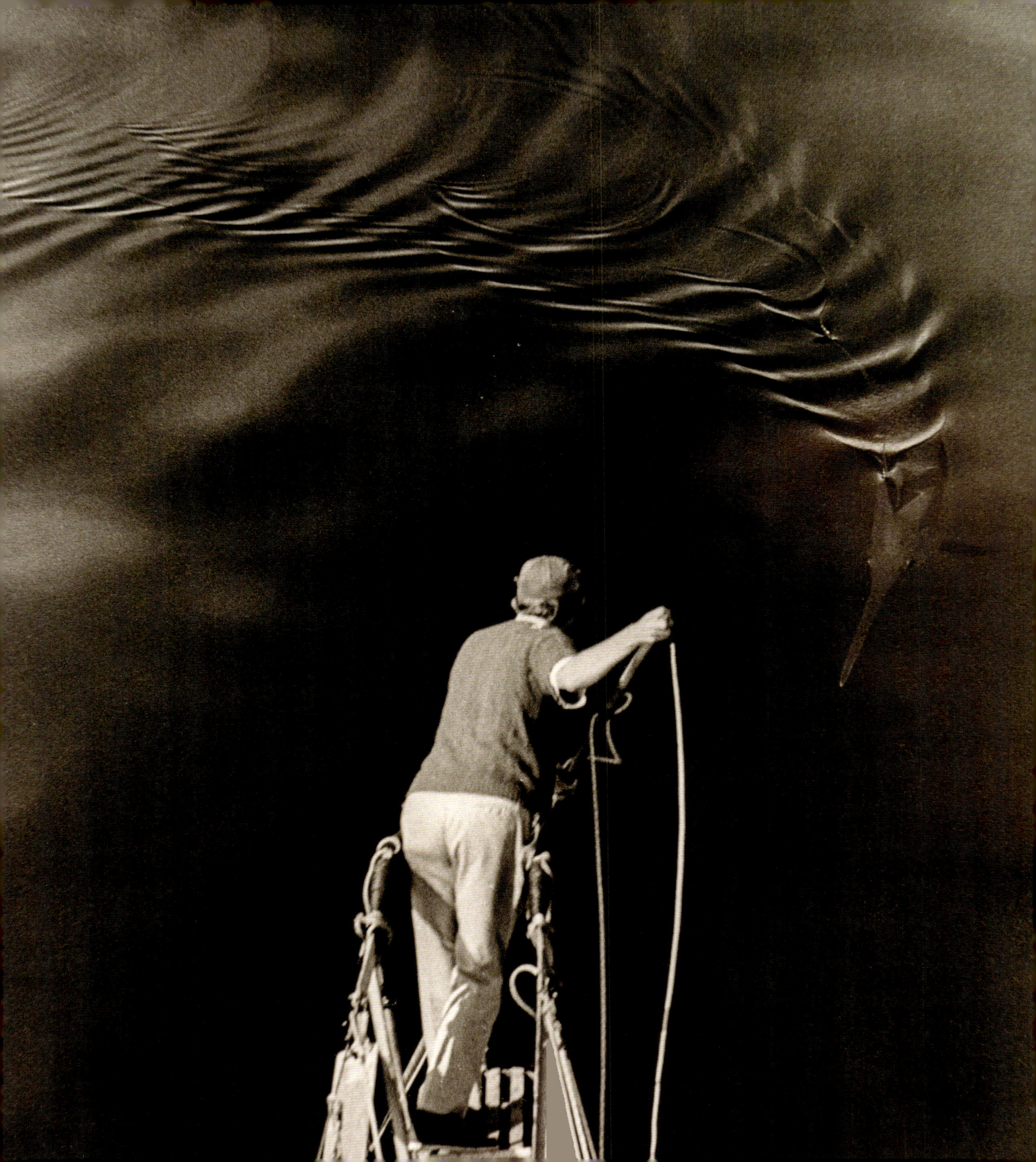

Harpooning

A swordfish harpooner only gets one shot and had better not miss. That's the situation facing Dave Brayton, owner and chief harpooner of the 65-foot *Harry Glen*, on the northeast peak of Georges Bank during a nine-day swordfishing trip in late August 1981. Brayton is standing on a small pulpit some 30 feet out from the *Harry Glen*'s bow, armed with a slender aluminum pole with a detachable dart on the end. That pole would be hard enough to hurl with any accuracy on dry land, but it was infinitely more difficult on a 65-foot boat moving through the ocean's swells.

Minutes before this image there hadn't been any swordfish in sight, although five crewmen secured to the top of the mast's rigging had long been searching. Another crewman was manning the steering station, using ropes connected to the main steering system instead of jog levers to control the boat. Then over the boat's loudspeaker comes the voice of the pilot in *Harry Glen*'s spotter plane: "O.K. 12:30 and about four boats." (That's using the "clock" for direction and boat lengths for distance.)

When it came time to commit, Brayton didn't miss. In fact, over the nine-day trip he *never* missed. The *Harry Glen* returned to port with thirty-two swordfish averaging 276 pounds each with a total dressed-out weight of 5,281 pounds. At a minimum price of about $3.50 per pound, the total payout came to at least $30,000, which made the crew's share about $2,000 each.

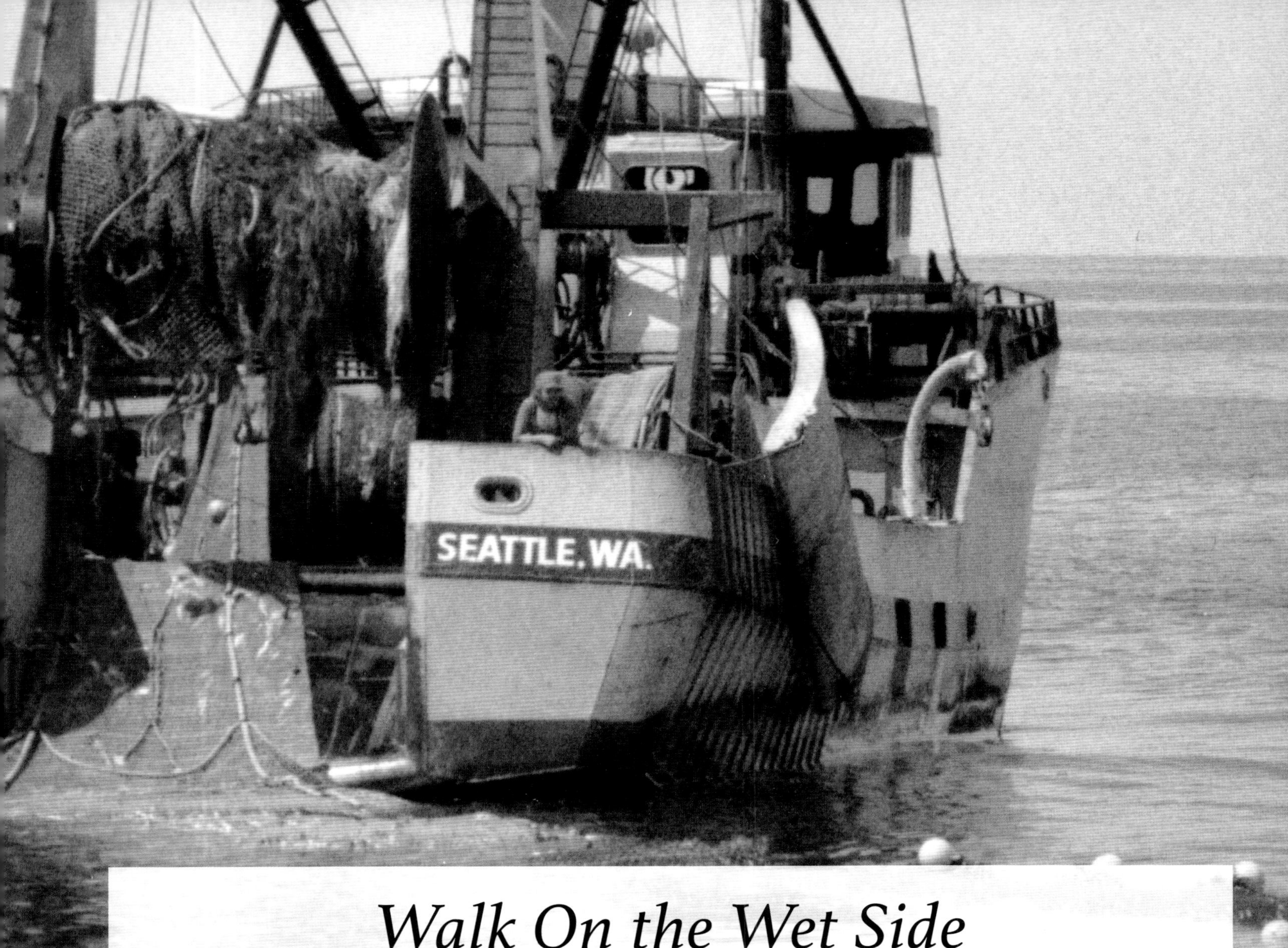

Walk On the Wet Side

There's not much in the way of diversions when trawling for pollock in the Bering Sea. It requires long hours—weeks and sometimes months at a time—while dealing with high winds and hellacious seas. So when you get a peaceful sunny day with blue skies and calm seas, as the 98-foot pollock trawler *Barbara Lee* seems to be enjoying, why not take advantage of it? That appeared to be the intent of the *Barbara Lee*'s skipper and deck boss on a June day in 1983.

They grabbed a beer and determined that a stroll along the cod end would be a good way to enjoy the day. The cod end is the business end of a fishing trawl, which is like a large funnel that tapers back to the cod end where the fish are contained. The photo appears to show that the trawl has been hauled back on the net reel over the stern ramp, and that only the cod end—full of fish—remains in the water. The fish that are in the net are providing the buoyancy that allows the two men to enjoy their saunter.

These photos were taken from another boat, the 123-foot *Sea Wolf*, which was fishing with the *Barbara Lee*.

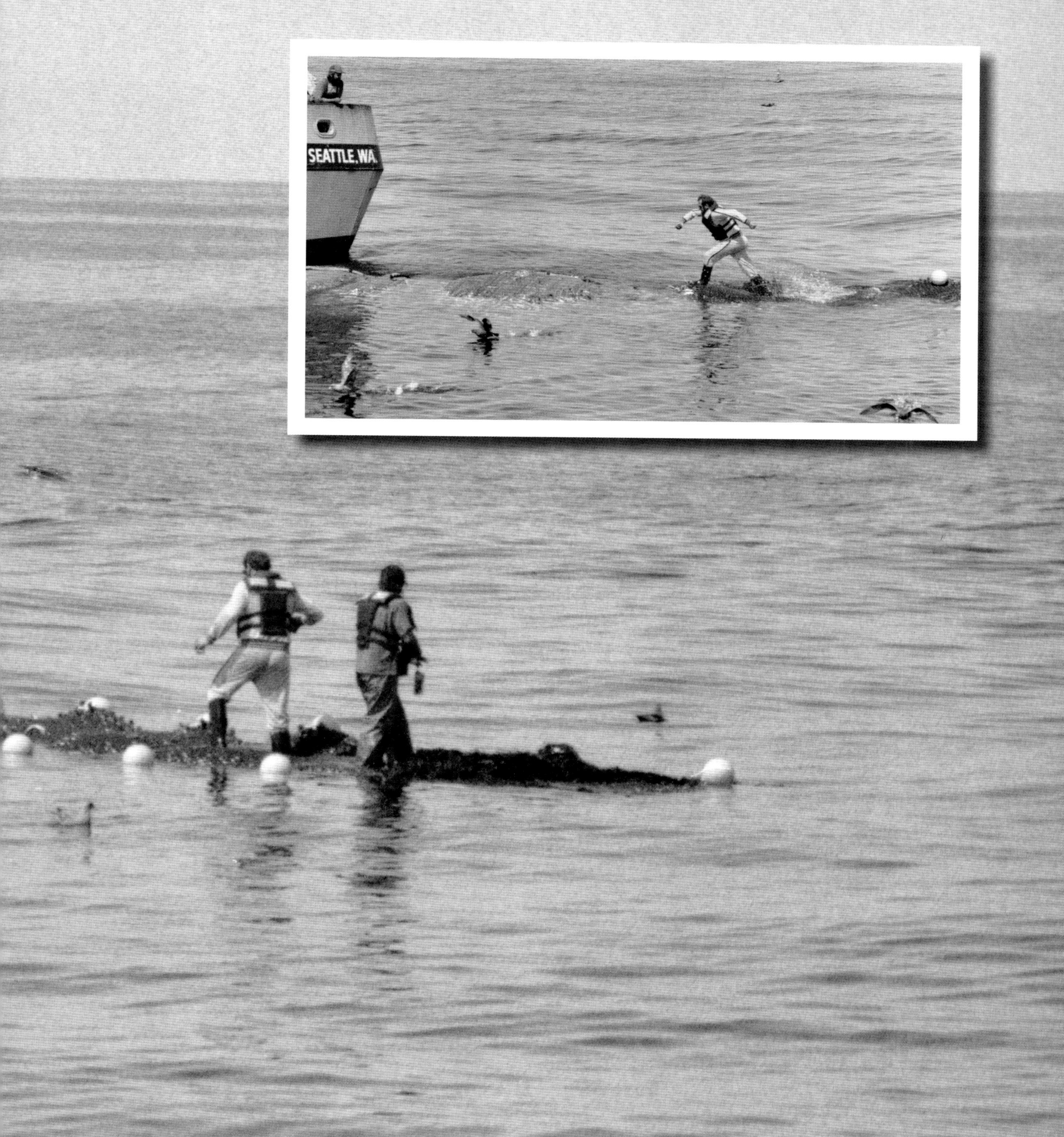
SEATTLE, WA.

St. Pierre Dory

This St. Pierre dory's roomy cockpit and ample cabin would seem to make it an ideal boat for coastal cruising. A number of St. Pierre dories like this one were built in the 1960s and 1970s from lines drawn by *National Fisherman*'s technical editor, John Gardner, as part of a seven-part series on the boat, beginning with the September 1962 issue.

The St. Pierre dory is a boat that appealed to someone satisfied with traveling at a leisurely five to eight knots while exploring coastal gunkholes and knowing they are doing it in one of the better sea boats. This boat's owner elected to go with wheel steering, though many stuck with a long tiller attached to an outboard rudder. That was the arrangement with the original St. Pierre fishing dories, introduced in the 1930s to the French islands of St. Pierre and Miquelon off the southern coast of Newfoundland.

Known as "la grande doris de St. Pierre et Miquelon," the heavy open boats were manned by two fishermen who relied on a low-speed make-and-break engine to get through the storms and ice of the waters they fished. Its tremendous sheer, a heavily rockered bottom, a bow that seems to tower out of the water, and sharp fore sections made the St. Pierre dory one of the most seaworthy wooden boats ever designed. Even though the dories might fish twenty miles offshore, Gardner found no record of a St. Pierre dory being lost or of any fisherman drowning while fishing in one.

The lines plan he came up with offered a 27-foot modified version of the fisherman's St. Pierre dory. The profile was unchanged, but extra inches were added to the beam and bottom, and the sides were slightly rounded. Those changes made it much easier to add a small house and cuddy cabin, as on this St. Pierre dory. There was enough room for two full-length berths, a head, and a Shipmate stove. The owner of a boat built to Gardner's design said the St. Pierre dory "takes rough, choppy water very easily with no fuss, is easy in head wind and heavy chop and nice to handle in a steep, following sea."

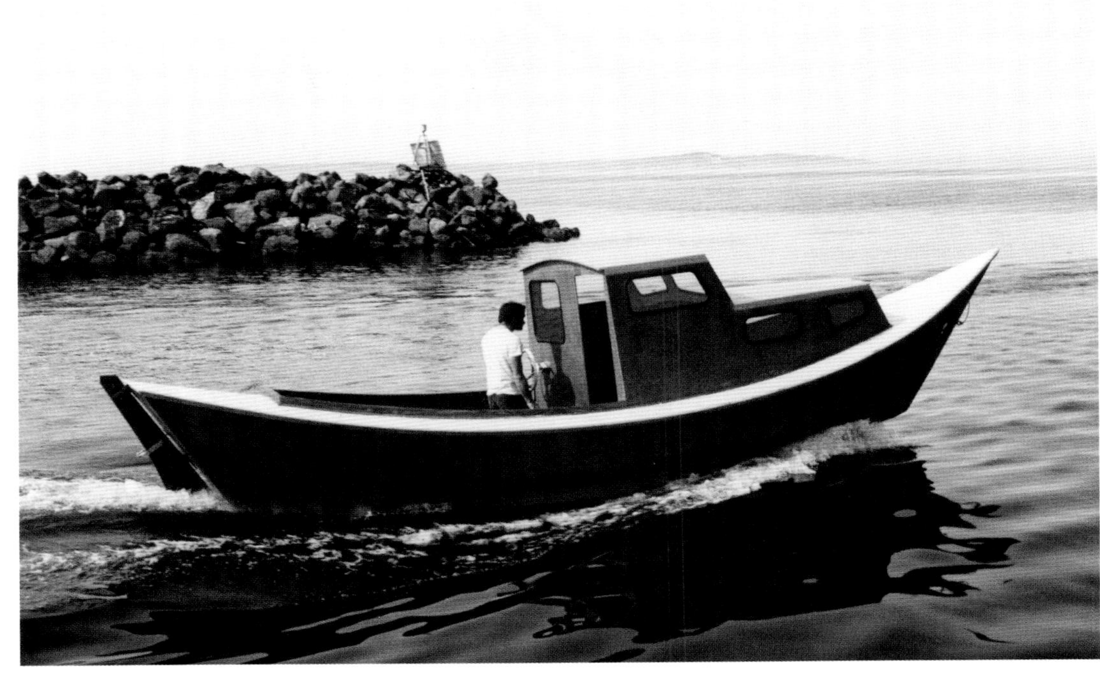

Dragging for Calico Scallops

After a twenty-minute tow, Luke Bowling yards back on a line and releases nearly a ton of calico scallops onto the deck of the 78-foot *Lady Barbara*. This is one of two trawls the *Lady Barbara* was towing on a sunny summer day in 1982 over a stretch of bottom eighteen miles off the east coast of Florida.

The trawl the scallops are tumbling out of is covered with black chafing material to protect its three-inch nylon mesh as the net is towed over firm, sandy bottom—a favorite habitat of calico scallops. A pair of wooden trawl doors maintains the net's 32-foot opening as it is towed across the bottom.

After setting and hauling a dozen tows over twelve hours, the *Lady Barbara* returned to Southern Seafoods in Port Canaveral, Florida, with about 22 tons of scallops, which would produce 174 gallons of meat. The haul was worth $1,392. Of that, the skipper got $181 and the two crewmen $125 and change.

Calico scallops were once abundant enough to support a commercial fishery on both the east and west coasts of Florida, with landings peaking in 1982 at about 43 million pounds of scallop meats. But the population has been too small to support a commercial harvest since 2000.

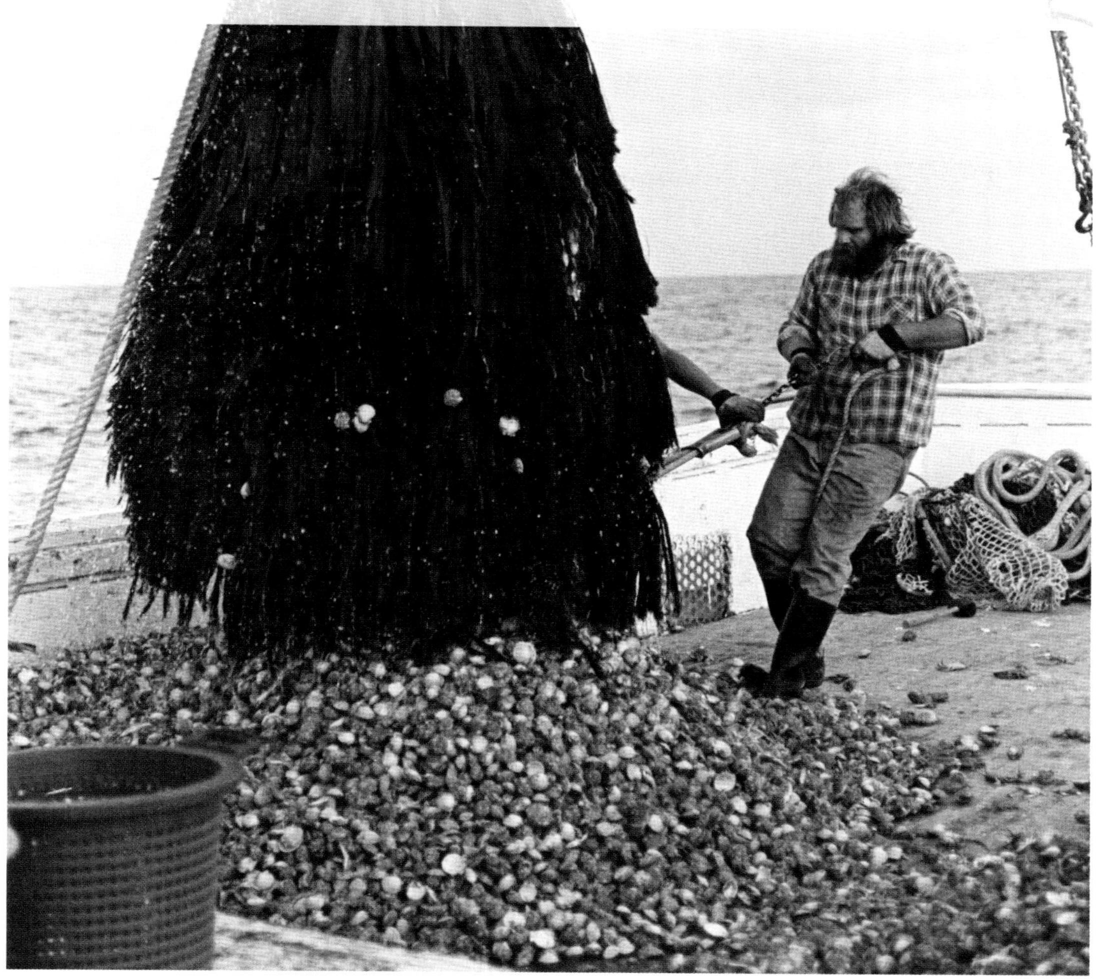

Alaskan Halibut Longlining

Judging by the grins of the crewmen on the *Grant*, a 68-foot halibut longlining vessel out of Seattle, all the fishing gear is aboard and they are finally relaxing after closing out a special four-day halibut season in May 1984 near the Semidi Islands in southeast Alaska.

Actually, the fishing was so good that the *Grant*'s hold and deck were both loaded up by the end of the third day. That would have been three days of intense activity for the six-man crew with maybe one or two three-hour naps each day. The rest of the time was spent hauling in halibut as the longline brought the fish up to the boat's railing one at a time, then dressing them, and icing them down in the hold. They also had to coil the longline as it came aboard and rebait the 7,140 Norwegian Circle hooks the *Grant* would set over the short season.

The *Grant*'s fo'c'sle served as both a galley and sleeping quarters with six bunks, three to the right of the galley table and three to the left. Three bunks served as storage space and three were used by the newer crew members. Two others slept in the stern and the skipper, Jack Knutsen, slept in the wheelhouse. The *Grant* was built in Seattle in 1925 as a halibut boat for Jacob Knutsen and was later owned and operated by his son, Jack. At the time of this photo, she was one of about twenty-five halibut boats in the Seattle fleet.

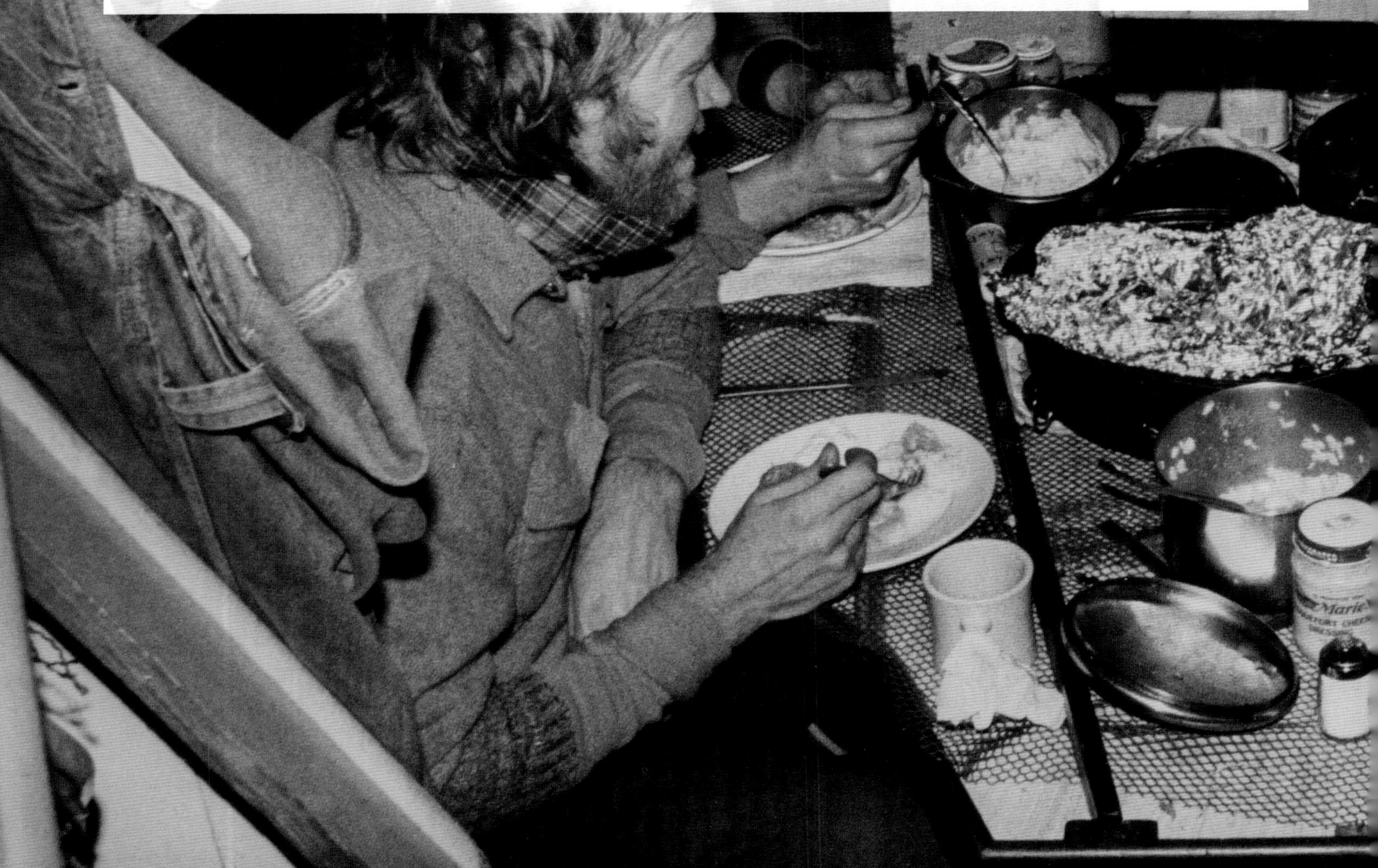

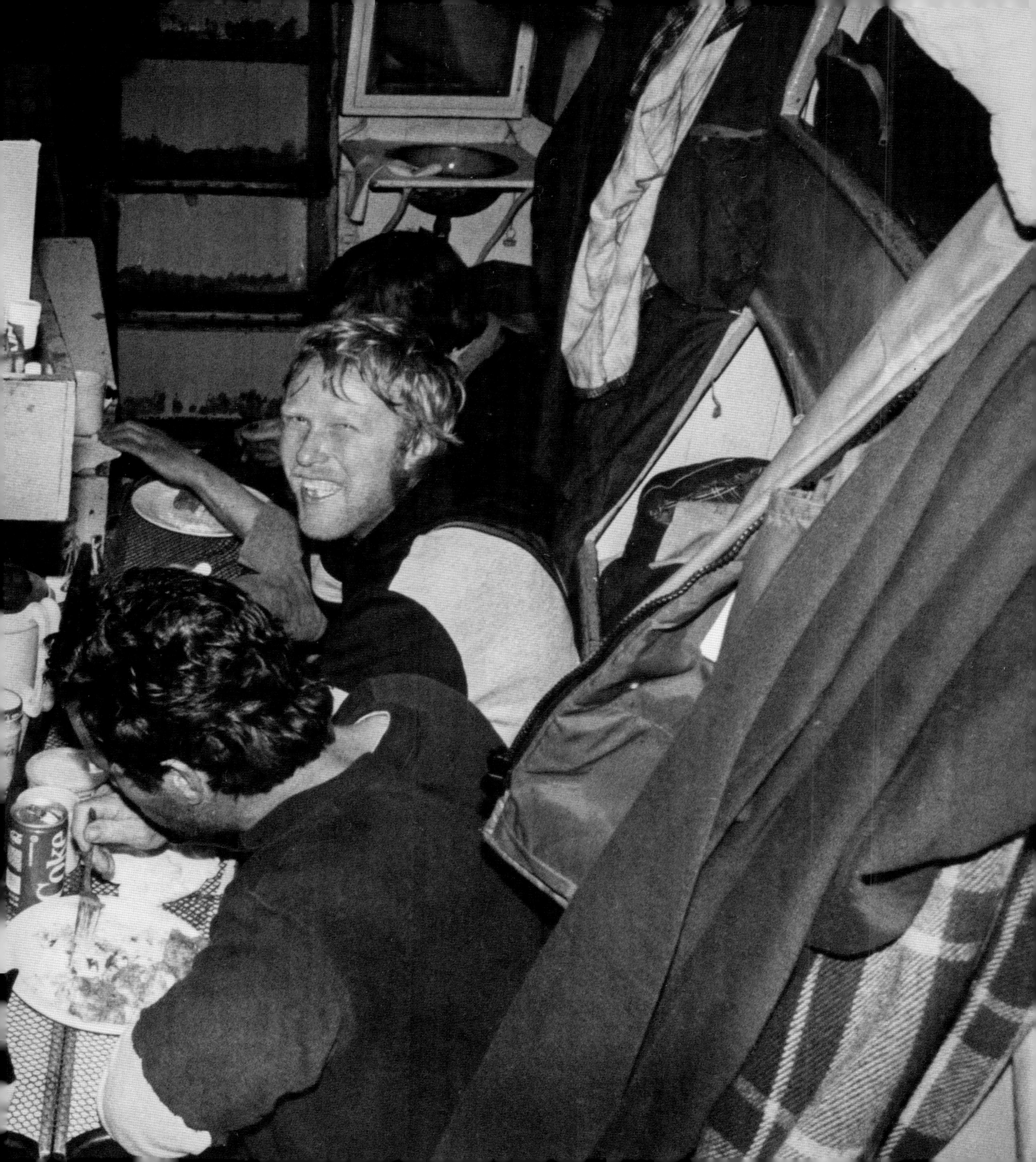

Coiling Gear

The most difficult task on a West Coast longlining halibut boat was coiling skates. A skate is a single three-strand quarter-inch nylon line about three hundred fathoms (1,800 feet) long with hooks attached to gangions fastened to the line on a becket every 20 feet or so.

Generally, boats set several strings of gear, each of which was made up of ten skates, with an anchor at each end and a buoy with a flag on it at the surface. Come time to haul back, the skates are pulled in over a roller on the side of the boat by the gurdy, a winch with a horizontal sheave that hauls in the ground line that's picked up by the crewman shown coiling down the skate.

The key to a successful coiling job is laying the line down in neat coils, about eighteen inches in diameter, except where the hook's gangion is connected to the becket. There, a tighter, narrower loop is formed and placed on the coils so it sticks out beyond the pile, while the hook is placed as flat as possible on the coiled line. This makes it easier to quickly grab each hook when rapidly rebaiting, which takes place as soon as the skate's last hook comes in, and while someone else coils down the next skate. Hauling, coiling, baiting, and resetting the gear could go on for hours and hours, and some fishermen might get three or four hours of sleep for every eighteen to thirty hours worked.

The man seen behind the coiler in this photo is dressing a halibut, which will go into the hold to be iced down.

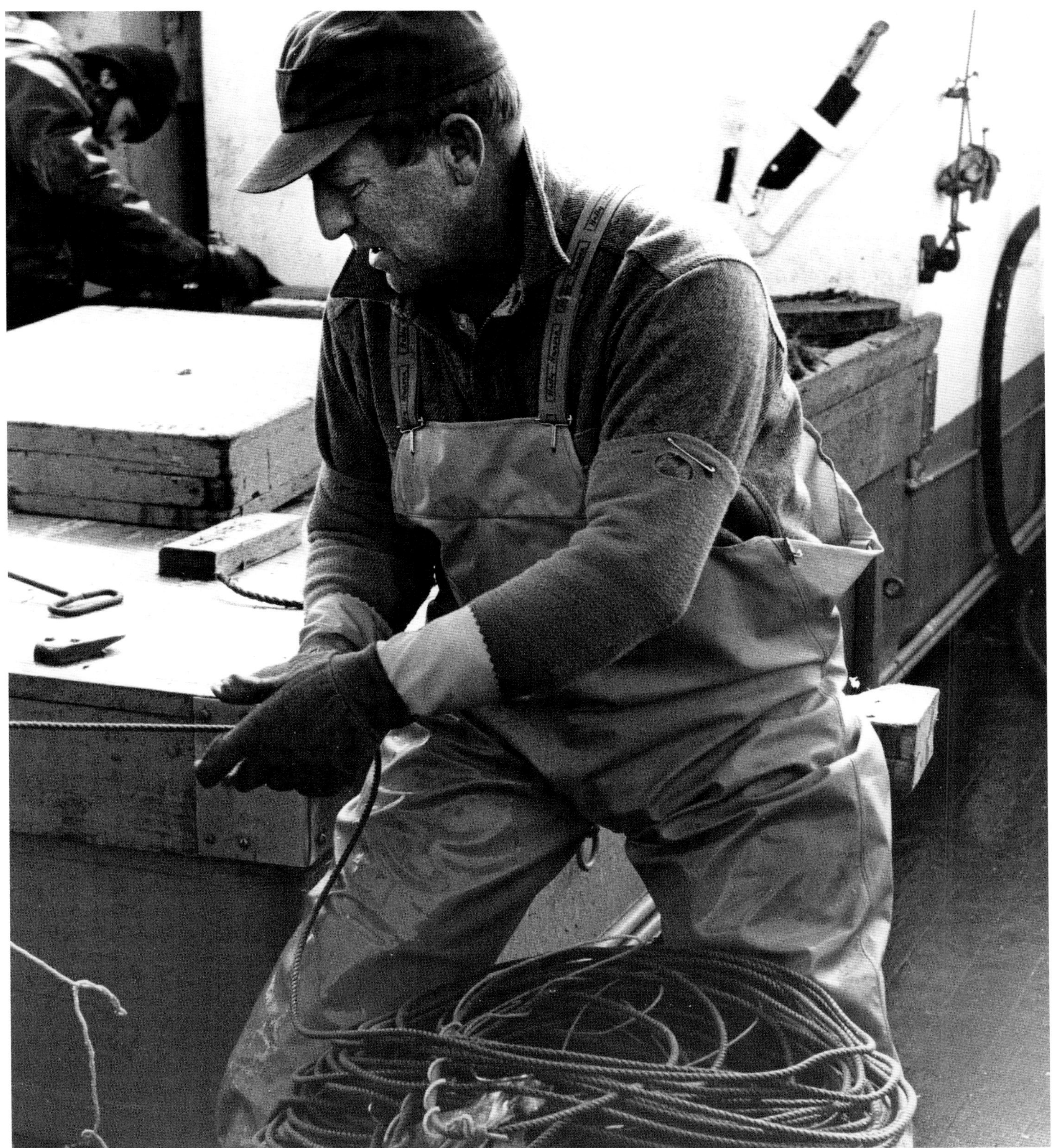

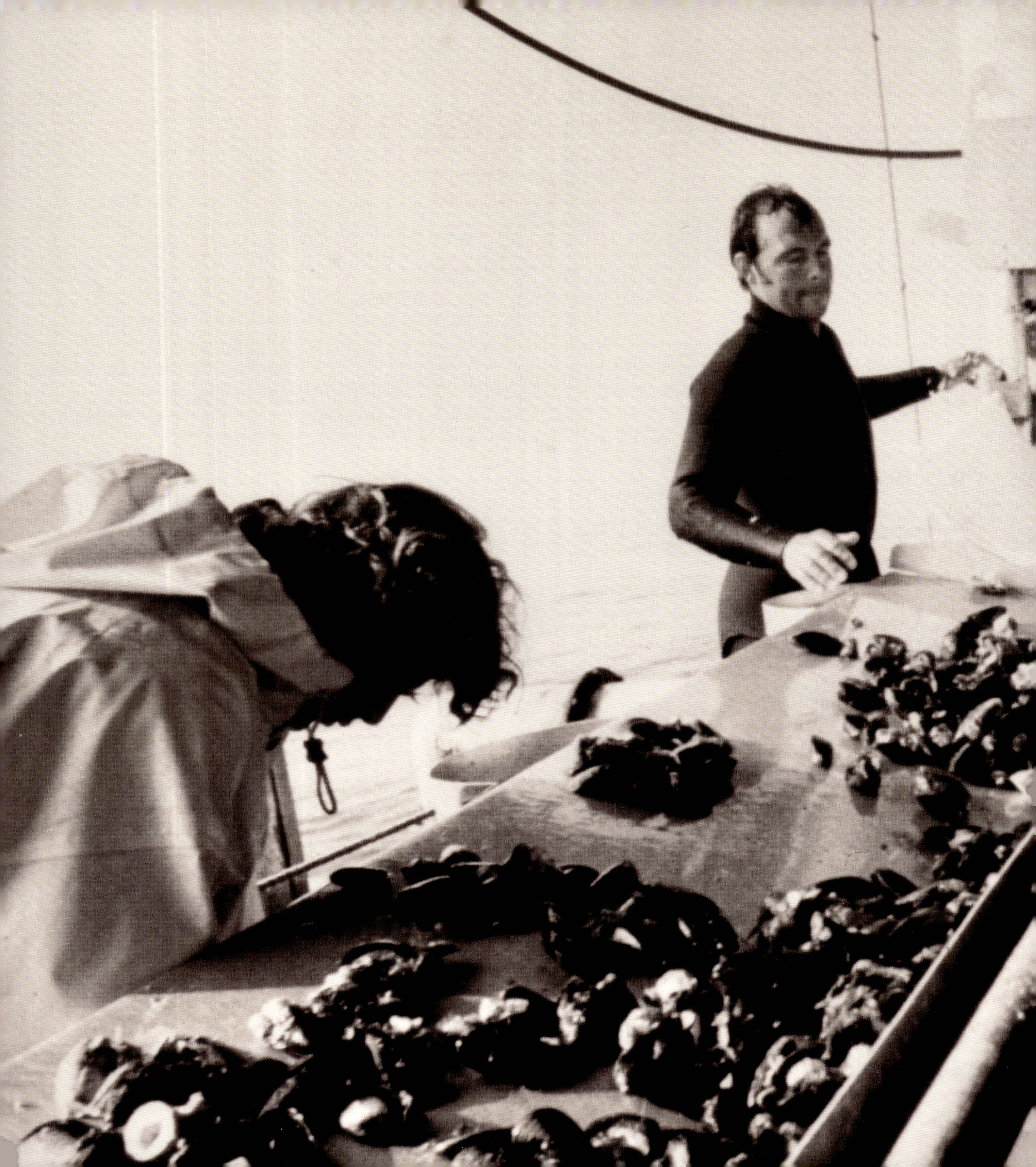

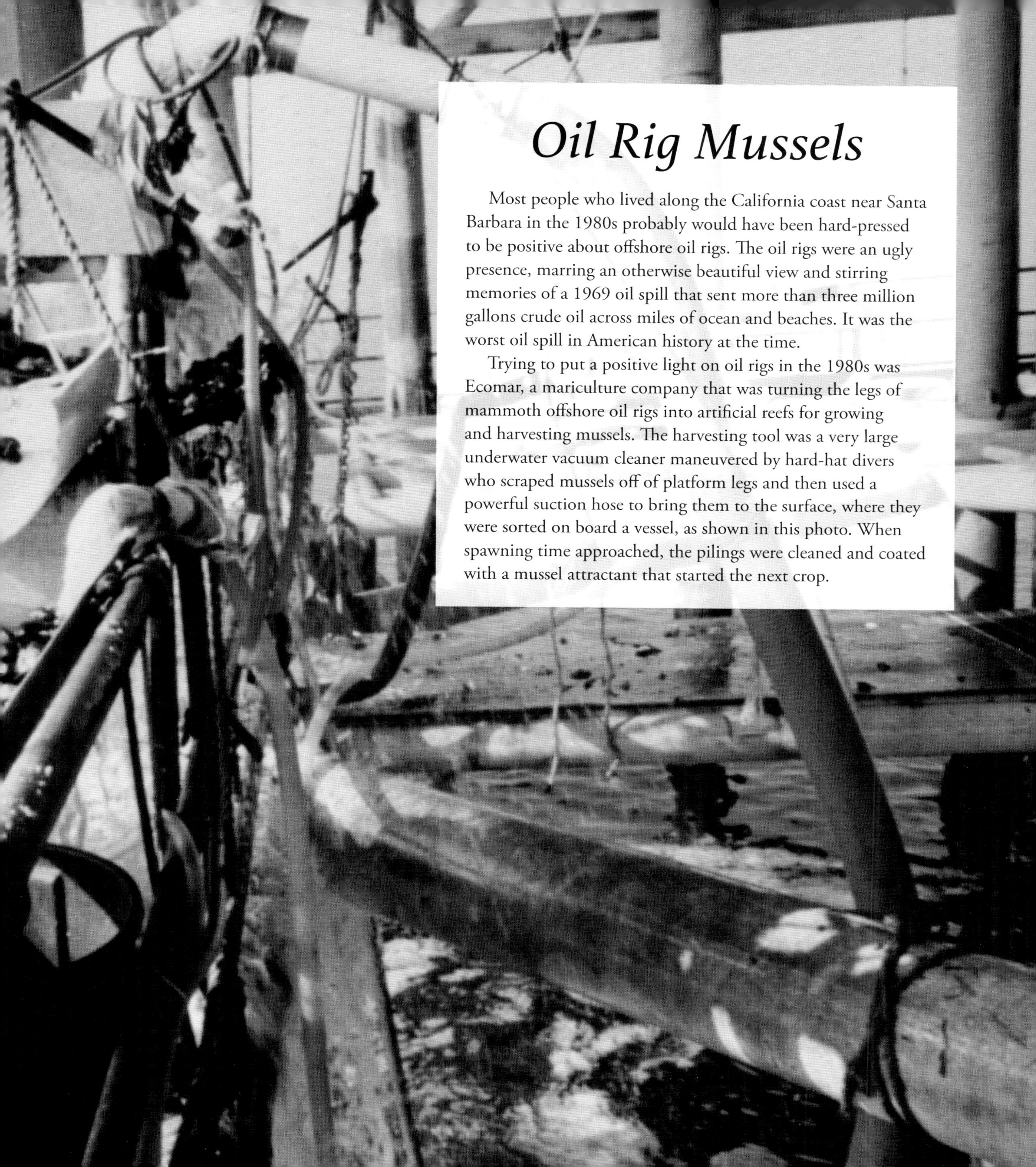

Oil Rig Mussels

Most people who lived along the California coast near Santa Barbara in the 1980s probably would have been hard-pressed to be positive about offshore oil rigs. The oil rigs were an ugly presence, marring an otherwise beautiful view and stirring memories of a 1969 oil spill that sent more than three million gallons crude oil across miles of ocean and beaches. It was the worst oil spill in American history at the time.

Trying to put a positive light on oil rigs in the 1980s was Ecomar, a mariculture company that was turning the legs of mammoth offshore oil rigs into artificial reefs for growing and harvesting mussels. The harvesting tool was a very large underwater vacuum cleaner maneuvered by hard-hat divers who scraped mussels off of platform legs and then used a powerful suction hose to bring them to the surface, where they were sorted on board a vessel, as shown in this photo. When spawning time approached, the pilings were cleaned and coated with a mussel attractant that started the next crop.

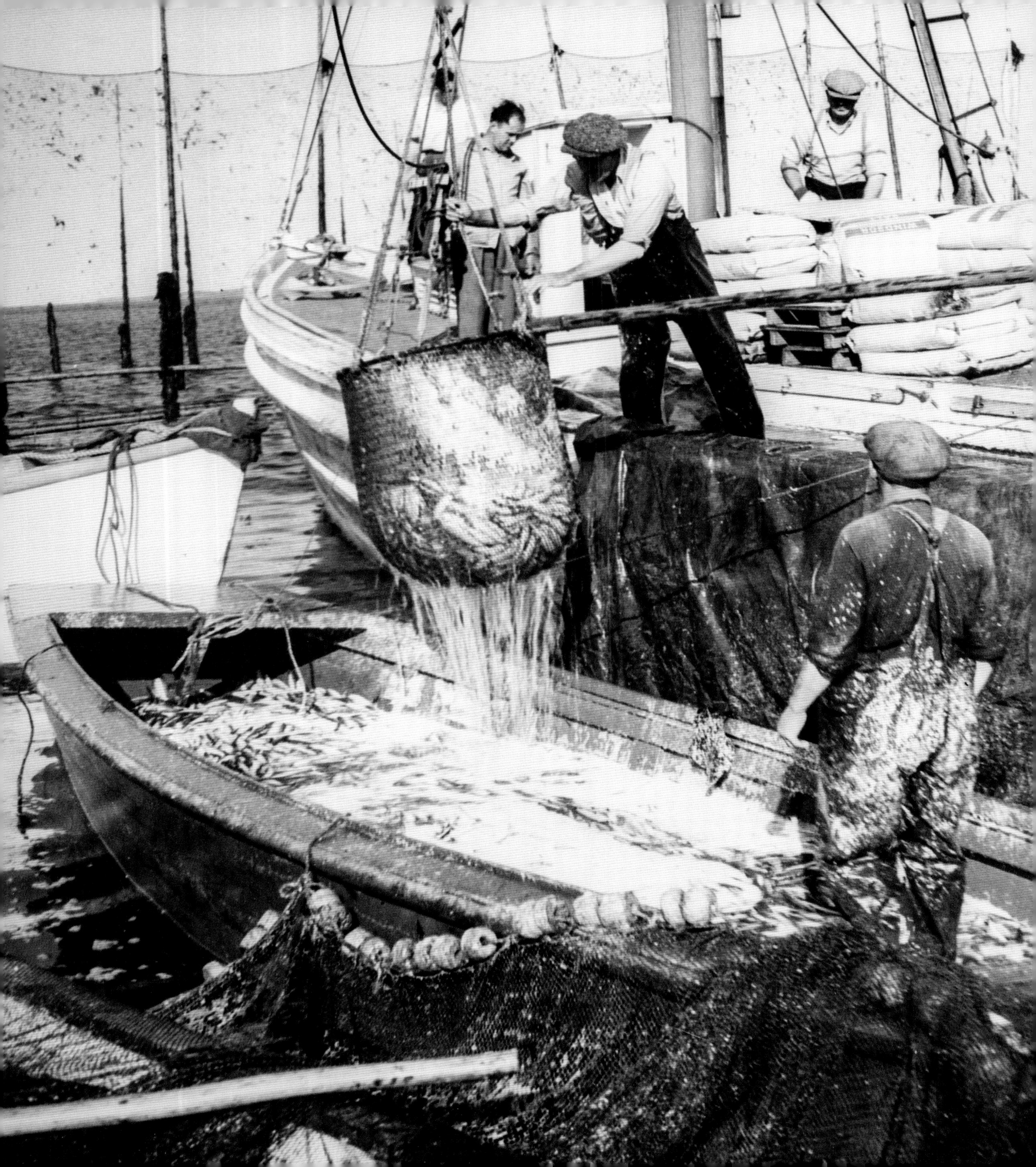

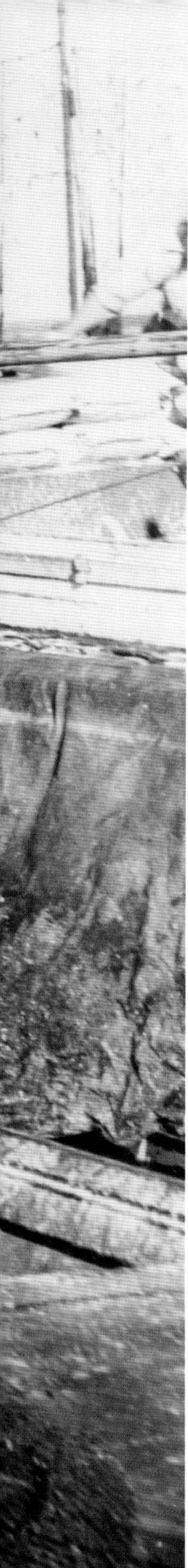

Selling the Catch

As long as men have worked the sea, they've been supported by infrastructure of support on shore. Seafarers, after all, need people on land to service their vessels, repair them when need be, and supply them with food, ice, gear, and other sundries so they can take to the ocean. When the boats return after being at sea, they need people to unload their cargo, process it, and market it.

The herring fisherman wouldn't bother catching the small fish if there weren't sardine packing plants to process the harvest. Wharf space is essential to dry fishing nets. Whether it's salt cod, sponges, or even turtle soup, somebody needs to turn the bounty of the sea into a product that can be sold.

And finally, members of the community—the public, shall we say—need to be willing to consume and celebrate the bounty of the sea. In fishing communities across the country, you can find people holding celebrations for the seafood that's embedded in their local culture, from lobster, scallops, and crab to oysters, salmon, and mackerel.

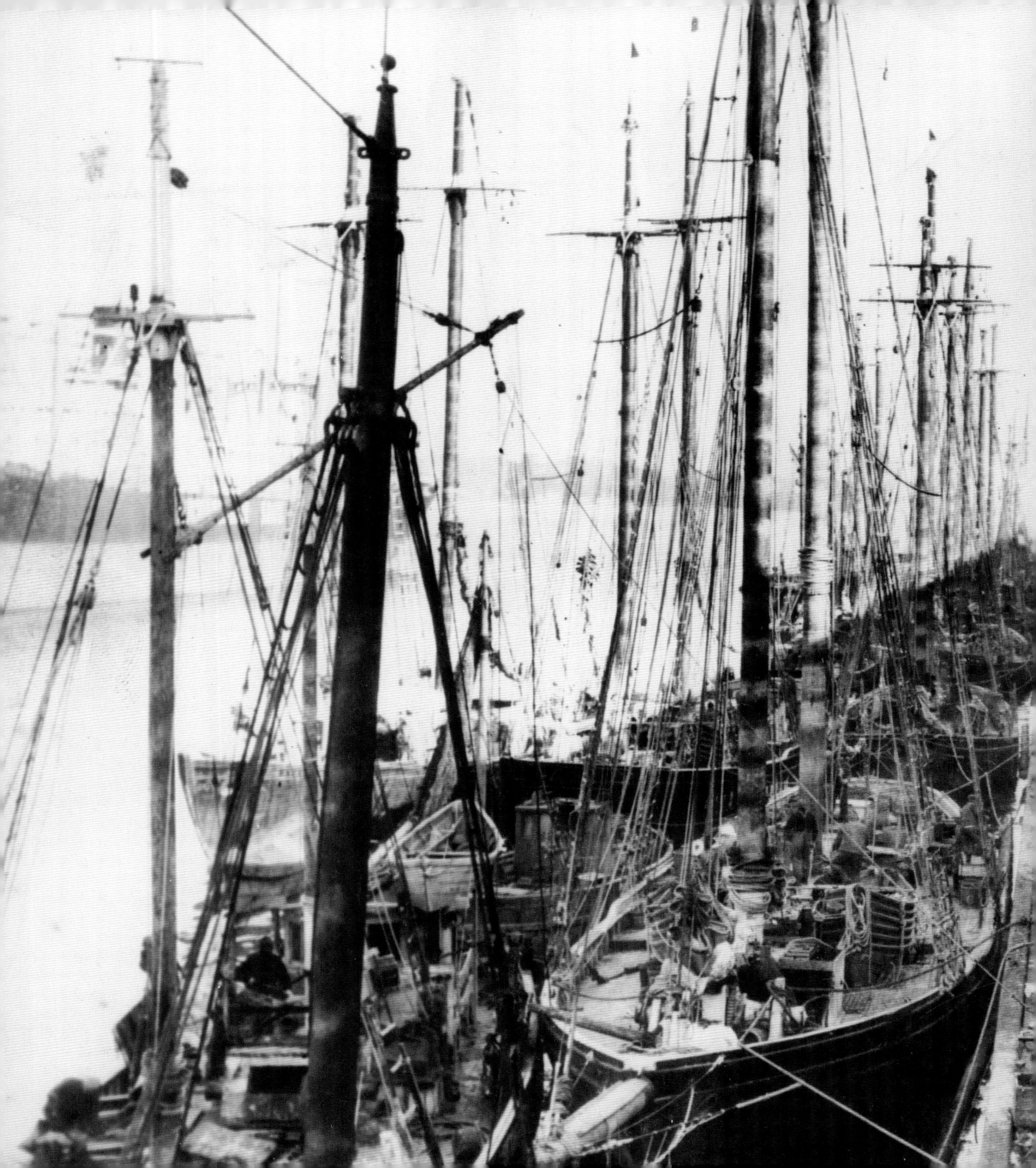

South Boston Fish Pier

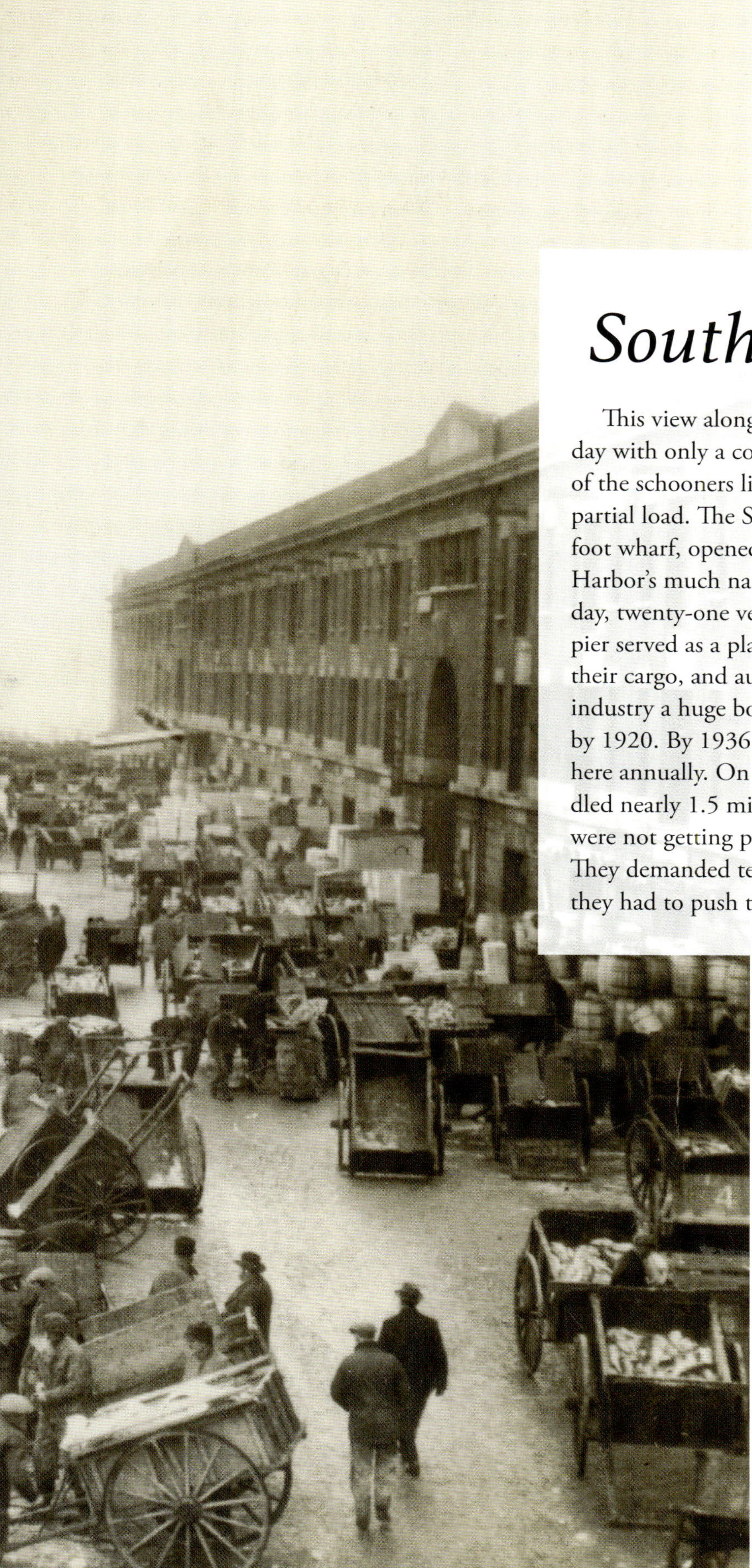

This view along the South Boston Fish Pier shows a relatively slow day with only a couple of hand carts full of fish unloaded from some of the schooners lining the pier, while other hand carts have only a partial load. The South Boston Fish Pier, with its substantial 1,200-foot wharf, opened March 30, 1914 as a replacement for Boston Harbor's much narrower and more crowded T Wharf. On its first day, twenty-one vessels delivered 1.45 million pounds of fish. The pier served as a place where fishermen could tie up their boats, unload their cargo, and auction their catch onsite. It gave Boston's fishing industry a huge boost, enabling it to become the nation's leading port by 1920. By 1936, nearly 350 million pounds of fish were unloaded here annually. On that first day, seventy-five hand cart haulers handled nearly 1.5 million pounds of fish, but evidently they figured they were not getting paid enough, and they went on strike the next day. They demanded ten or twenty cents per load, depending on where they had to push the cart. The fish dealers agreed to the deal.

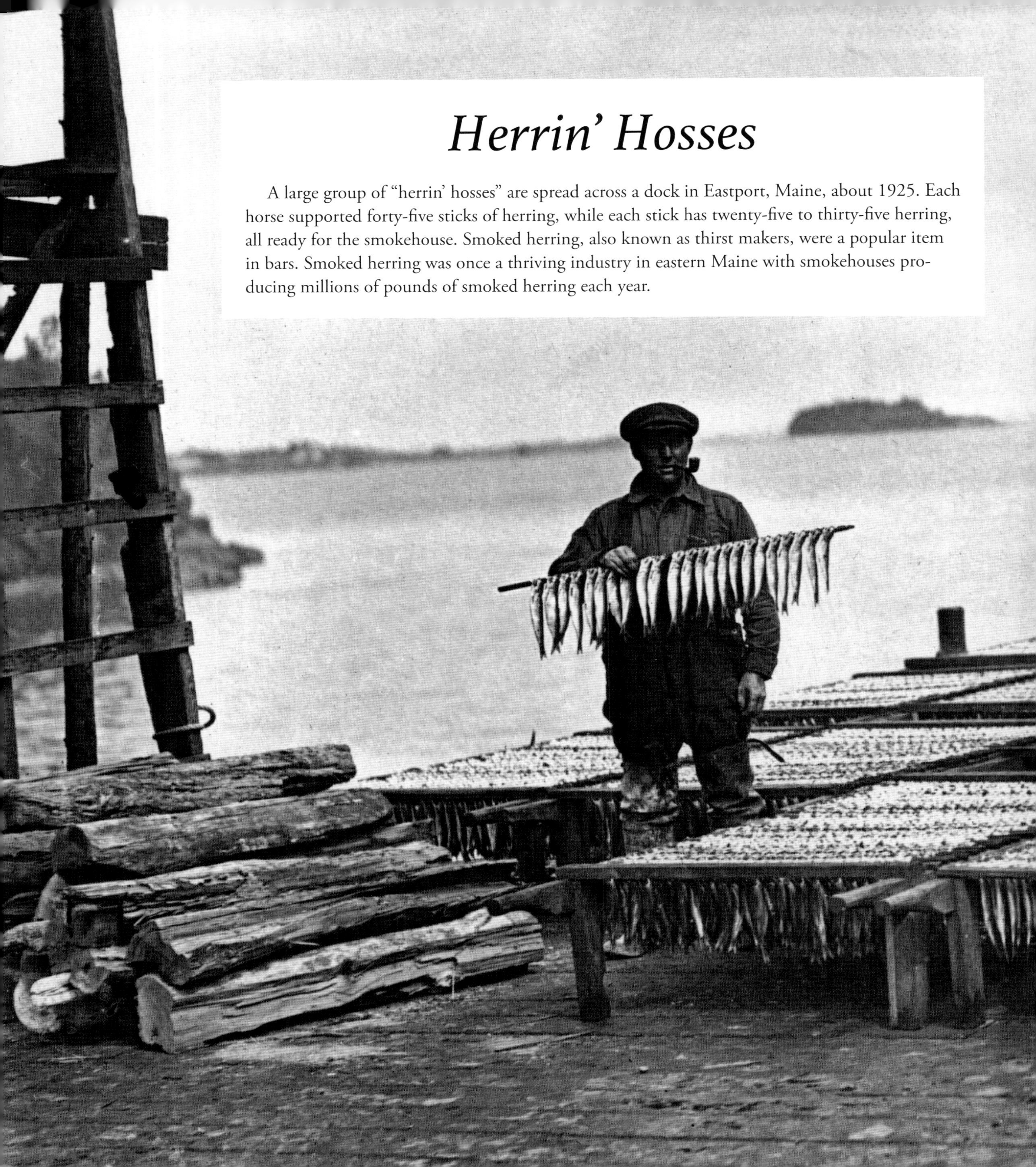

Herrin' Hosses

A large group of "herrin' hosses" are spread across a dock in Eastport, Maine, about 1925. Each horse supported forty-five sticks of herring, while each stick has twenty-five to thirty-five herring, all ready for the smokehouse. Smoked herring, also known as thirst makers, were a popular item in bars. Smoked herring was once a thriving industry in eastern Maine with smokehouses producing millions of pounds of smoked herring each year.

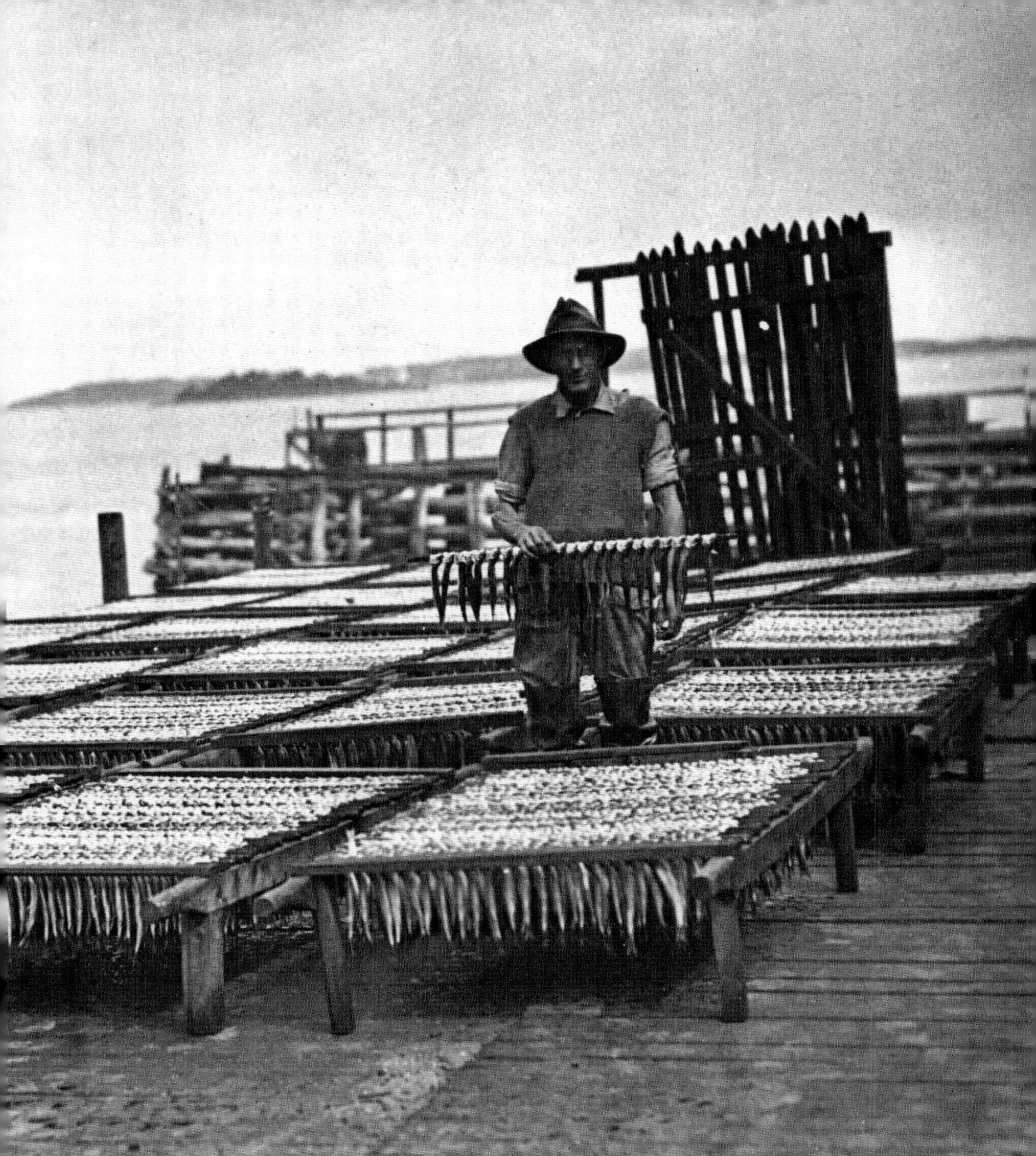

Humongous Hauls of Herring

Herring ruled the sea. Or so it must have seemed to boats fishing off Yarmouth, Nova Scotia, in October 1929, when the sea was said to have been "a great mass of life, so thick and immense were the schools of herring." It had to have been that "mass" that forty boats—none of them longer than 40 feet—encountered one night when hauling back their gillnets. Some fishermen had set four to eight gillnets, but only needed to pull one or two before filling their boats. The remaining gillnets sank, they were so jammed with herring that the fish drowned. The dead fish were used later for fertilizer when the nets were recovered.

When the boats arrived at the Yarmouth Cold Storage docks the next morning to unload, each was carrying between fifteen and twenty-five barrels of herring. Some of those boats are shown in this photo side by side against the dock while offloading their herring.

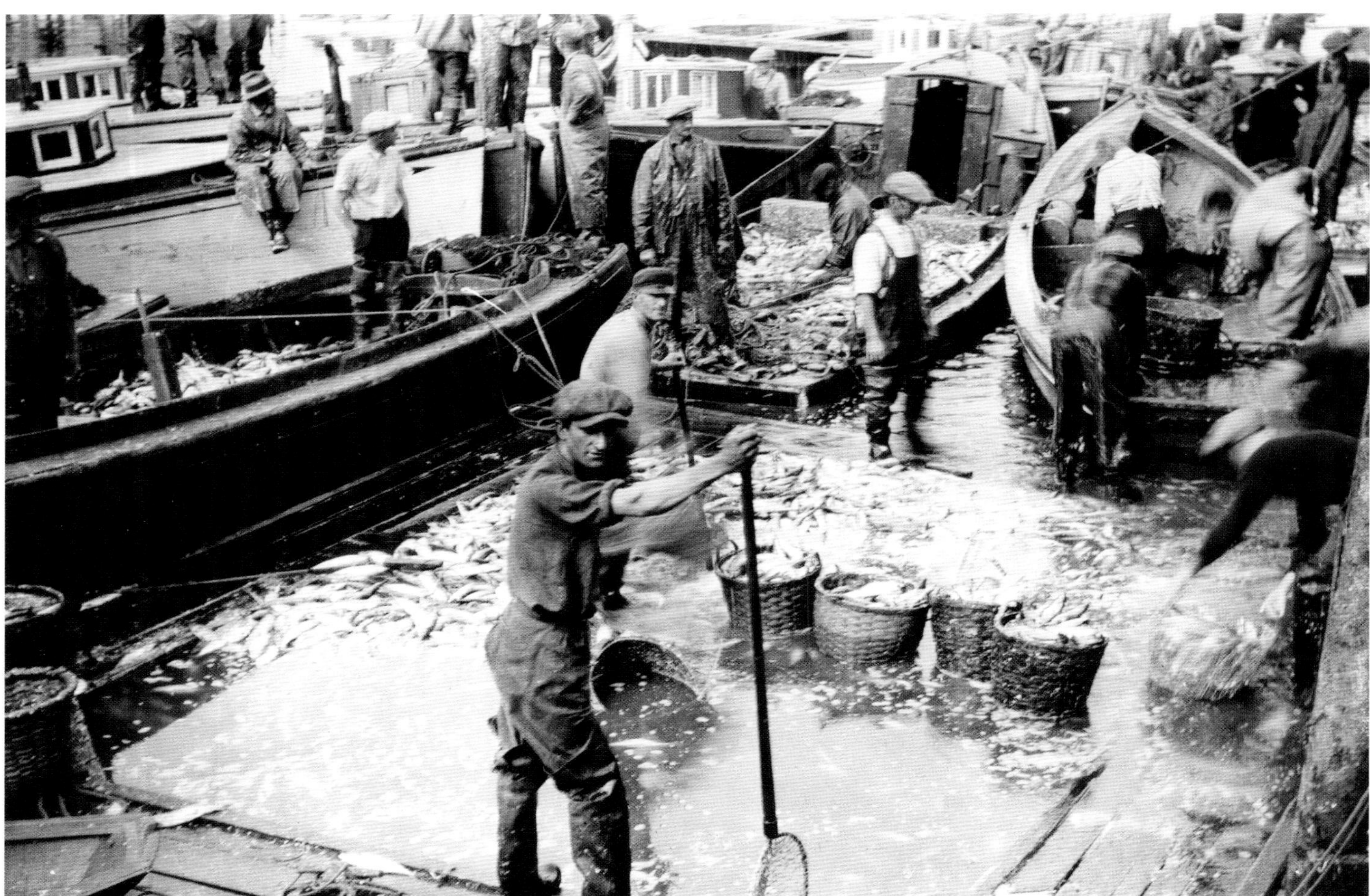

Turtle Soup

A crowd of tourists are shown gathered on a Key West, Florida dock in this late 1930s photograph. They are watching a cargo of green sea turtles being slid, one-by-one, down a chute into a pen, known as the crawl. Here the turtles stayed until they were processed and made into canned green turtle soup at the A. Granday Canning Co.

The turtles came from the waters of Miskito Cays off the Nicaraguan Coast. They were transported to Key West on the *A.M. Adams*, a two-masted, white-hulled schooner. The turtles were off-loaded from the schooner onto barges with a block and tackle, as some of the bigger turtles tipped the scales at 500 pounds. The barges took the turtles to a dock behind the cannery—see the turtles behind the crowd—and from there they went down into the crawl. Green turtle soup remained a signature product of Key West until the early 1970s.

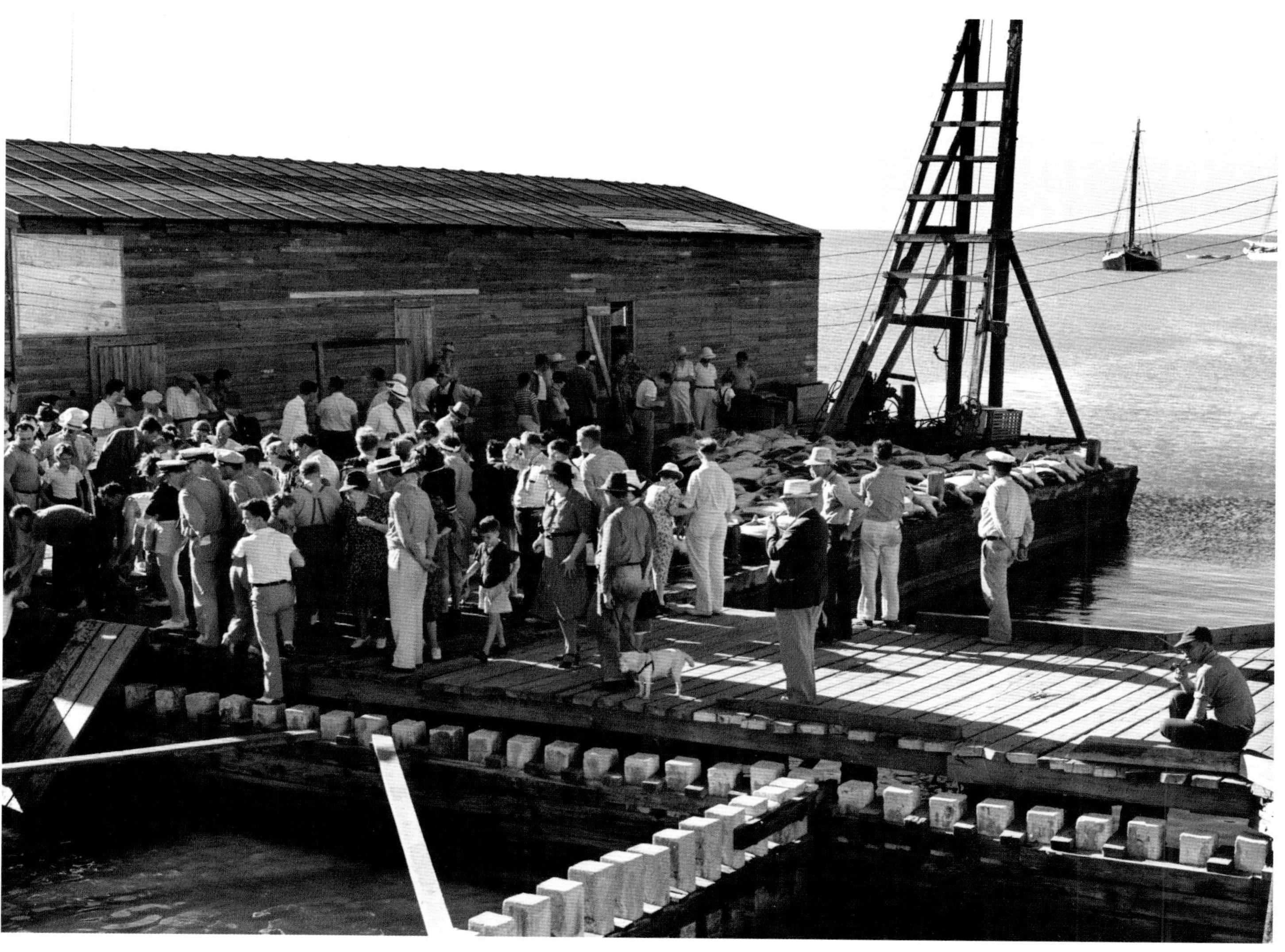

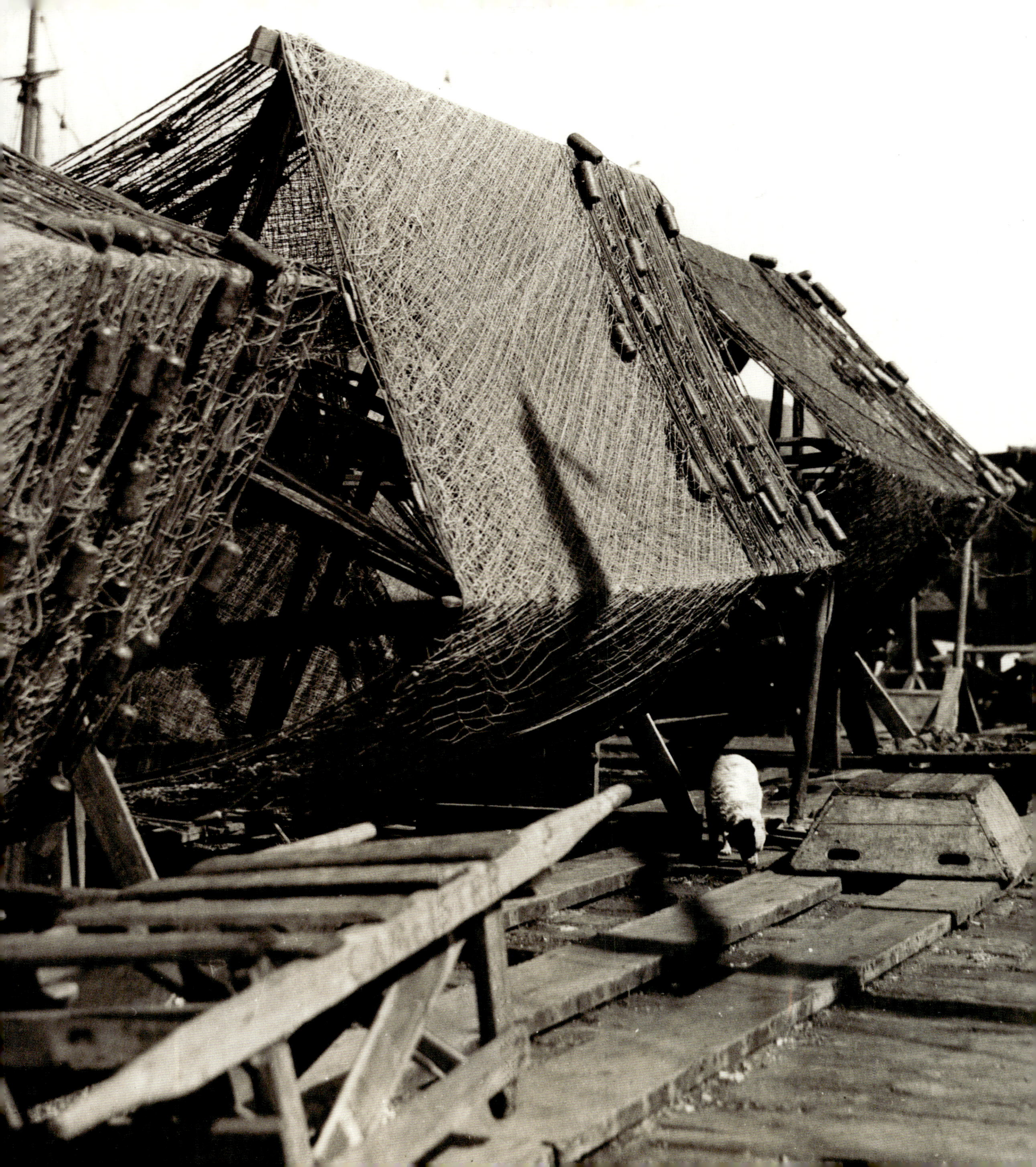

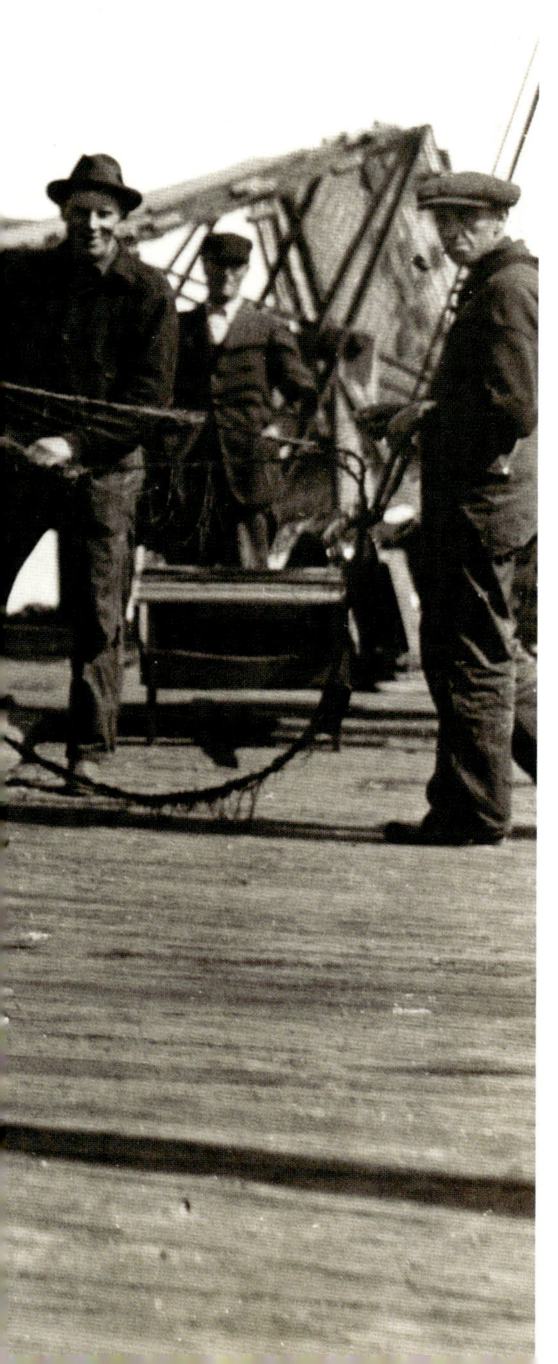

Growth of Gillnetting

As gillnet fishing grew in popularity, it was not uncommon to find fishermen checking out their Italian gillnets as they hung drying on Portland, Maine's commercial wharf, as this 1926 photo shows. Maine fishermen were said to be the first in New England to set out gillnets—nets that hang in the water column and catch fish by their gills—beginning in 1906. Fishermen working the waters off Cape Ann, Massachusetts, were quick to follow, and by 1912 some thirty-eight boats were setting gillnets. Initially sets were made close to shore, but within a few years gillnetters were working eight to twelve miles offshore.

Salt Fish

Gorton-Pew Fisheries Co. was founded on salt fish. From the time the company was formed in 1906 in Gloucester, Massachusetts, that's all that was produced until 1911 when frozen fillets, smoked fish, and fresh fish were added to its lineup. Salt fish, however, remained the prime seller. This 1935 photo shows long rows of drying racks that are covered with salt fish at Gorton-Pew's East Gloucester plant.

At the end of a fishing trip, fish were split, cleaned, washed, and salted in large barrels holding 1,200 pounds each. After thoroughly curing, the fish were stacked in piles until the pickling brine drained. Then the fish were wheeled to the flake yard and spread flesh side up on wooden racks with a daily drying capacity of 125,000 pounds.

Depending on the weather, drying could take several days. Afterward, the side and back fins, the skin, and all the bones were removed. Then each were then cut into half- to one-pound pieces that were molded into brick-shaped objects, wrapped in wax paper, and boxed for shipping. Gorton-Pew Fisheries is now known as Gorton's and continues to produce a variety of frozen seafood products.

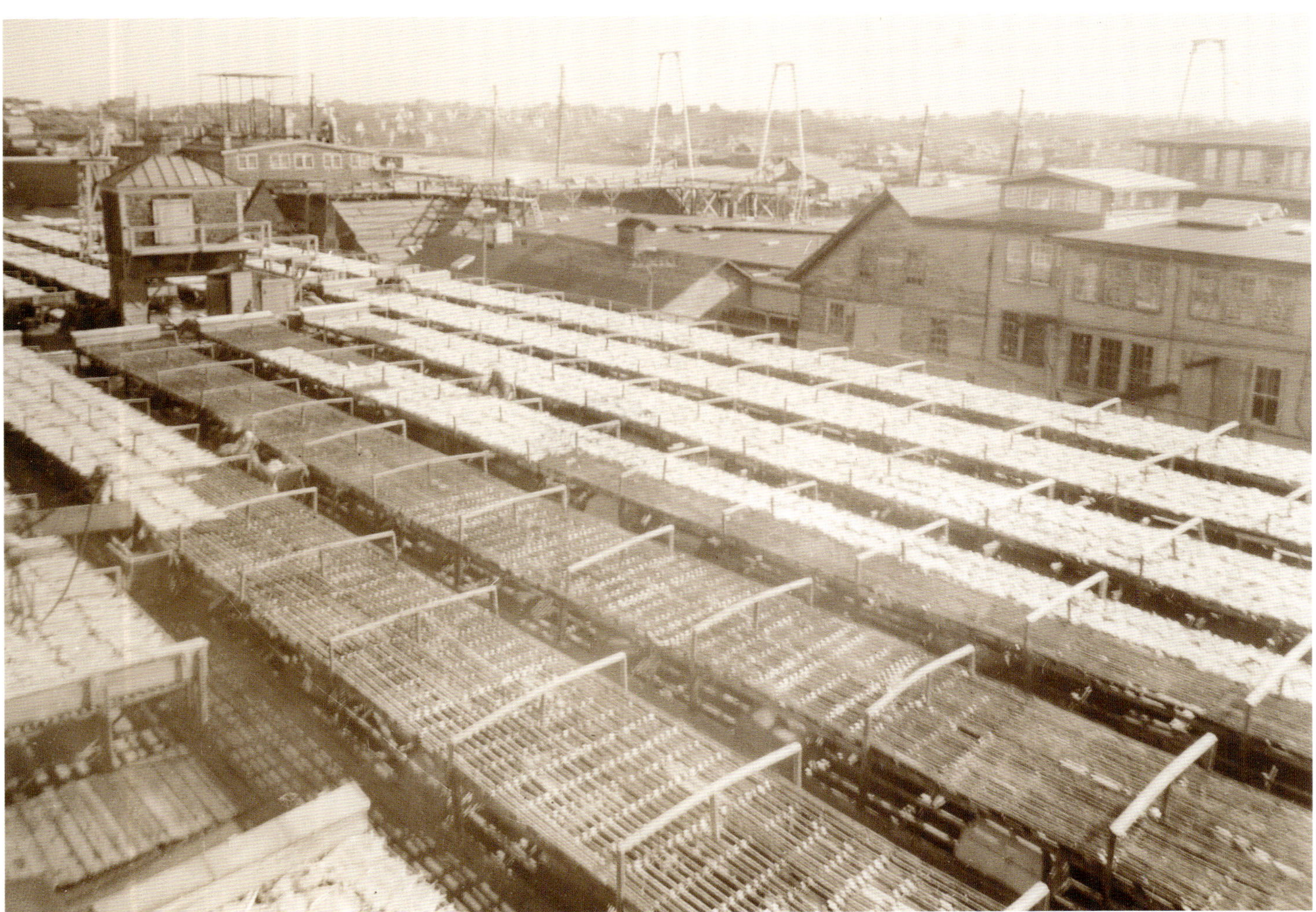

Celebrating Scallops

Long before the internet and social media, one of the best ways to promote your seafood product was an open-air, everyone-welcome seafood festival. That was certainly a benefit of New Bedford's Scallop Festival in Massachusetts, which was first held August 8, 1958. That first festival served 8,200 people, but only ten years later, it had become a three-day event and the women dishing up a "fried scallop meal with all the fixings" were feeding ten thousand people a day. The $14,686 in proceeds went to local charities. More importantly, the festival brought national attention to sea scallops and New Bedford, with food editors from national publications discovering the deep-sea delicacy and sharing it with readers.

The New Bedford Scallop Festival became the New Bedford Seafood Festival in 1968 after the scallop harvest declined and yellowtail flounder landings went up.

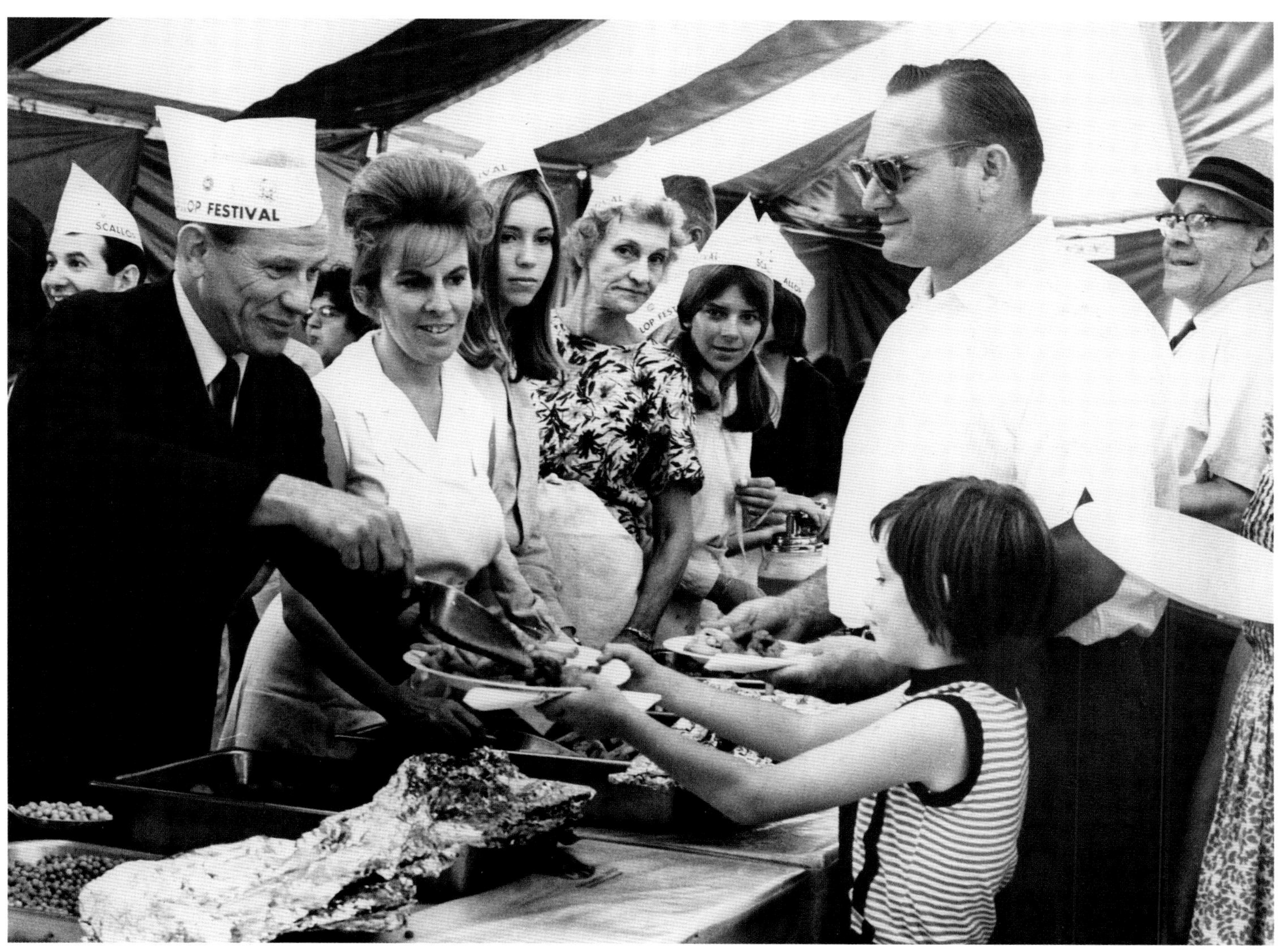

Wooden Lobster Boats

Freddy Lenfesty stands in front of his lobster boat the *Laura W.*, and behind him are the lobster traps he'll set from his boat come lobster season. Lenfesty was born and raised in Jonesport, a region in eastern Maine that has been known for its wooden boats and skilled boatbuilders since the early 1900s.

As a kid coming home from school, Lenfesty often stopped at the shop of local boatbuilder Freeman "Frem" Beal to earn a dime for helping out. When not in Frem's shop, he might be found building a small boat model or pulling a model boat on a string in the shallow waters of Moosabec Reach, which separated Jonesport from Beals Island. Later in life he would say, "That's how I developed my present models, pulling them on a string."

Lenfesty emphasized that his lobster boat designs were not like others, saying if you copy someone else, you "won't get a boat that goes any faster than the boat you copied." Lenfesty liked to race in the annual Moosabec Reach lobster boat races, where the *Laura W.* was a dominant force in the 1970s. Lenfesty was so ready to race that it's been said there were a couple of times when he was offshore lobstering and encountered a Navy destroyer, he raced the destroyer, keeping up with it for maybe a mile. Lenfesty was inducted in the Maine Lobster Boat Racing Hall of Fame in 2013.

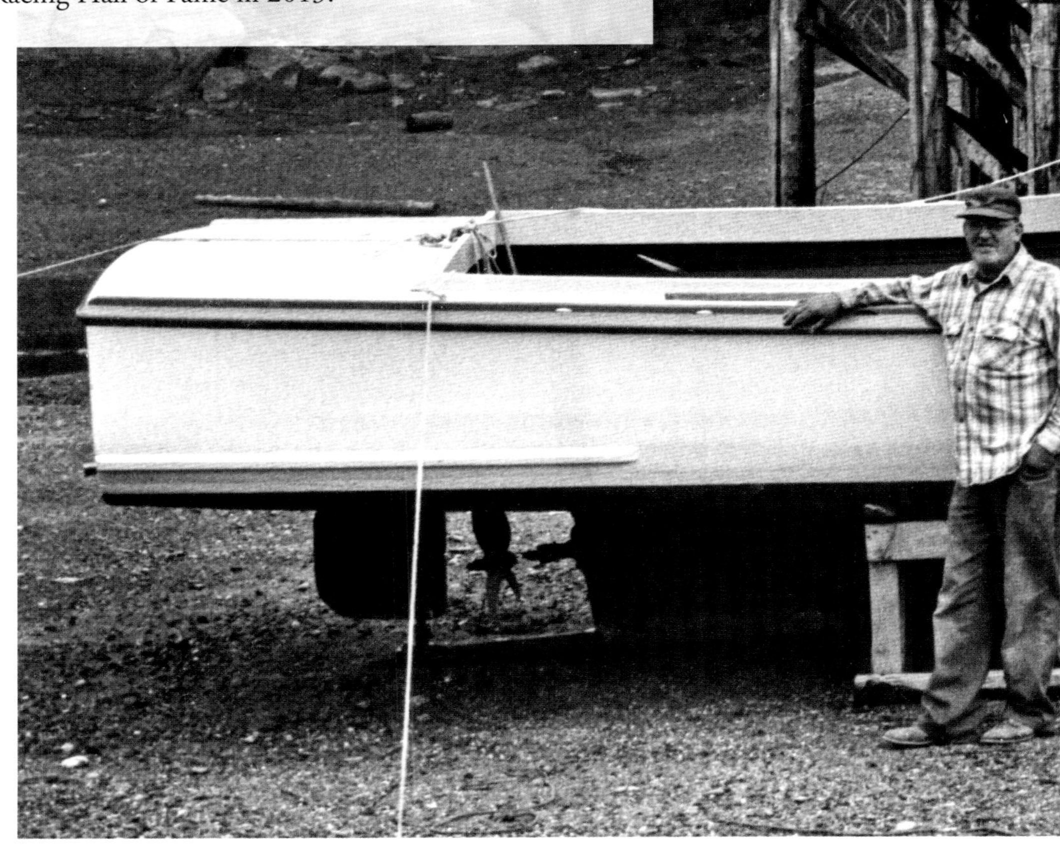

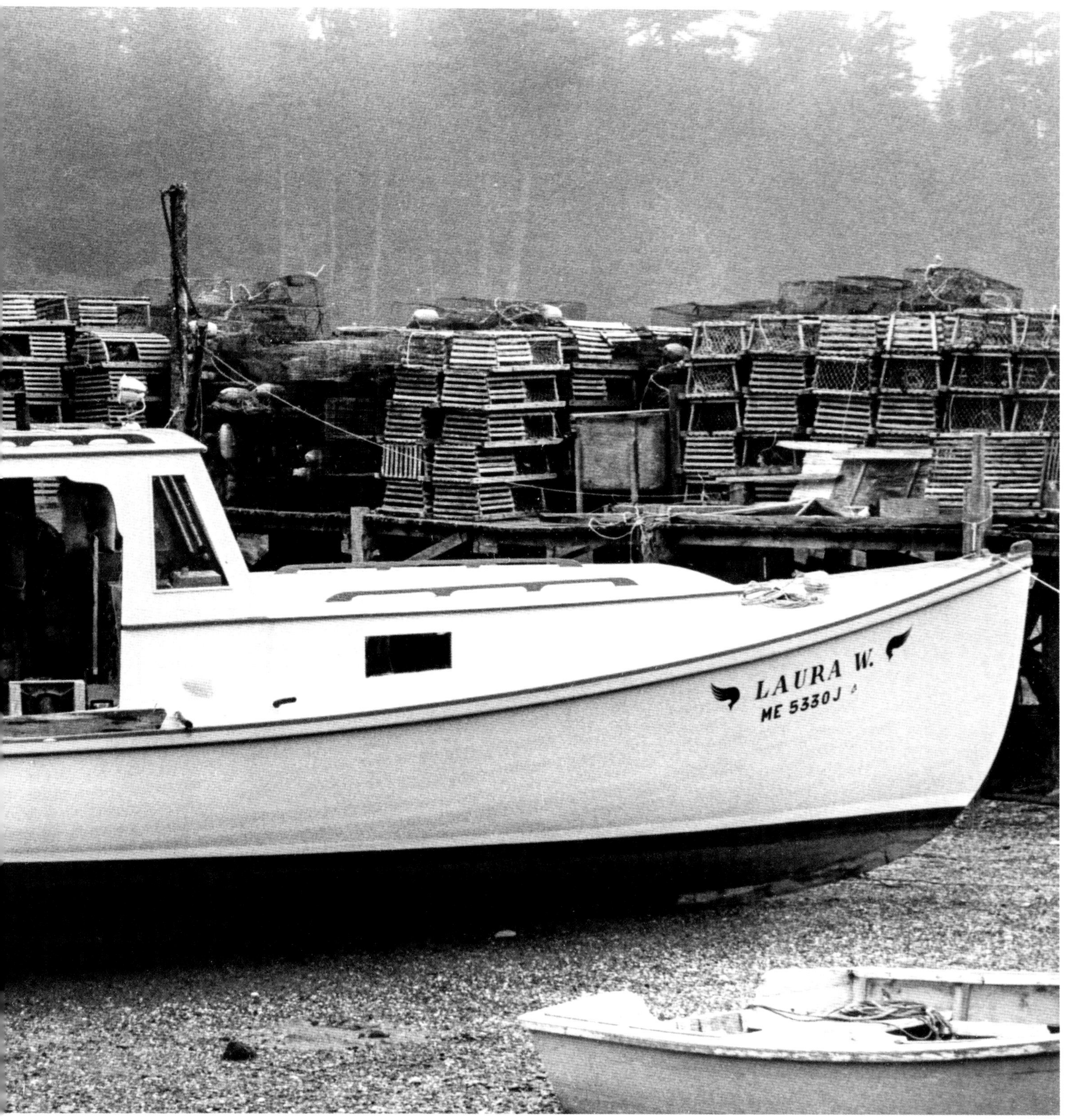

LAURA W.
ME 5330 J

Sponge Capital of the World

The sponge dive boat *Eleni* arrives in Tarpon Springs, Florida, after a seven-day trip in the late summer of 1970 loaded with 4,300 grade-A wool sponges, from nine to twenty-four inches. The waters off Florida's western coast were one of the few places suitable for the growth of natural sponges for commercial use. Since its first sponge fishing boat was launched in 1890, Tarpon Springs has been the epicenter of Florida's natural sponge industry.

Sponges were initially hooked off the bottom until diving was introduced in 1905. Three years later, in 1908, the Tarpon Springs Sponge Exchange was incorporated, which is where the *Eleni*'s sponges were sold for about $8,000. At the time, the *Eleni*'s trip was labeled "one of the best hauls of sponges ever brought into Tarpon Springs."

While most sponges used today are synthetic, natural sea sponges are still being harvested in Tarpon Springs, sometimes called the Sponge Capital of the World.

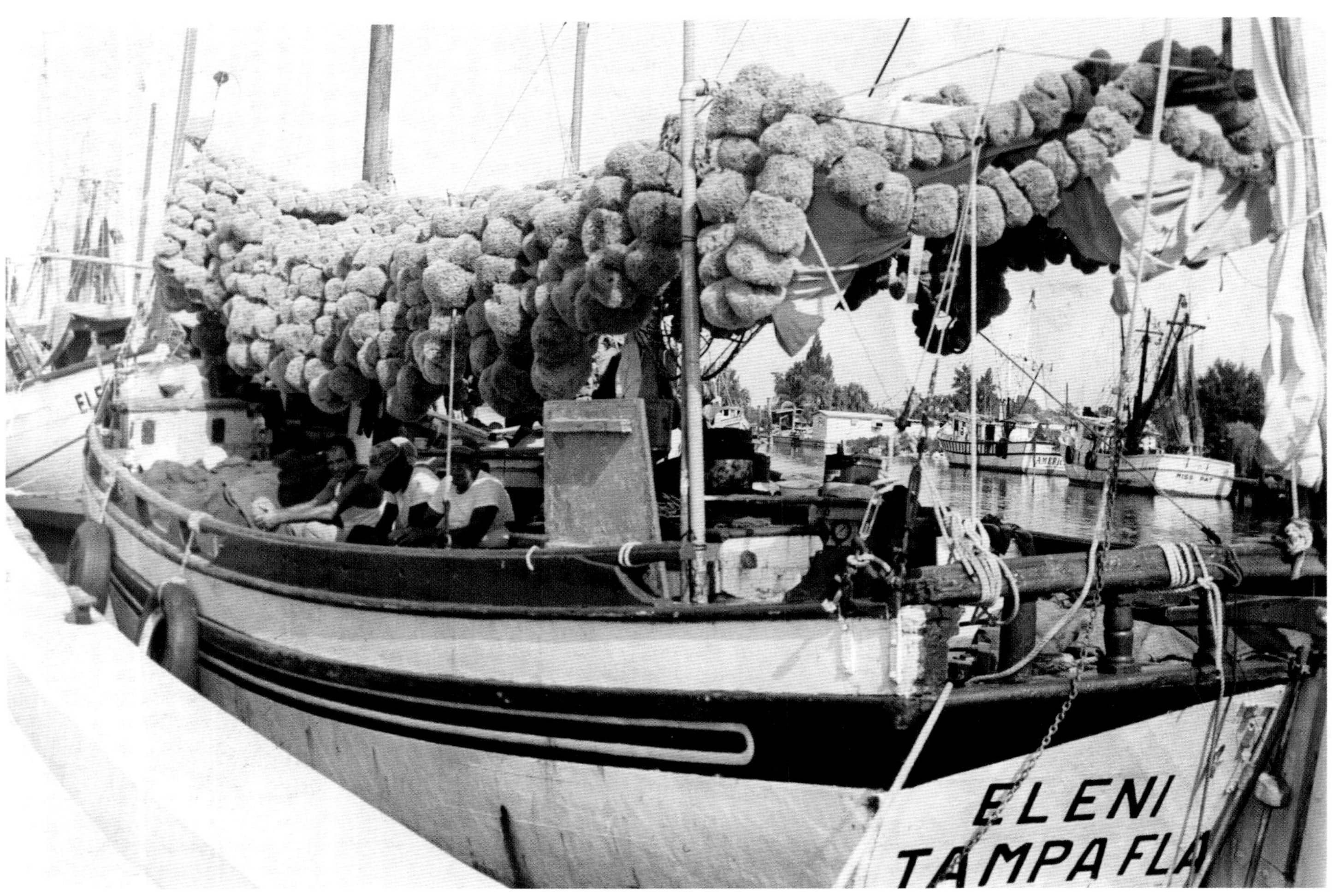

Record Shrimp Haul

How many shrimp does it take to make 350,000 shrimp cocktails? Figuring six shrimp to a cocktail, probably about two million shrimp. That was an estimate given by the skipper of the 80-foot *Warrior* when he delivered 62,000 pounds of pink and rock shrimp to St. Petersburg, Florida, in the early summer of 1972.

At the time, it was believed to be the largest shrimp haul ever in Florida by a single boat. It represented forty-eight days of working eighteen to twenty hours, with the catch bringing in $55,000 for the skipper and two crewmen. That's a long trip with long hours, but it was a relatively young crew, which might have made the task a little easier. The captain, Fred McGinn, was twenty-five. Sharing in the work were Buddy Dennis, twenty-six, and Gerry Derbyshore, thirty.

In addition to the shrimp, there were about 40,000 pounds of red snapper and black grouper were handlined when the *Warrior*'s crew wasn't shrimping. That's called "fish money," which pays for some expenses and on-shore recreation. After the shrimp were caught, they were cleaned off on deck with a high-pressure hose and then put into in a chill tank for an hour to remove the "animal heat." From there, the shrimp were glazed in a solution of corn syrup, common salt, and salt water before being put into mesh sacks and refrigerated. Even though the *Warrior* was out just shy of seven weeks, the catch was described as being "in beautiful condition" by the fish broker.

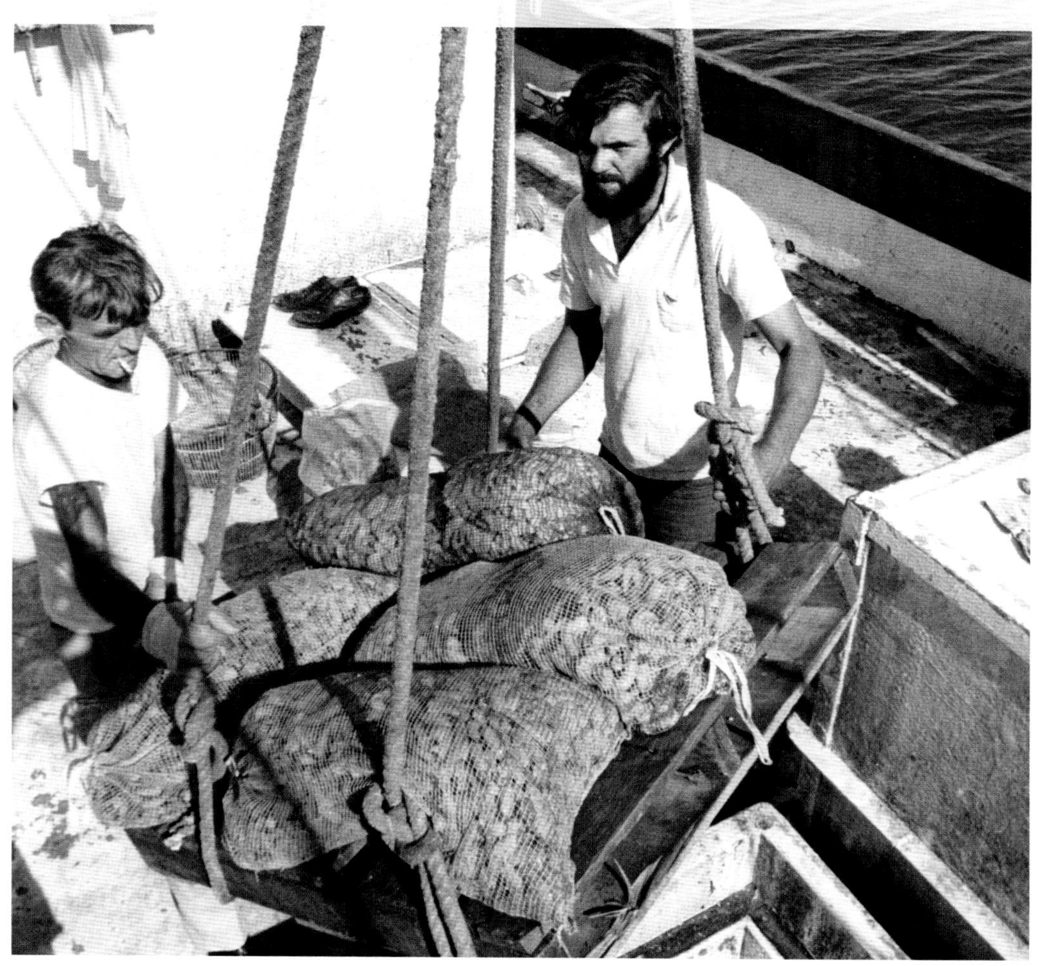

The End of the Serafina N

There's really no dignified way to close out the career of your family's fishing boat, no matter how attached you've become. That was the case with the 104-foot *Serafina N* on January 3, 1974, as she was broken up by a backhoe on Pavilion Beach in Gloucester, Massachusetts and carted away to the dump, fifty-seven years after being built.

Those fifty-seven years were a lot longer than the *Serafina N*'s builders expected. They had pegged her life expectancy at six months to a year, for the *Serafina N* was built in World War I to be a subchaser, with the job of destroying German U-boats lurking off the East Coast to sink merchant convoys departing from American ports.

After the war ended, the *Serafina N* was one of twenty to twenty-five Gloucester subchasers that joined the local mackerel fleet. Her best years were in the 1930s and 1940s when the Nicastro family took ownership. In 1944, she landed 1,418,000 pounds of mackerel.

When Gloucester's herring fishery was revived in the 1960s, it was determined the *Serafina N* was too old and worn out to participate. That's when Captain Philip Nicastro decided to break up the *Serafina N*. At the end, Nicastro couldn't watch what would happen and didn't attend the demolition. Other Nicastros attended and one was seen trying to "focus the movie camera with red eyes as the backhoe ripped the boat apart."

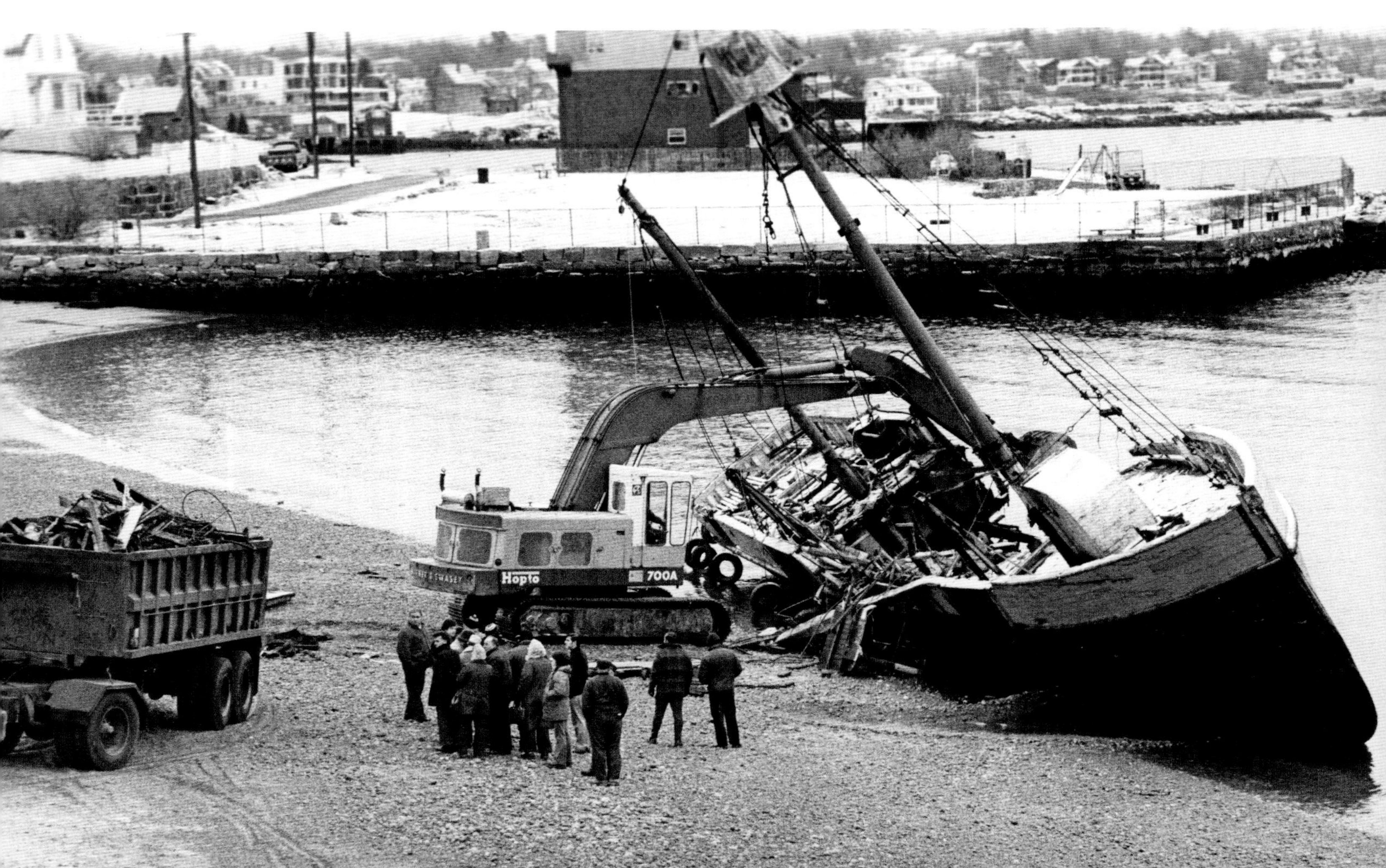

Sardine Packing

Sardine canneries (see page 104) in Lubec, Maine, produced 456,000 cases of sardines in 1901. But by 1980, the eastern-most town in the United States had just two sardine canneries that produced only 100,000 cases.

One of those facilities was the R.J. Peacock Canning Company, shown here in 1981 when many packing tables were empty and often only a boatload of fish a day was processed into canned sardines. Seven other Lubec processors had closed in the previous twenty years, and those that remained had trouble hiring enough workers.

R.J. Peacock's packing line was comprised mostly of women between fifty and eighty years old with a few of high-school age. Whether sitting on stools or standing, a woman would sweep a group of sardines off the conveyor belt passing between two packing lines and onto her worktable.

She then picked up a sardine, placed it between her fingers and cut its head off with a very sharp pair of household scissors. The sardine was then set in the can, but not just a casual placement, for sardines had to be arranged as carefully as possible because they were one of the few canned products that needed to have an attractive appearance when the can was first opened.

Sardines at one time were considered a delicacy, and it's been estimated that more than four hundred canneries have come and gone along the Maine coast since the first cannery opened in 1875 in Eastport. Faced with declining demand and a changing business climate, the plants went by the wayside one by one after the 1950s until the last Maine cannery closed in 2010.

A sardine is not a species of fish, but instead can be any of dozens of small, oily, cold-water fish that are part of the herring family and sold in tightly packed cans.

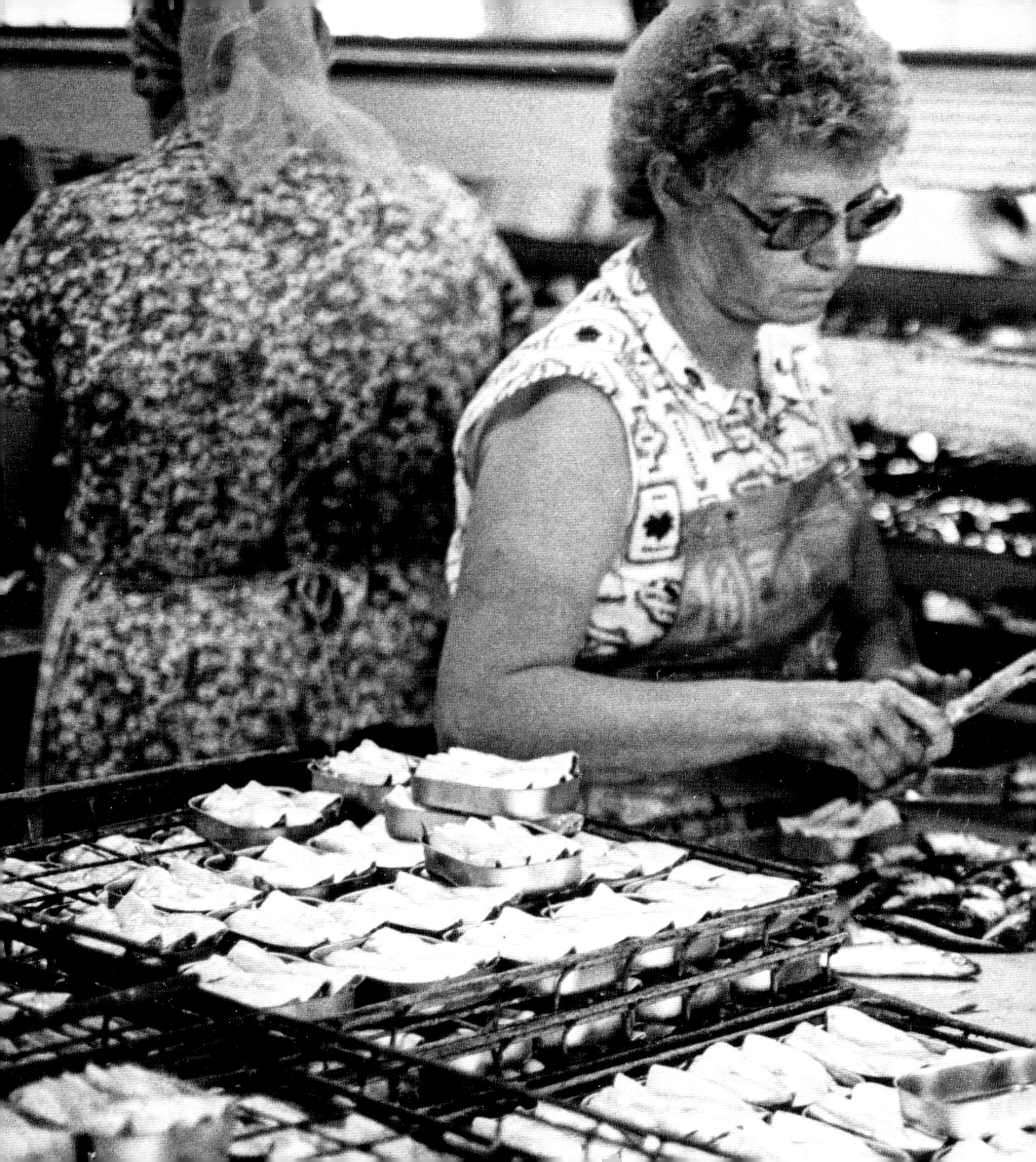

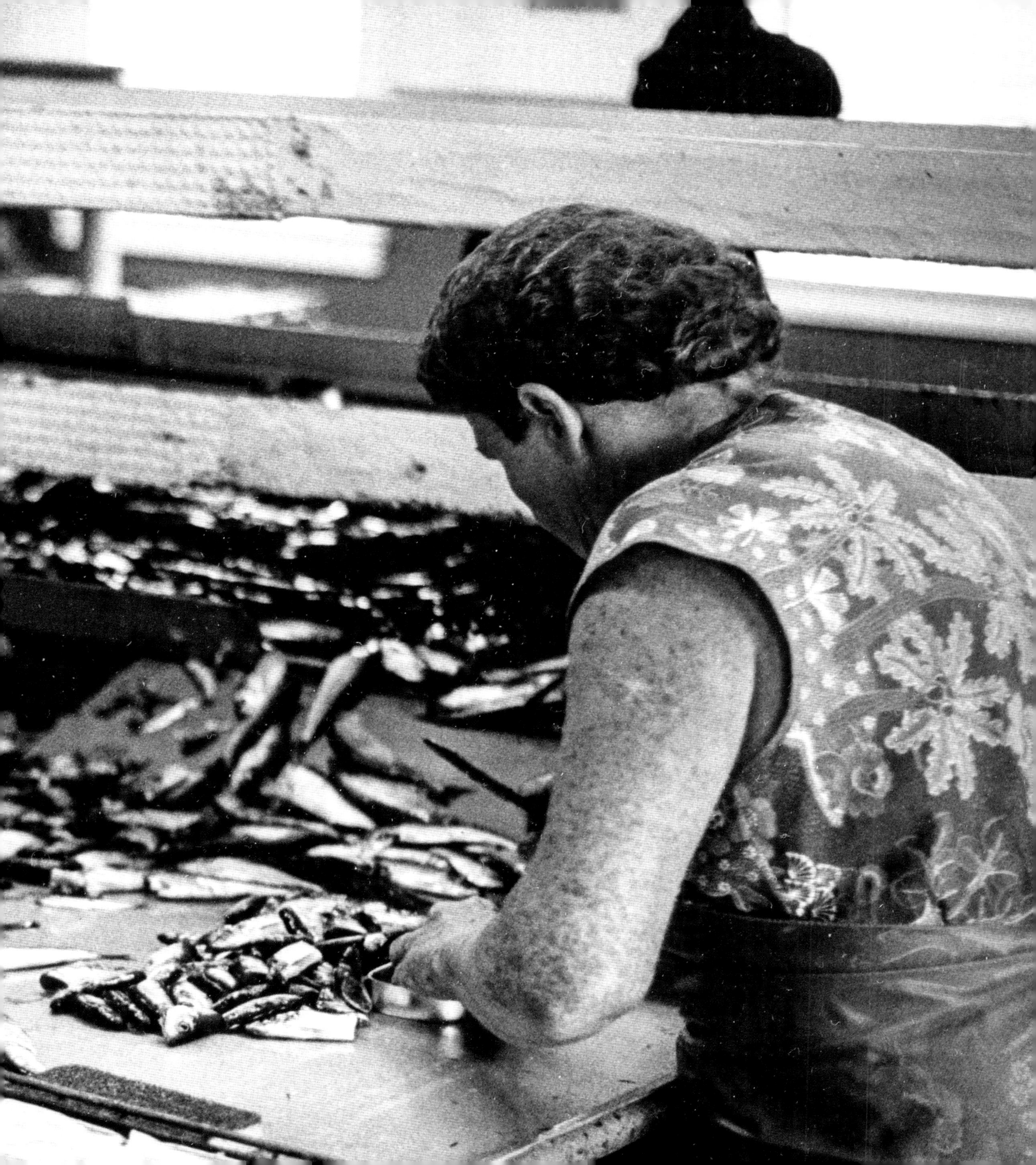

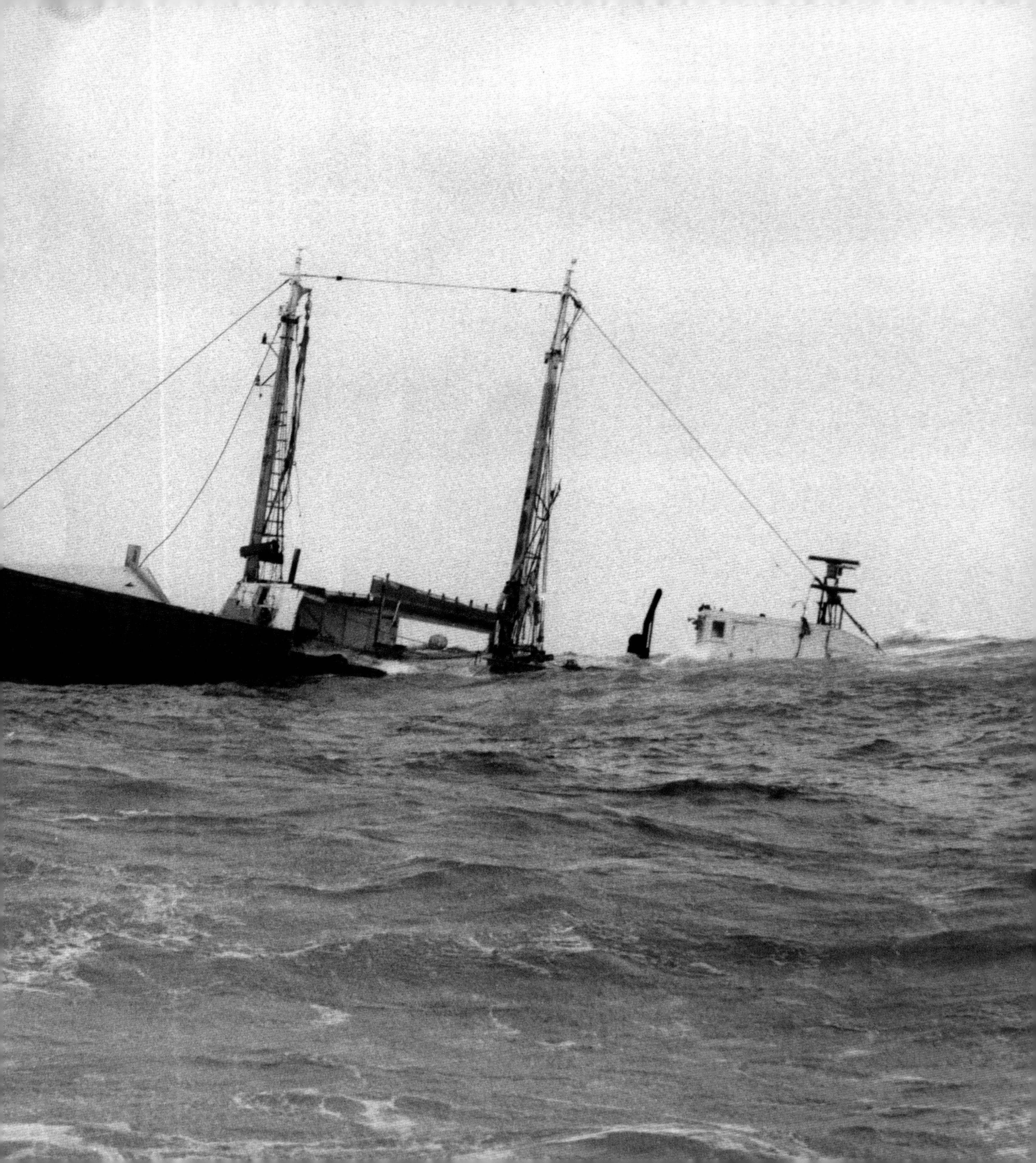

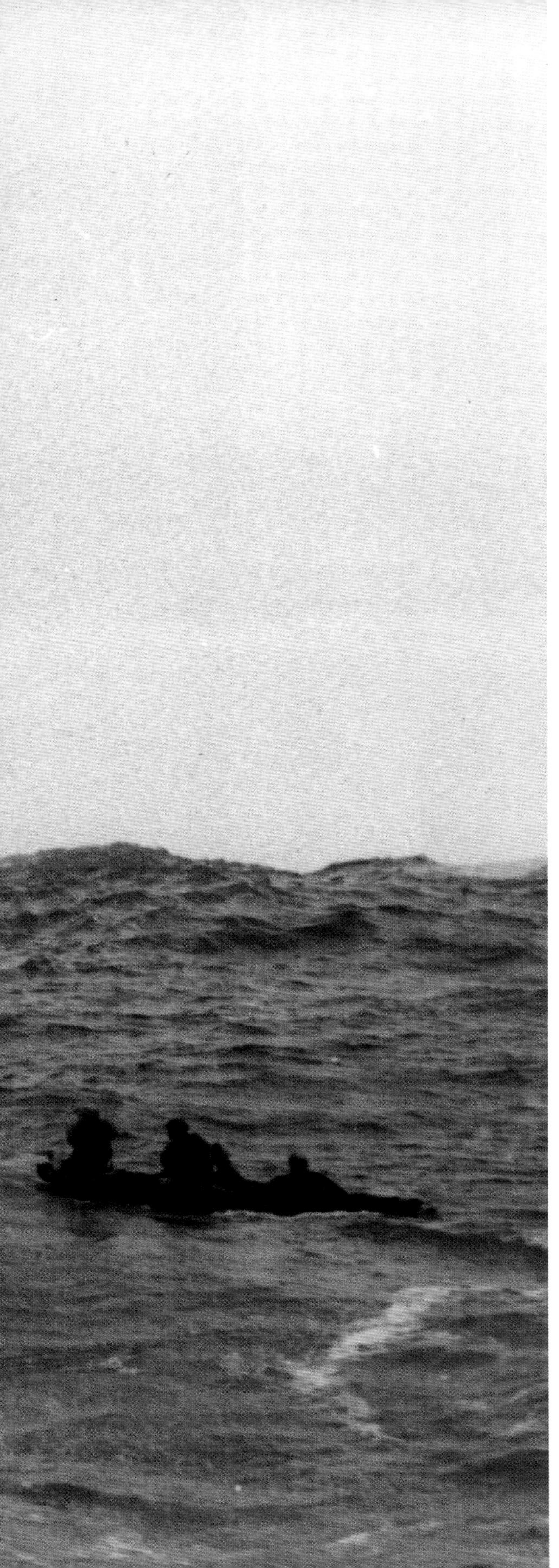

Drama at Sea

The ocean can be unpredictable, volatile, and inherently dangerous. And beyond the weather and ledges and other hazards that can sink a boat, you never know when you might be staring down the wrong end of a revolver or at the badge of law enforcement officer.

As long as men have been sailing ships, they've been losing them at sea to adverse weather, to collisions with other vessels, to rocky shores and sandbars, and even to torpedoes fired by German U-boats. Fishermen have faced threats to their lives and their livelihoods in territorial disputes, in high-seas rescues, and in political squabbles that can jeopardize their way of life. And they've also been known to confront lawmen, protesters, and regulators in matters such as illegal fishing, taxes on booze, and fishing rules they deem unfair.

End of the Whaling Era

The commercial whaling industry in the United States began in the 1600s and peaked in the mid-1800s, when more than seven hundred vessels engaged in whale hunting. Whales were prized for their oil—used primarily in oil lamps but also as a lubricant for clocks, typewriters, guns, and other machinery—and whalebone used in tools, buggy whips, corset stays, and other products.

Launched on April 16, 1878, the 300-ton *Wanderer* was the last whaleship built in Mattapoisett, Massachusetts. It was 116 feet long and had a 27-foot beam and 15-foot draft. It generally carried a crew of thirty during the next forty-six years. In that time, the *Wanderer* logged twenty-three whaling voyages, catching twenty-four whales. Many of those whaling voyages were out of San Francisco, while others took it around the Azores in the North Atlantic.

The *Wanderer* appeared in the 1922 silent film *Down to the Sea in Ships*, reportedly with very realistic whaling scenes. She has also been called the most beautiful whaleship and was a featured subject in an oil painting by well-known artist Irving Ramsey Wiles.

The *Wanderer* was well-known for being the last square-rigged whaleship to sail out of New Bedford, Massachusetts, on August 25, 1924. The following day, she was caught in a gale and wrecked on the treacherous rocks of Cuttyhunk Island in Buzzards Bay.

The whaling industry was made famous by the 1851 novel *Moby Dick*, whose author, Herman Melville, spent three years aboard a whaler a decade earlier. The *Wanderer* was the last sail-powered whaling vessel, and her demise marked the symbolic end of an industry that once fueled the economies of Nantucket, New Bedford, and other New England ports.

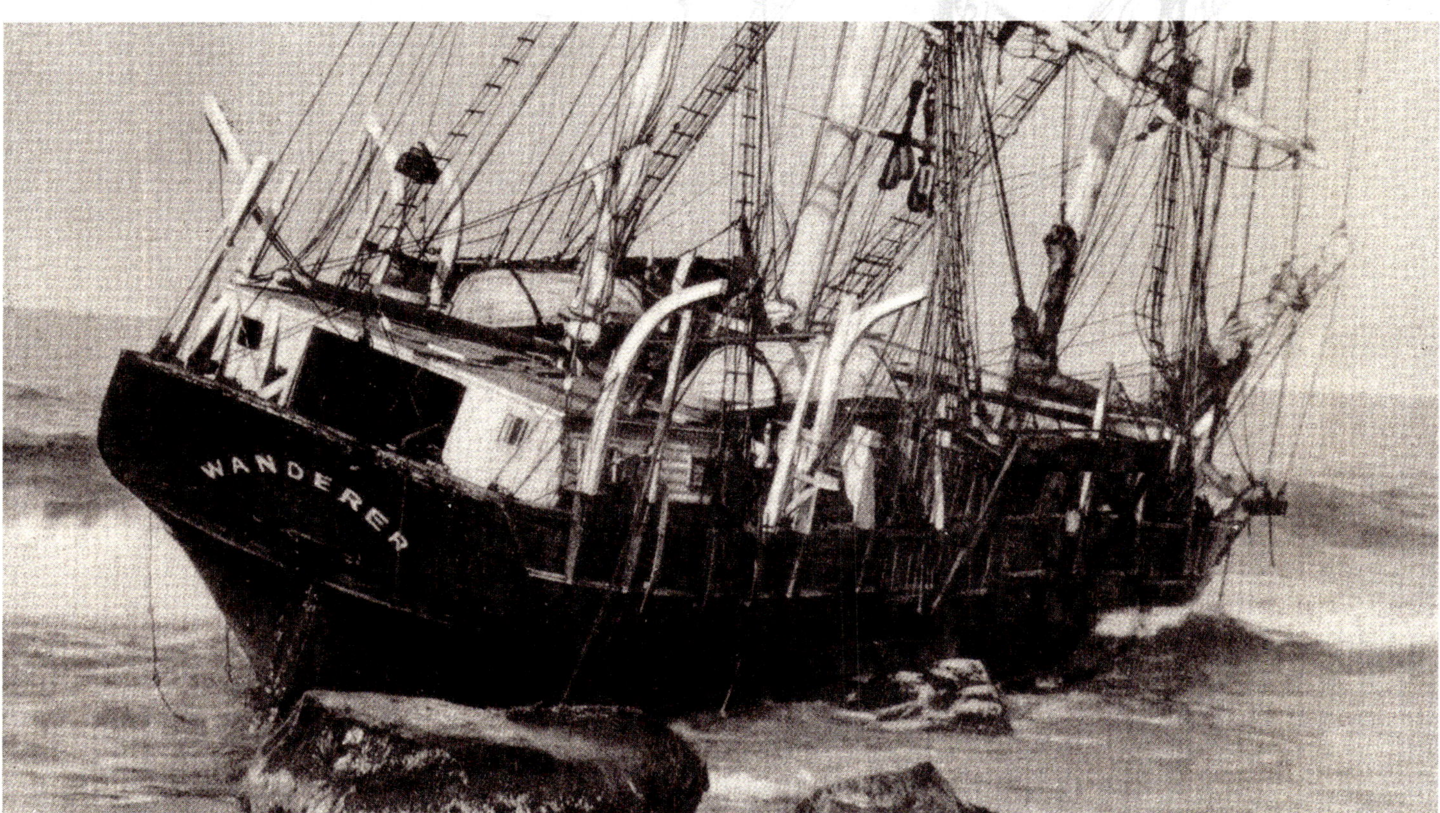

Mutiny on the Chisholm

The crew of the 77-foot schooner *Mary F. Chisholm* (see page 110) is shown cutting bait at a dock in Portland, Maine, before heading out on a fishing trip in 1931. That's about twenty-five years after what might be the only mutiny on a New England fishing boat. The *Mary F. Chisholm* was fishing out of Gloucester, Massachusetts, in 1906, but crews were scarce. So that April, the schooner swung up to Portland for additional crew before heading to the Virginia Capes at the entrance to Chesapeake Bay for the first mackerel of the season.

It might have been another forgotten fishing trip if the regular skipper hadn't broken his leg and Sylvester Durost, "a six footer, black as a Spaniard and with a long red scar over his right eye," hadn't been hired as his replacement, recalled Johnny Kern, one of the Portland fishermen onboard. Looking back on the trip, Kern said, "We wished whoever put that scar on his forehead had hit him twice as hard."

The *Mary F. Chisholm* chased mackerel for ten weeks on the Virginia Capes. But finding little luck there, Durost headed back to Portland, only to suddenly decide to go to the Bay of Fundy in Canada. "Right then," Kern said, "is when the rebellion or mutiny really began."

After a thick fog bank forced the *Chisholm* into Monhegan Island Harbor, four of the Portland crewmen rowed ashore in a dory looking for a way out. A mail and freight packet was going to Boothbay in the morning, and they borrowed the packet's dory to bring their gear back with them. They came out of the *Chisholm*'s fo'c'sle with their dunnage bags just in time to see Durost cut the dory's painter, sending it drifting off into the fog. "Then the fun began," said Kern.

The Portland part of the crew was made up of Americans and Irishmen while the rest were Frenchmen from Nova Scotia who tended to line up behind Durost. He gathered his Frenchmen while "our crowd . . . gave Durost a good understandable idea of what we thought of him."

In response, Durost broke one fisherman's arm with an oar. "Durost was wild," said Kern. "He cursed and threatened us all." He aimed a blow at another fisherman who grabbed a swordfish harpoon and yelled, "Come on you and I'll drive this beanpole clean through your damn gizzard."

That stopped Durost, and the Portland crew then agreed to go along on a few more days of fishing. However, with no mackerel to speak of, Durost threatened to head out to Georges Bank two hundred miles away. The cook told Kern there was only a "peck of beans, three pecks of flour and three barrels of water." They consumed a barrel a day.

"That's when we really mutinied," said Kern.

They confronted Durost, repeated what the cook had said, and told him, "We refuse to help handle the vessel or to fish a lick. Put us ashore. We demand it and the law's with us." When Durost called them "a damn liar," twelve suits of oilers and twelve pairs of hip rubber boots went over the starboard railing and into the sea. Durost ended up backing down, telling the helmsman to "jibe her over and head North by West" toward Cape Elizabeth, Maine.

Durost knew that he could be in trouble for breaking the fisherman's arm and not taking him ashore for treatment. So he offered hush money: $100 each to forget what had happened.

"What was we to do?" said Kern. "No use borrowing money for a sea-lawyer just to get square. So we pocketed the $100 apiece and never mentioned our experiences to the reporters. That's why the story . . . never got out."

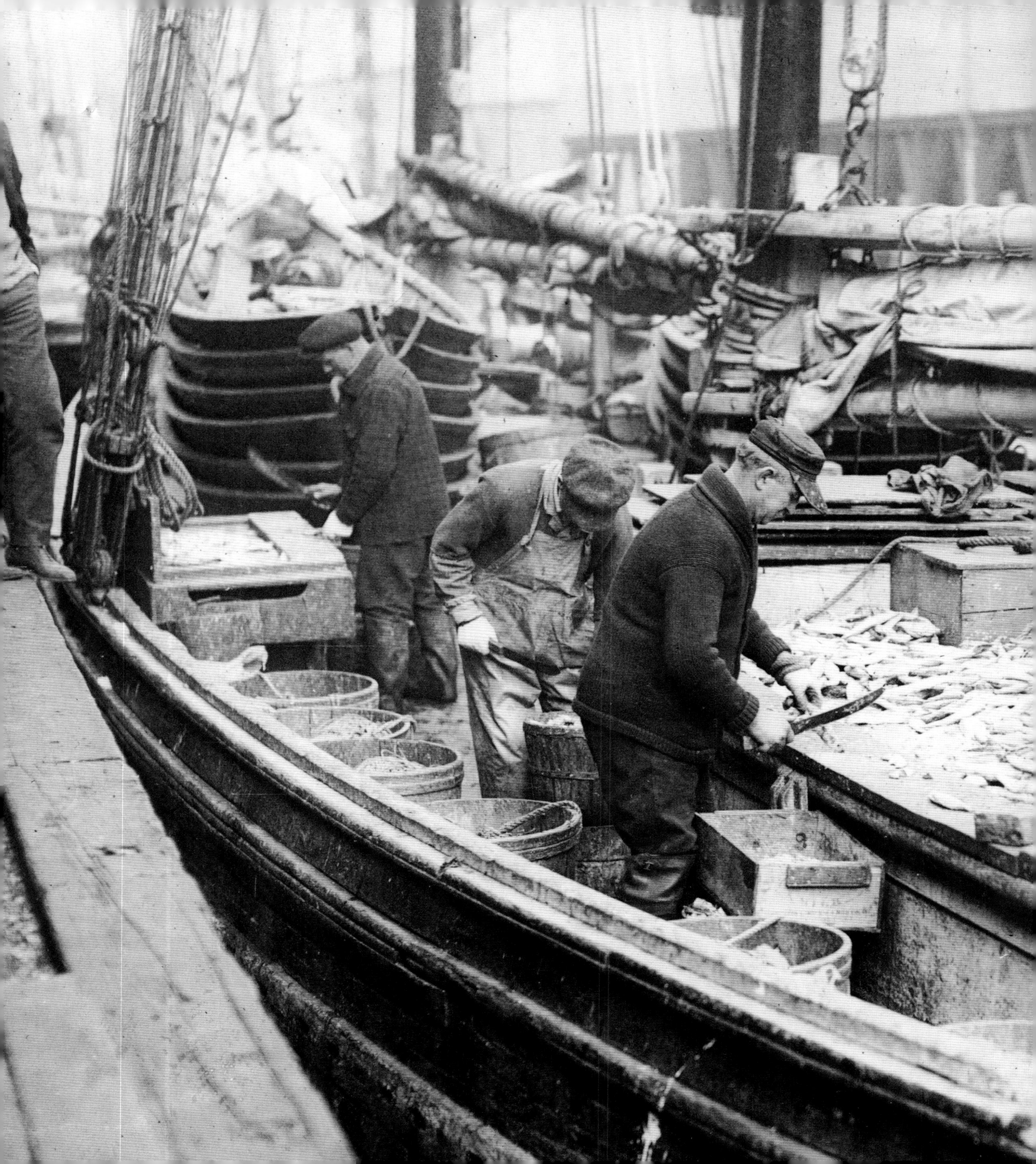

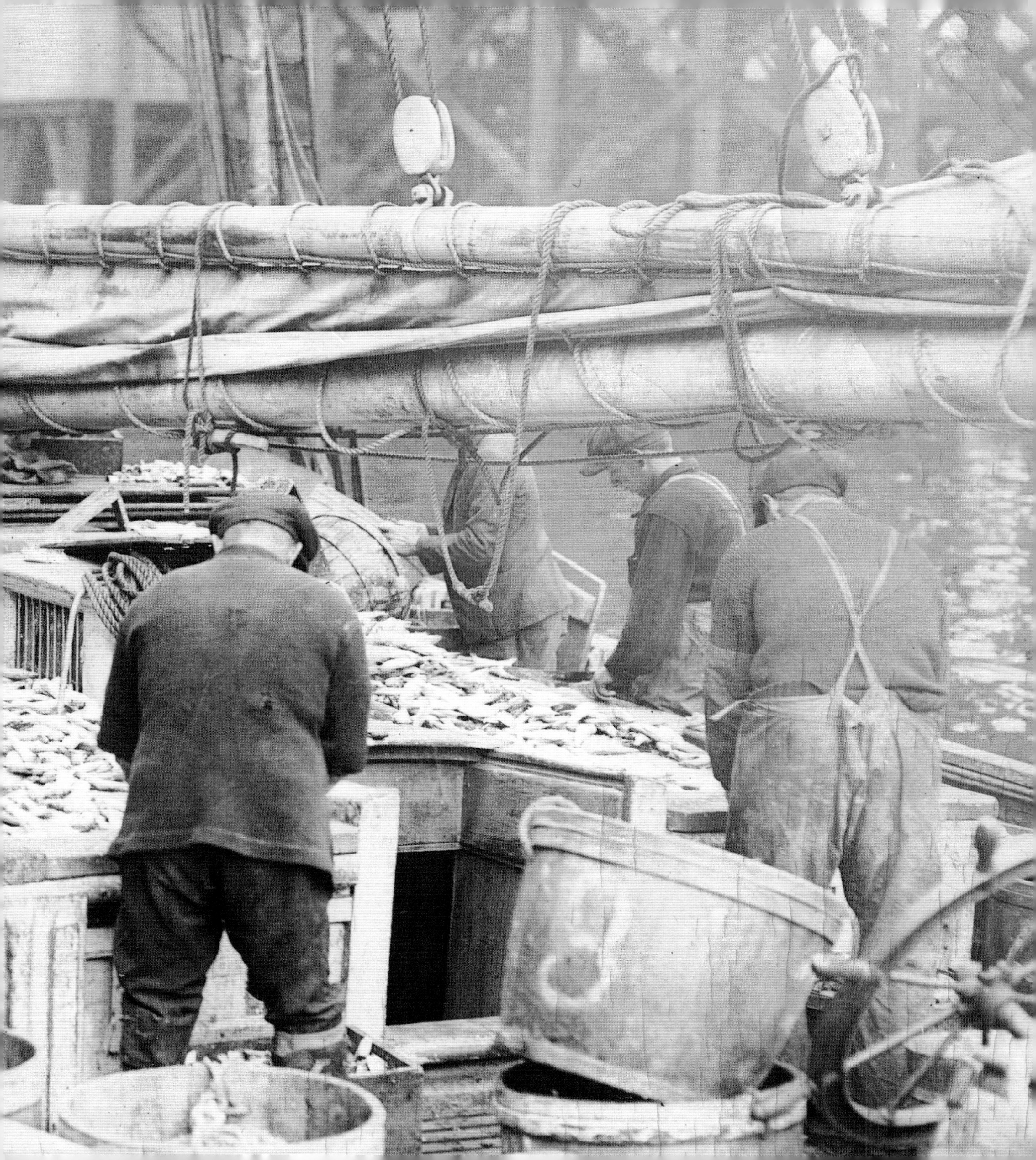

Boat Fire Rescue

The Boston-based dragger *Star of the Sea* was fishing the waters off Martha's Vineyard the night of February 2, 1960 when it was rocked by two below-deck explosions, setting it afire. Luckily for the *Star of the Sea*'s seven-man crew, the Stonington, Connecticut-based dragger *America* was nearby and took them aboard. However, nothing is easy in any rescue, and that was true in this case when lines from the *Star of the Sea*'s life raft got caught up in the *America*'s prop, causing the two vessels to pound against each other.

Fortunately, the *Luann*, another Stonington dragger, was nearby and pulled the *America* away from the fire. The *Star of the Sea*'s skipper, Kevin Cleary, said the rescue succeeded with only moments to spare.

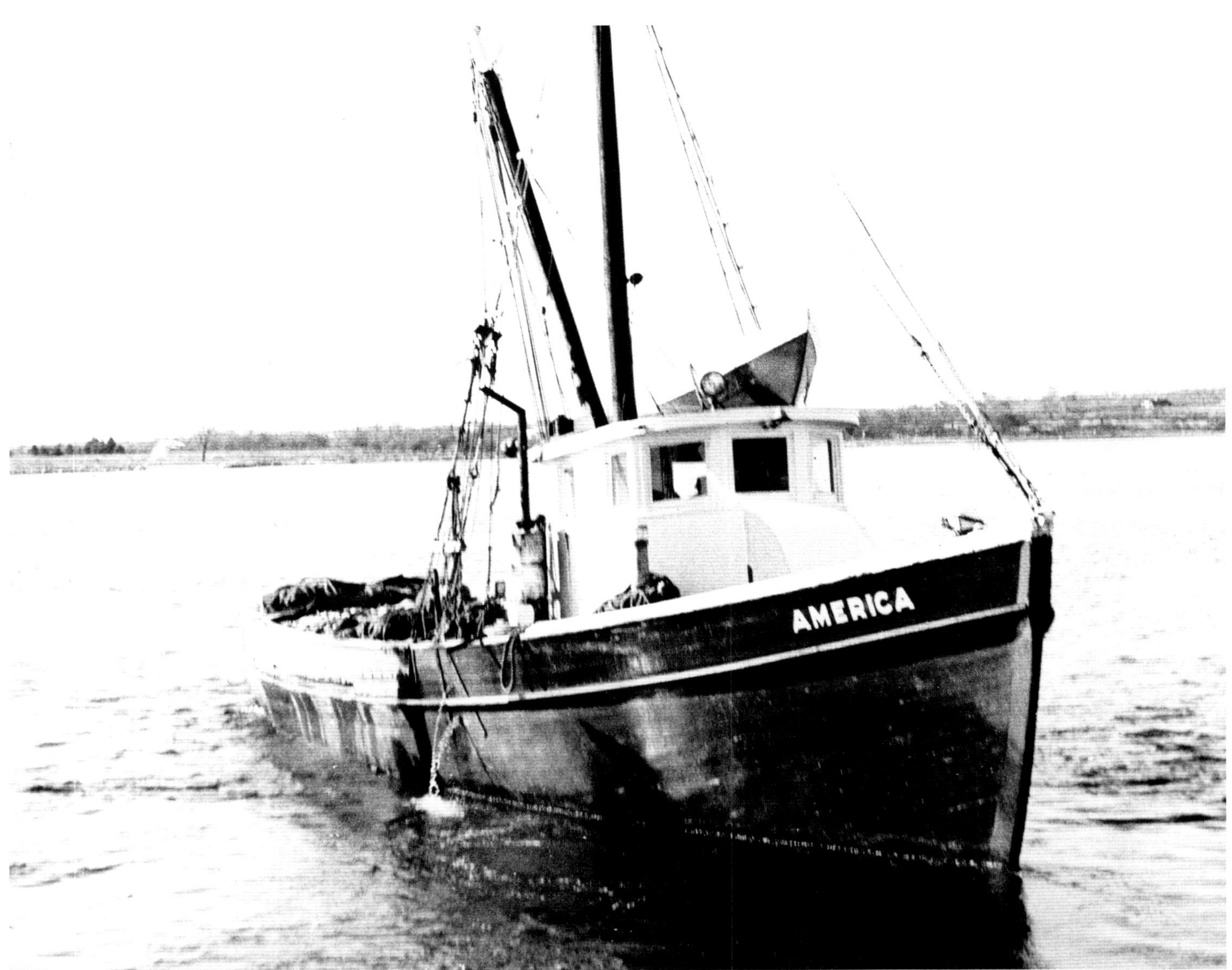

German U-boats

The *Ben & Josephine* (see page 114), shortly after she was launched, is shown tied to the dock at Morse Boatbuilding in Thomaston, Maine, in March 1941. She was built as a 92-foot side trawler, targeting mostly redfish, with a 130,000-pound hold capacity. Then World War II intervened, ending the career of the *Ben & Josephine*—and many other fishing boats— before it had barely begun.

The *Ben & Josephine* left Gloucester, Massachusetts, on June 2, 1942, bound for the Seal Island fishing grounds off Nova Scotia. The *Aeolus*, another side trawler, followed about five miles back. At 3 p.m. the next day, the two boats noticed an unmarked submarine some two miles away. The crews on both boats assumed it was friendly, at least until it closed within a couple of hundred yards and machine-gunned the *Ben & Josephine*'s wheelhouse. That was the German U-boat *U-432*.

The *Ben & Josephine*'s crew quickly launched two dories and abandoned their vessel as the Germans shelled them, sinking the vessel at 4:30 p.m. As soon as the *Ben & Josephine* went down, the sub went after the *Aeolus*, ordering it to stop and the crew to leave in dories before shelling and sinking the vessel. Crewmembers noticed the Germans were filming the shelling.

Once the submarine departed, the four dories headed for Maine's Mount Desert Rock, which they reached two days later. That was neither the start nor the end of the German submarine war with fishing boats. On May 17, the same U-boat sank the Boston-based trawler *Foam,* killing one crewman. On July 25, the fishing schooner *Lucille M* out of Lockport, Nova Scotia, was sunk at three a.m. by a German submarine's shelling and machine-gunning. About twenty shells were fired into the schooner and four crewmen were wounded.

Three days later, a sub sank the Boston-based trawler *Ebb,* killing five fishermen and wounding seven about thirty miles from the *Lucille M*'s demise. A Canadian destroyer rescued the survivors. The *Ebb* was the last fishing vessel sunk by Germans off the New England coast.

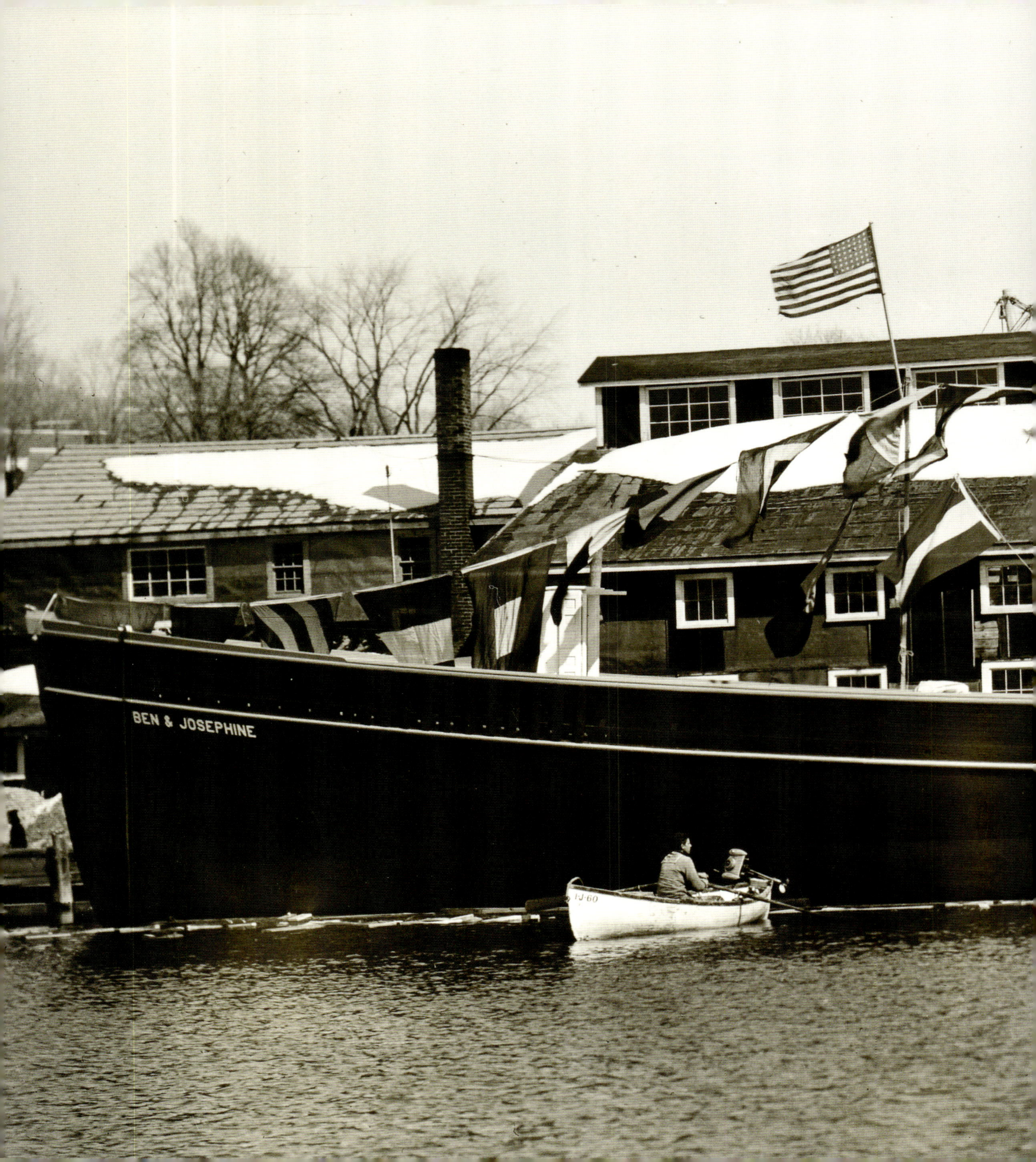

BEN & JOSEPHINE

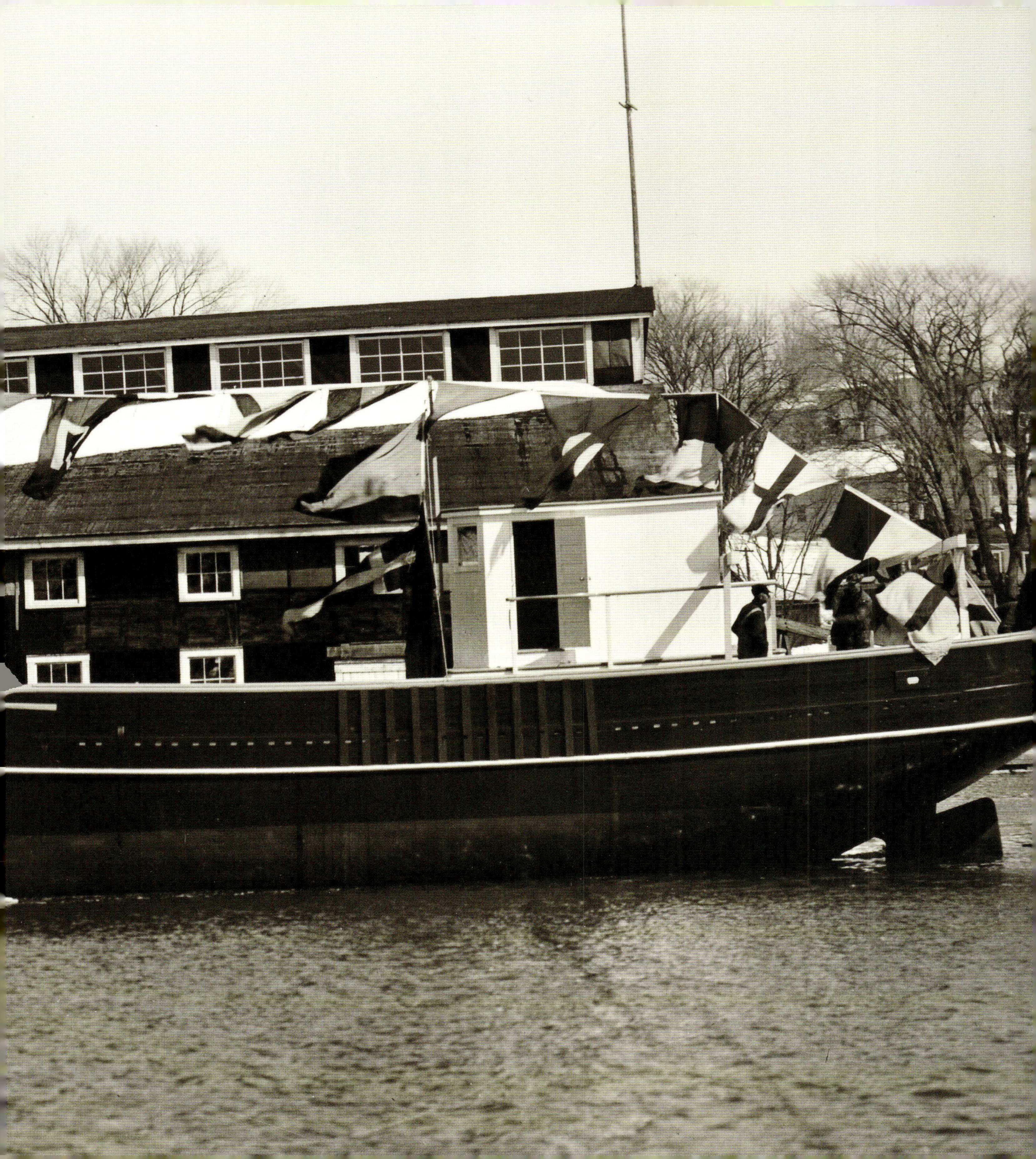

Plane Crash at Sea

The *Sovereign of the Sky*, a Pan American Clipper with twenty-four passengers and seven crew, lost its tail section when making an emergency landing in the Pacific Ocean. Amazingly, everyone survived after a Coast Guard cutter helped with the landing and rescued the passengers and crew before the plane sank.

The cutter *Ponchartrain* was assigned to a forty-square-mile chunk of ocean between Hawaii and California known as Ocean Station November, where it reported weather information, served as a navigational aid to passing aircraft, and relayed emergency messages by radio.

With the threat of World War II and submarine warfare looming, the Coast Guard instituted so-called "ocean stations" in 1940, thereby allowing merchant vessels to stop making weather reports. By 1943 there were eight ocean stations in U.S. waters, each with its own name.

The *Ponchartrain* received the *Sovereign of the Sky*'s distress call at 3:30 a.m. October 16, 1956, reporting that two of its four engines were down. In darkness, the plane circled the *Ponchartrain*, making dry runs in anticipation of ditching. In preparation, the *Ponchartrain* laid down a two-mile trail of foam on the water to mark the best place for the plane to land. When the plane landed at about 6:15 that morning, the impact was so great the tail section completely sheared off.

Passengers in life jackets quickly exited onto the wings and were picked up by boats from the *Ponchartrain* and transferred to the cutter. Twenty minutes later, the *Sovereign of the Sky* sank. Something as intense as an emergency plane landing at sea was unusual for Coast Guard crews who patrolled the ocean stations. In fact, life was often monotonous, so much so that a Coast Guard cutter stationed in the Atlantic held beauty contests—by radio with stewardesses in aircraft passing overhead participating.

One category was Miss Heavenly Body, chosen by body measurements that were readily given over the radio. The other category was Miss Heavenly Voice, based on the alluring qualities of the stewardesses' voices. Five hundred stewardesses entered in all, with the winners later feted on the *We the People* television show. The Coast Guard's Ocean Stations were discontinued in the 1974.

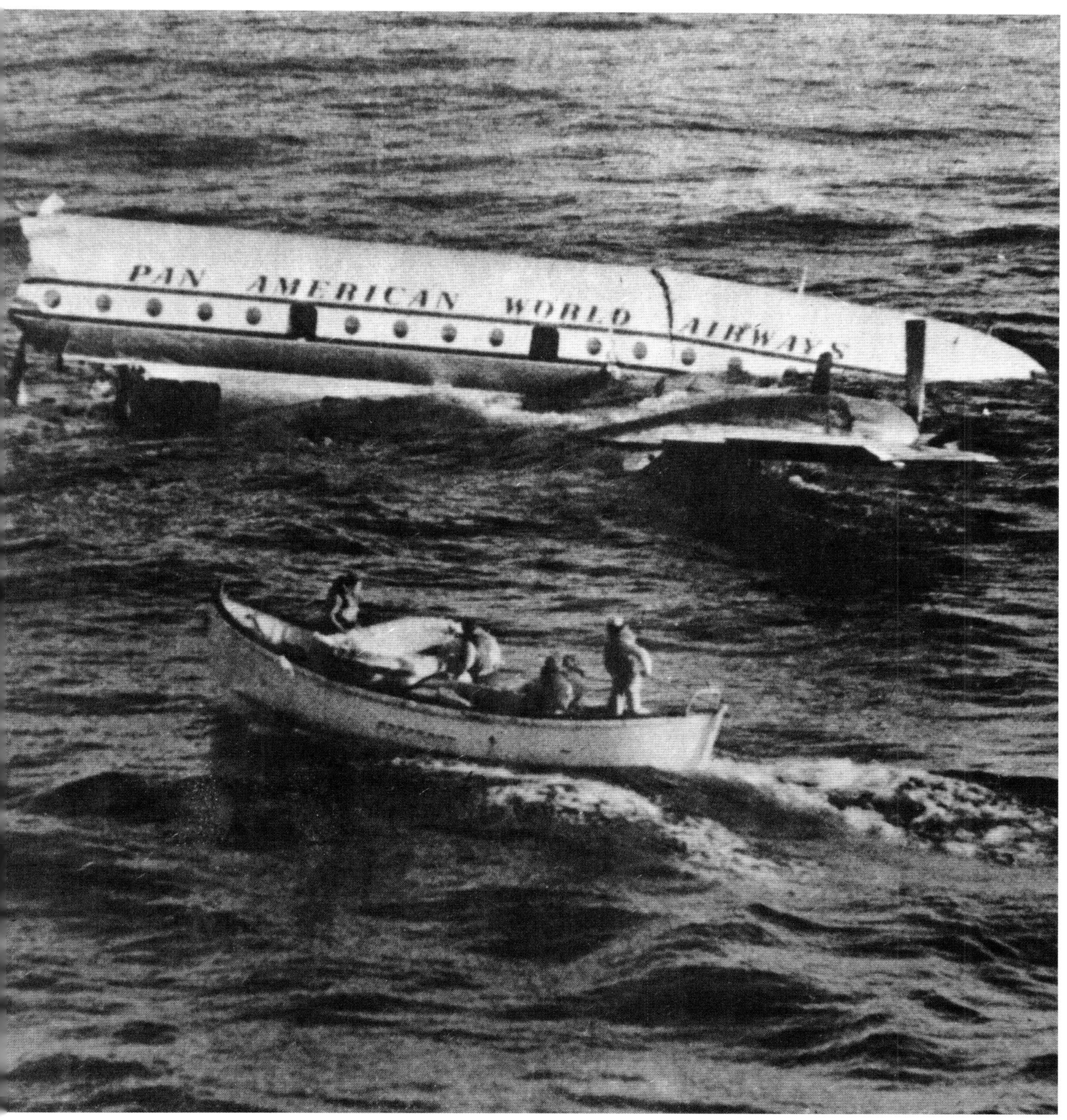
PAN AMERICAN WORLD AIRWAYS

High Seas Rescue

The 310-foot Coast Guard cutter *Castle Rock* operated out of Portland, Maine in 1967, patrolling a 210-mile area of New England waters for three weeks at a time.

On one of those patrols, the *Castle Rock* was in rough seas, ninety miles southwest of Cape Race, Newfoundland. So too was the Canadian 82-foot wooden trawler *Maureen & Michael* when she was struck broadside by a huge wave and began taking on water. For three days, her eight-man crew did the best they could to repair the damage, but to no avail.

The *Castle Rock* came upon the scene on February 22, but as the seas were too rough to launch a rescue boat, two Coast Guardsmen volunteered to take the crew off the trawler in a rubber raft. The last two crewmen to board the raft were only fifty yards from the *Maureen & Michael* when she disappeared beneath the waves.

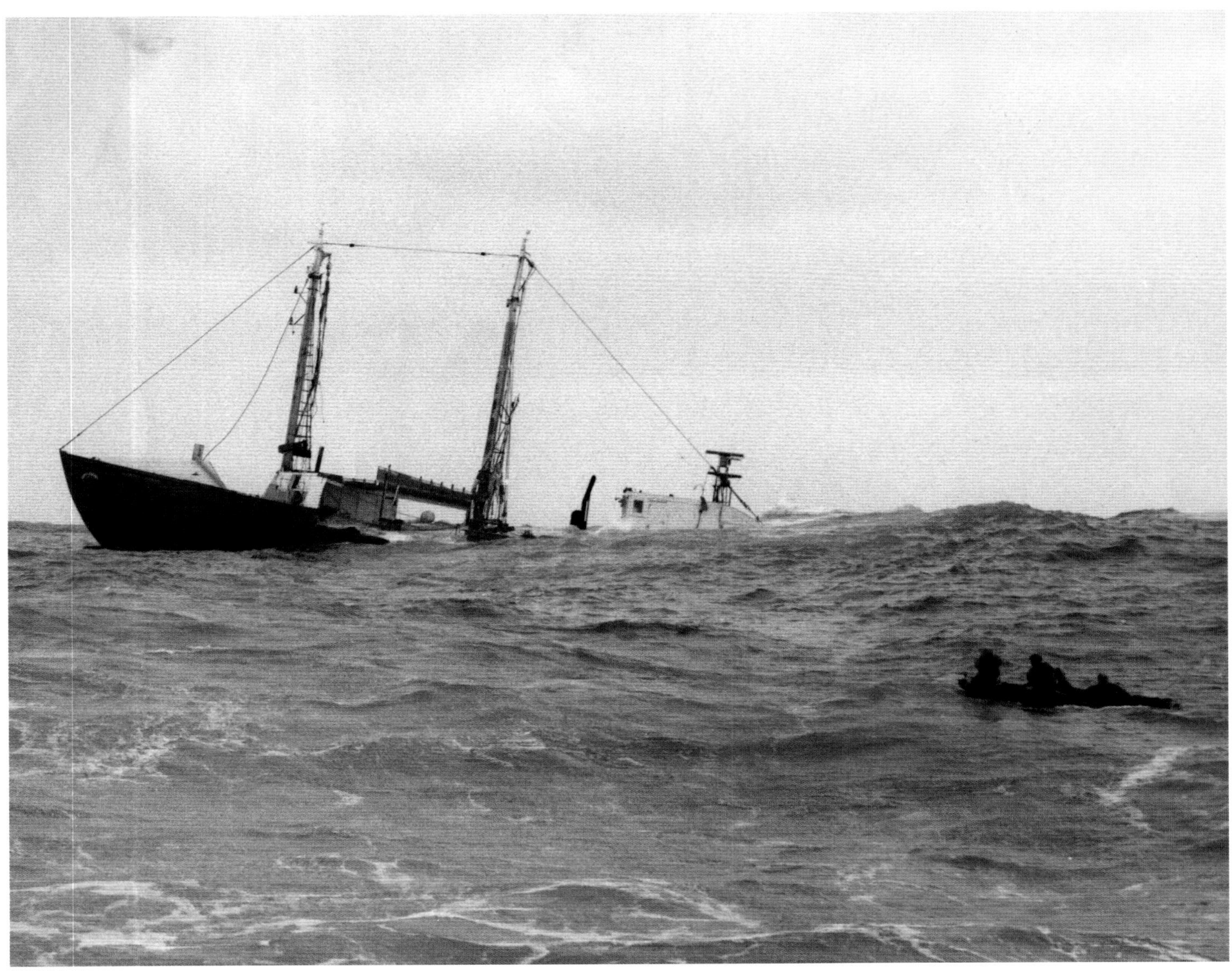

San Juan

Through much of the 1960s, Peru was a fisheries powerhouse and the world's leading producer of fish meal. Peru was not about to share its fishing grounds. Two American seiners fishing twenty-five to fifty miles off the Peruvian coast discovered this on February 15, 1969, when they were attacked with .50 caliber machine gun fire from a Peruvian warship. The *San Juan* was hit at least sixty-six times. No injuries were reported but there was $50,000 in damages. The *Mariner* was captured and released, but only after paying a fine.

Relations had been tense between the Peruvian military government and America after Peru seized an oil company that was a subsidiary of Standard Oil Company and claimed jurisdiction up to two-hundred miles out to sea. At the time, the United States only recognized a three-mile limit with an additional nine-mile fishing zone.

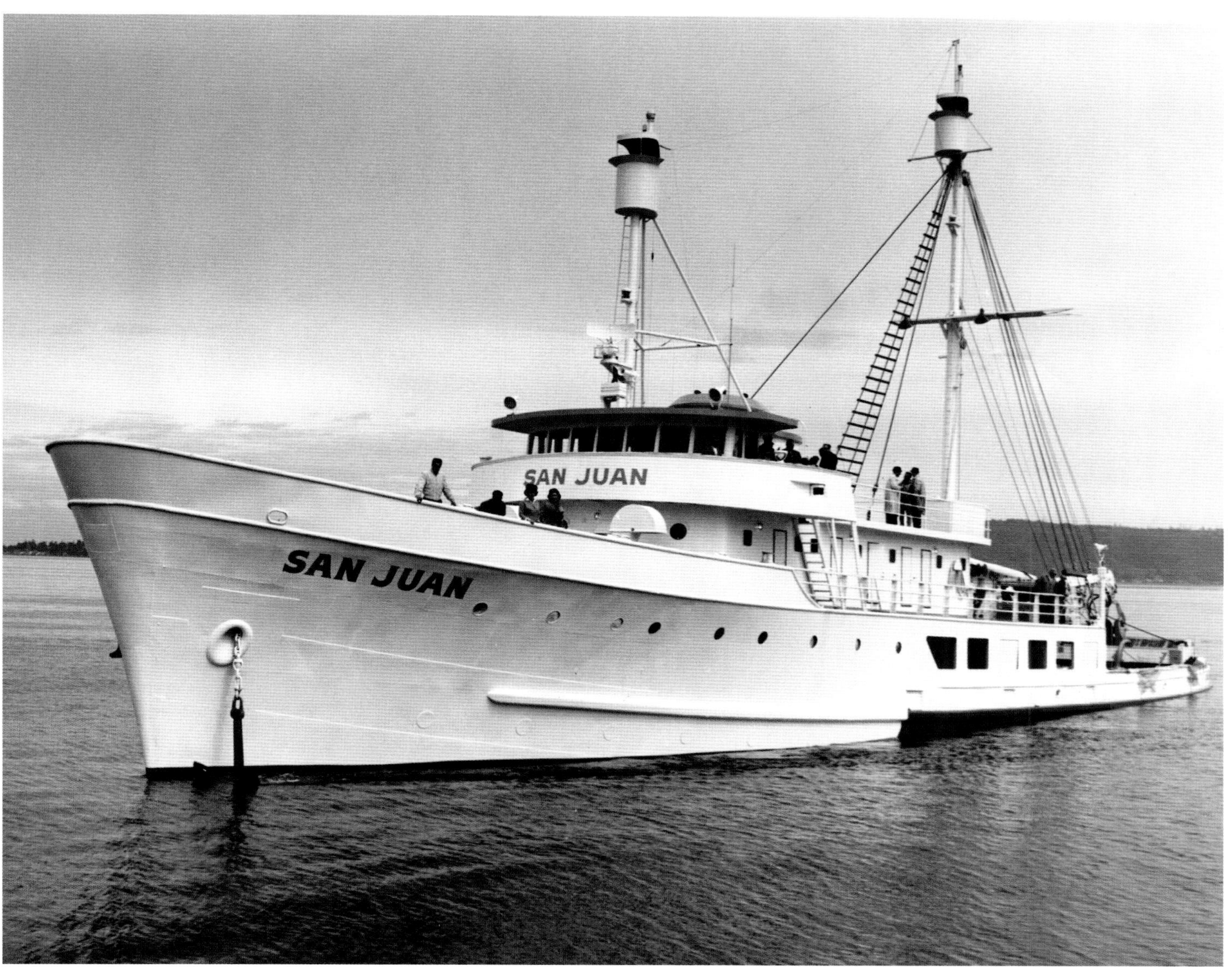

Hurricane Tragedy

Eighty men and teenage cadets were lost at sea after the *Pamir*, a fifty-two-year-old, four-masted steel barque sailing across the Atlantic with 3,780 tons of barley, was overwhelmed by Hurricane Carrie on September 21, 1957.

The *Pamir*, sailing from Buenos Aires, Argentina to Hamburg, Germany was no match for Carrie's 70-foot waves and winds estimated at 127 knots. Roughly two hours after Carrie struck, the *Pamir* listed at forty-five degrees, prompting the captain to lead the crew in prayer and issue cigarettes and liquor. At 1:03 p.m., the 377-foot ship capsized six hundred miles west of the Azores.

Twenty-year-old Gunter Hasselbach, shown here struggling to reach the cutter *Absecon*, was the only survivor of the twenty-one men in his lifeboat. The *Absecon*, a Navy weather station vessel, was 260 miles away when the distress call was received and took twenty-two hours to arrive.

It wasn't the only vessel on the scene: some fifty vessels from thirteen nations—along with U.S. Air Force rescue planes based in the Azores—searched for survivors, but only four crewmen and two cadets were rescued out of eighty-six who were aboard.

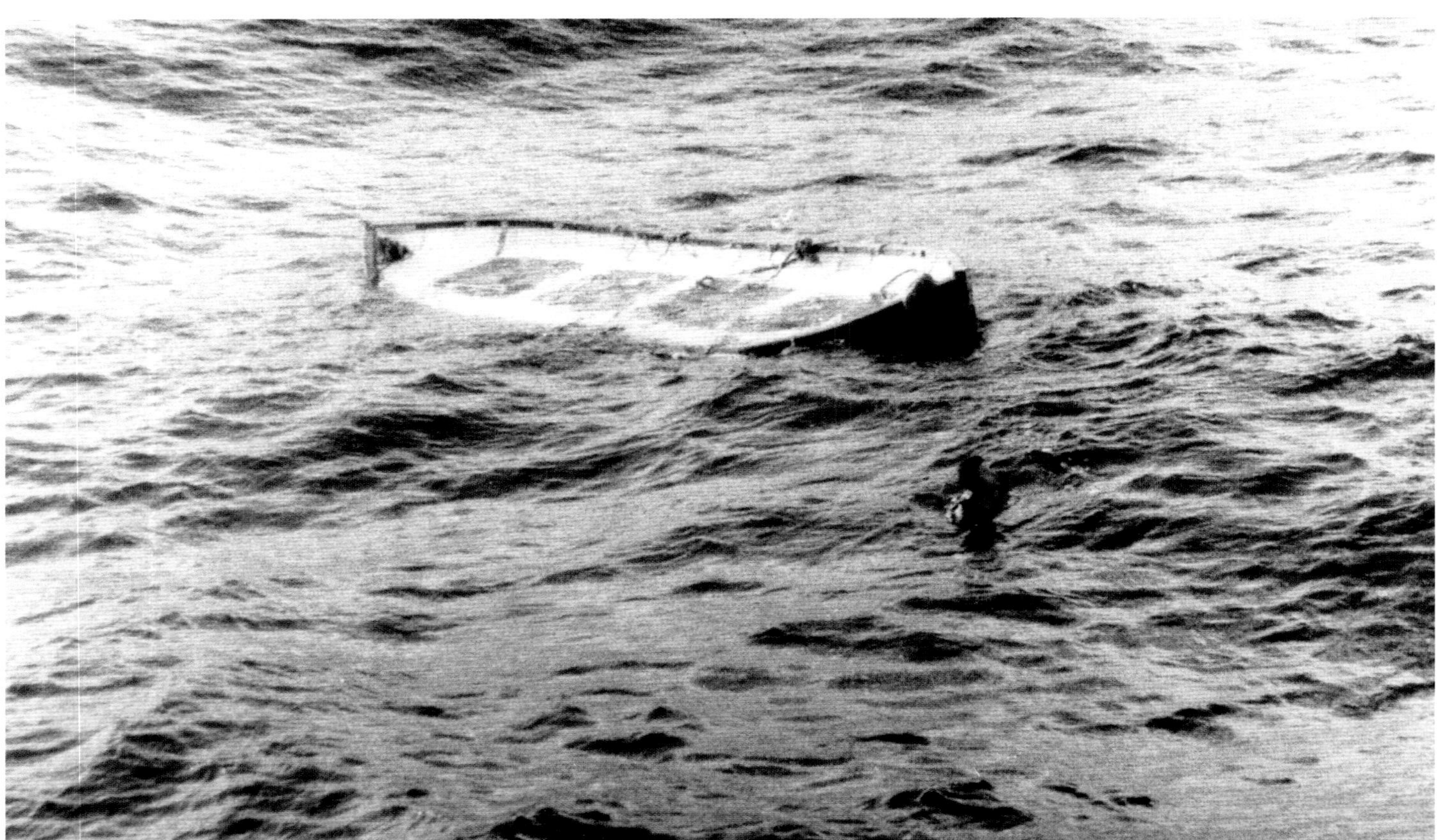

Booze Smugglers

Monterey, California and the surrounding area is known for many things including being the home of the Motery Jazz Fesival and of noted authors such as John Steinbeck and Henry Miller. But it's also known regionally for the drama that took place on June 18, 1972, when agents busted a bunch of fishermen and seized their boats.

On that day, twenty-five U.S. Treasury officers, along with agents from the Bureau of Alcohol Tobacco and Firearms and the California Alcoholic Beverage Control, arrested seven fishermen and seized nine fishing boats and a half dozen cars and trucks. The number would soon grow to ten fishermen and sixteen boats, shown with the Coast Guard cutter *Cape Wash* in this photo. The charge: smuggling booze. It was called "the largest seizure of illegal alcohol since Prohibition."

Commercial fishermen could legally buy liquor and cigarettes from duty-free "sea stores," which had to be sealed and not consumed until the vessel was outside U.S. territorial waters. But an investigation revealed that in many cases, boats never left the harbor and the liquor and cigarettes were illegally brought to shore for onshore consumption.

Furthermore, the amount of cigarettes and liquor that could be bought was based on the number of people on a boat, but officials found that the documents listing the number and names of crewmen on a boat were often "heavily padded" with nonexistent individuals. The smuggling operation resulted in a loss of more than $250,000 to the government in customs duties and revenue taxes. One uninvolved fisherman reacted: "This has been going on ever since Prohibition ended. Why the big deal now?"

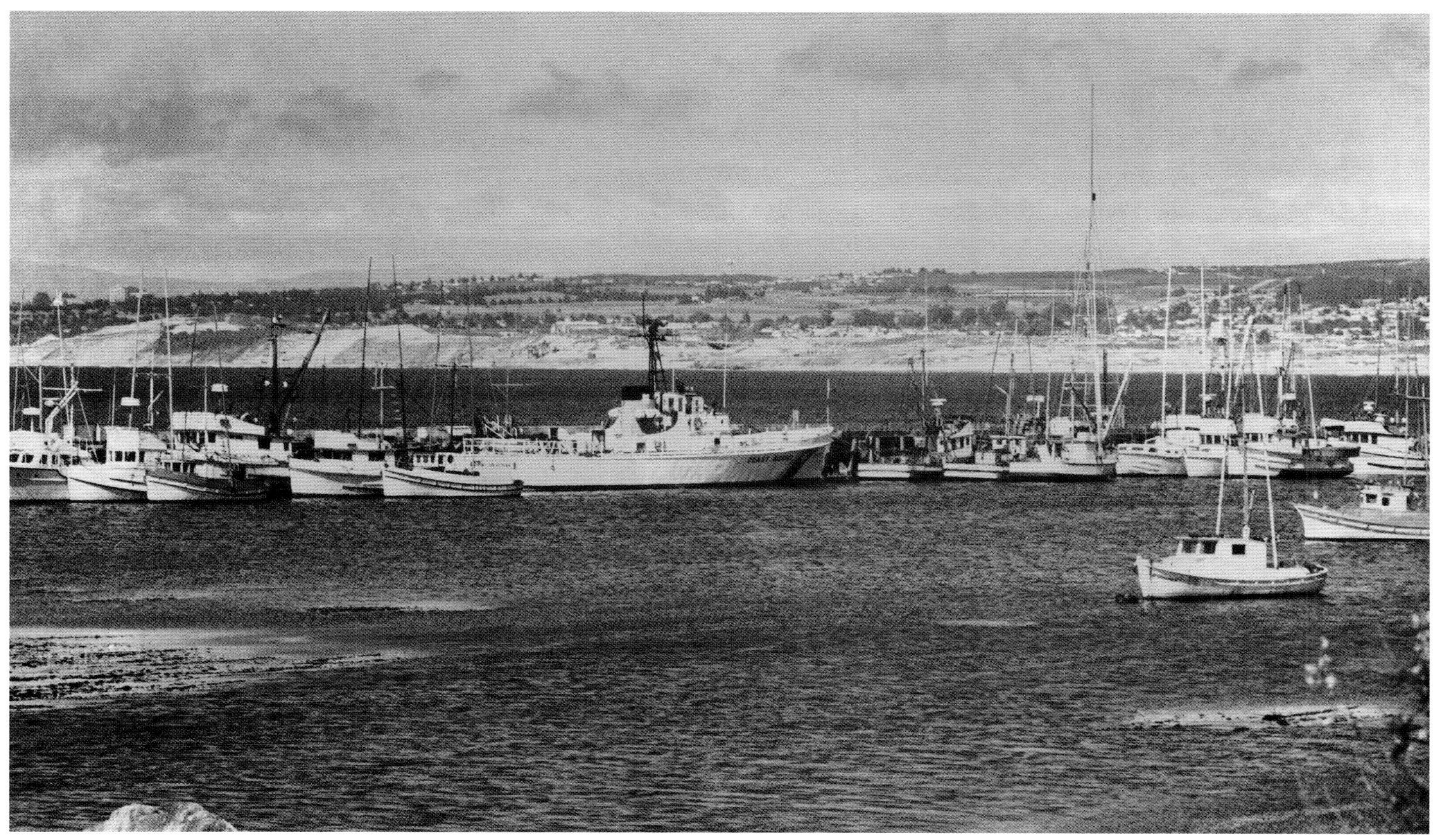

Face-Off

One-on-one it would be a ridiculously stupid jostling match for a small salmon troller to take on a 600-foot-plus steel cargo ship. The same goes for five, ten, or even fifty wooden salmon boats. But what about 115 salmon trollers? That's the number of boats that faced off against the *Falstria*, the 637-foot steel Danish container ship weighing in at 20,325 tons, and a second container ship, the *Zhang Jia Kou* of China, on June 2, 1981. Both vessels were trying to pass under the Golden Gate Bridge and enter San Francisco Bay.

The salmon fishermen were blockading the huge ships in an effort to draw attention to the plight of their fishery—three years of shortened seasons, three years of fruitless industry negotiations, and a cancelled June 1981 offshore salmon season. The protesters sent out a plea to the container ships: "We are the fishing fleet. Please respect us. Please respect our right to work and support our families."

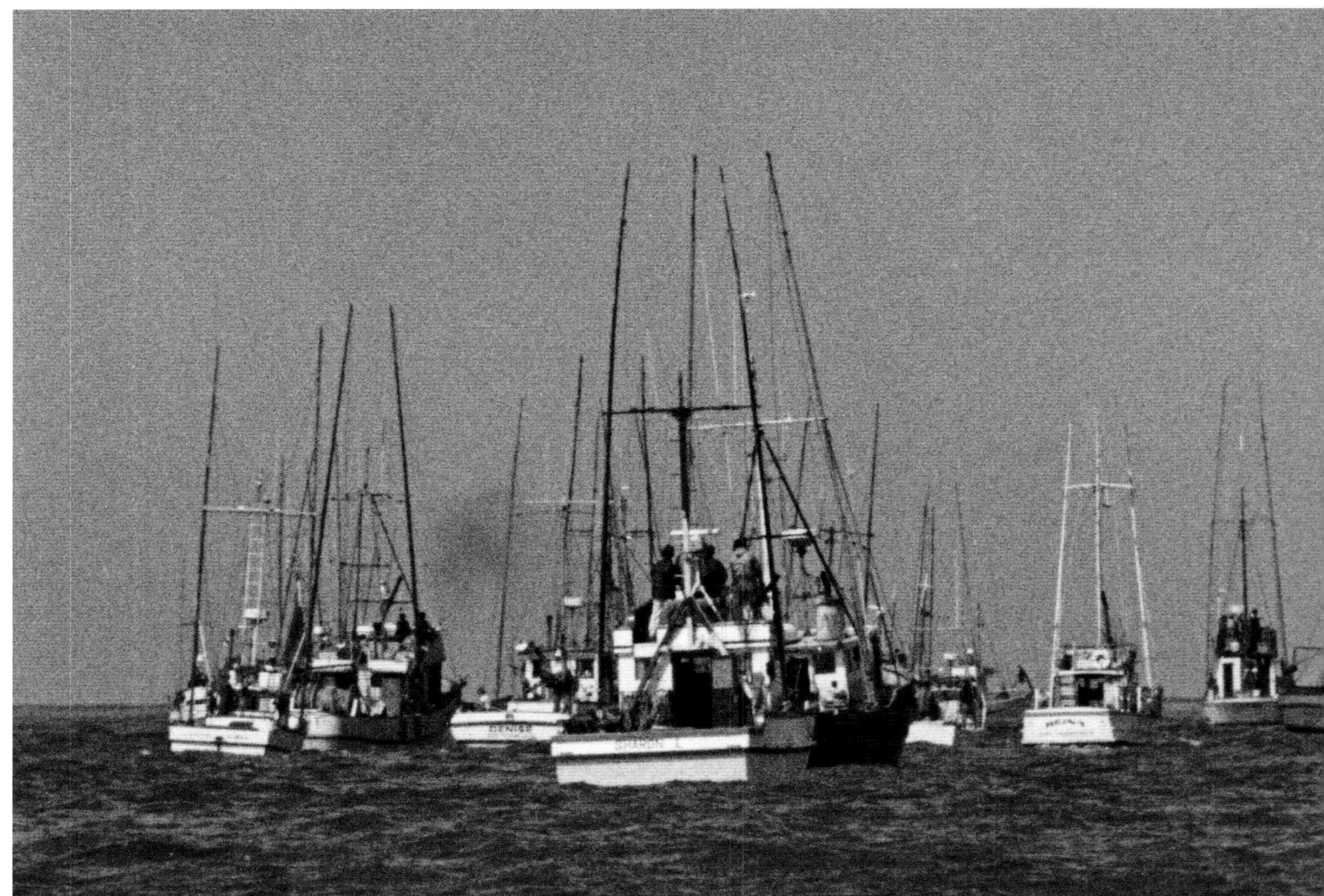

A 95-foot Coast Guard vessel and a patrol boat tried to lead the containerships into the harbor, but soon the trollers came bow-on-bow and flank-on-flank with the cargo ships. Fishermen fended off from the *Falstria* with their hands, with a mast or trolling pole catching on a containership's flaring hull and snapping off.

Eventually, the container ships cut their engines and were guided in by the Coast Guard. All the while helicopters were overhead, looking for the best camera angle, which gave the fishermen what they wanted—live television and newspaper coverage from Los Angeles to New York. "Man, looks like we got the coverage," one fisherman said during the skirmish. "The whole country is going to know about this!"

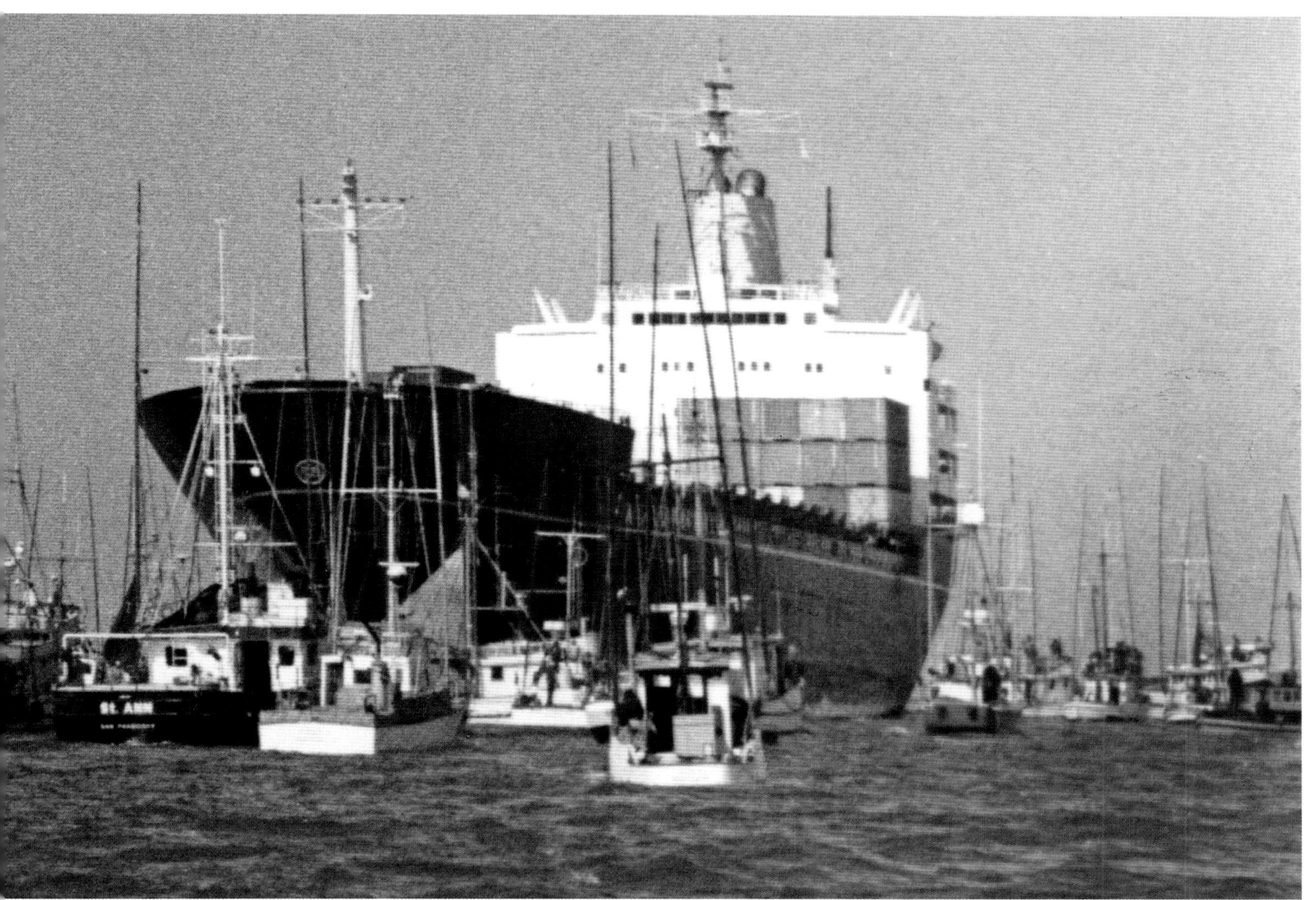

Sinking of Rosanne Maria

It was a clear, calm June night when the 86-foot, wooden Gloucester dragger *Rosanne Maria*'s bow was opened up by the *Brandenburg*, a 214-foot steel-hulled East German trawler that struck while the *Rosanne Maria* was anchored.

She was anchored near two other fishing boats near the Isles of Shoals, small islands and tidal ledges that straddle the Maine and New Hampshire border. Her anchor lights were on and, except for a crewman in the wheelhouse, everyone was asleep. The skipper was in his wheelhouse bunk and two crewmen in the fo'c'sle. The *Brandenburg*'s blow came within two feet of the two sleeping in the fo'c'sle.

The *Rosanne Maria*'s crew used their pumps, and a Coast Guard helicopter dropped two men to try and keep the dragger afloat, but it was no use. On the morning of June 4, 1972, the *Rosanne Maria* went down in 550 feet of water. The Gloucester dragger *Frances R.* took the *Rosanne Maria*'s crew to port. The East German skipper blamed the accident on the *Rosanne Maria*. But Steve Biondo, the *Rosanne Maria*'s skipper, reacted otherwise: "Our lives aren't worth two cents when these big boats are around."

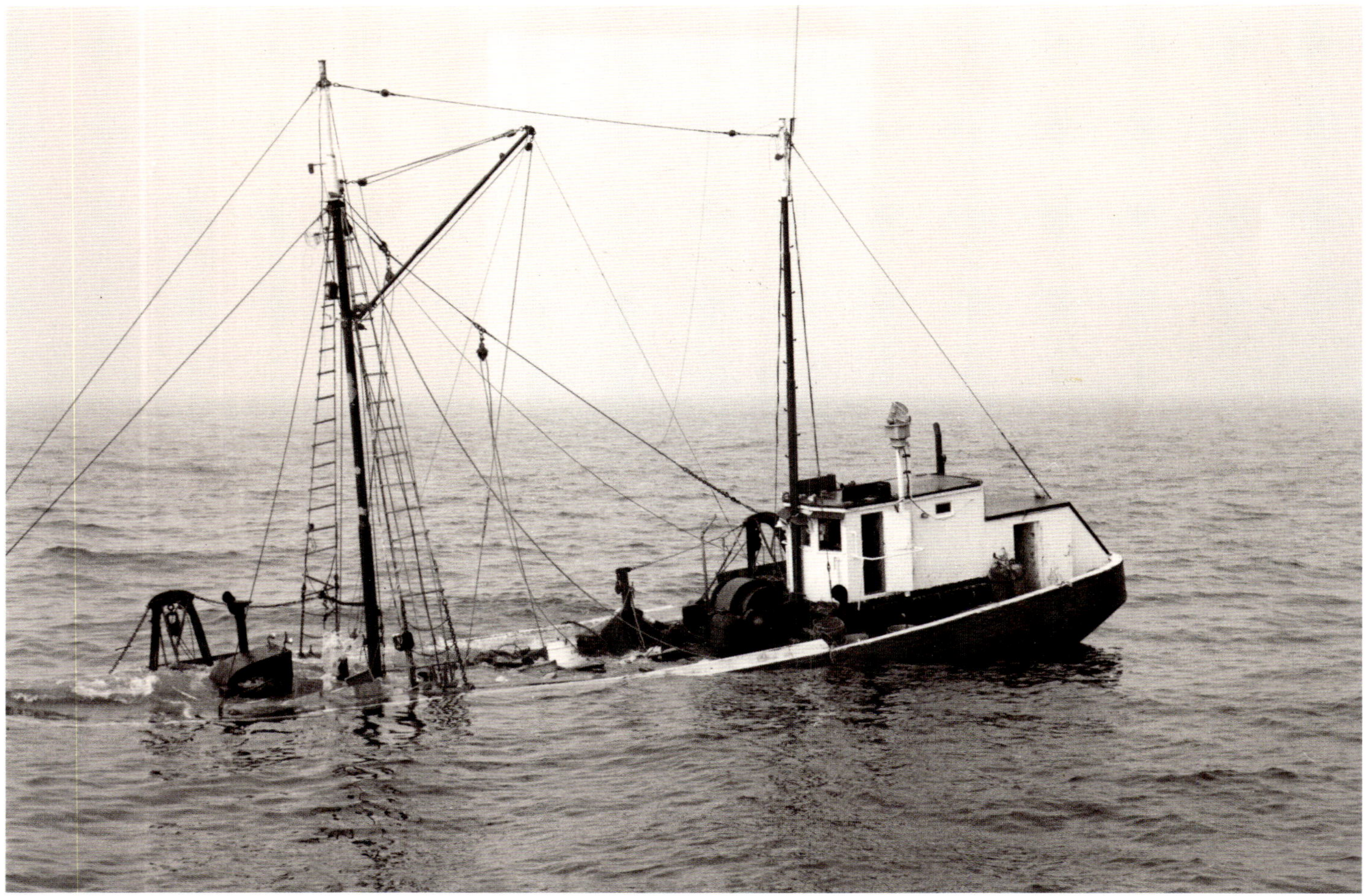

Florida Lobster Shooting

Territorial disputes are not uncommon within America's fishing communities and can manifest themselves in vandalism, poaching, personal confrontations, and even sunken boats. But lobsterman Richard Mager encountered an extreme situation shortly after dawn on November 5, 1972. Mager, out of Palm Beach, Florida, was hauling traps on the Great Bahama Bank in the 54-foot *Diamond Head II* when a number of 16- to 22-foot outboard powered boats surrounded his lobster boat. Bahamians manned the smaller boats and one of them fired on the *Diamond Head II*, hitting it several times, with one shot shattering the wheelhouse window.

Mager called out to his crew to hit the deck, grabbed a revolver, and fired several shots. The Bahamians left when another lobster boat, the 55-foot *Diamond Head* skippered by Dick Wolfferts, the owner of both boats, showed up. The shooting was preceded by numerous incidents of Bahamian trap poaching that cost Mager and Wolfferts six hundred traps. Just two days before the shooting, Wolfferts was on Walker's Cay, the northernmost island in the Bahamas, talking to a customs agent when twelve to fifteen Bahamians looking "like a lynch mob" with hoses, ropes, and knives went after Wolfferts, who hid out in the Bahamian Custom Office for several hours.

Shortly after that encounter, Wolfferts and Mager took both boats out to recover the remaining traps that hadn't been stolen, triggering the November 5 shooting. Ignoring advice from the U.S. State Department, they went out the next day and retrieved their remaining lobster traps, but not before purchasing semi-automatic guns and ammunition—"just in case."

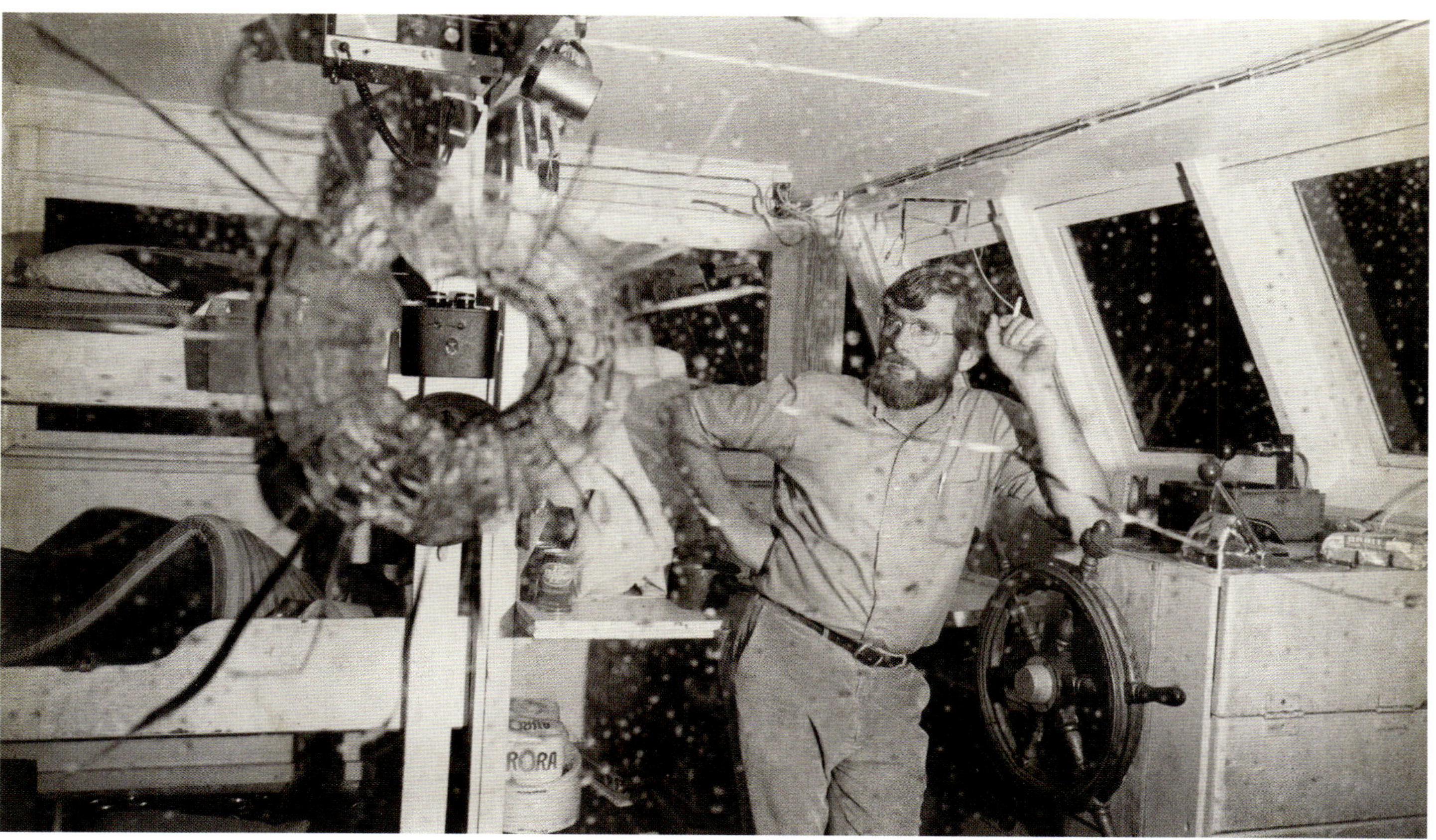

Explosive Catch

The *Pam Bay* was a mid-sized coastal trawler out of Coos Bay, Oregon. The *CG 007* was an old plywood skiff with a crummy little cabin that was part of the playground equipment at the Coast Guard station in Brookings, Oregon. On November 9, 1974, one of them—and almost both—was blown up.

The culprit was a Japanese mine that had ridden the Pacific's easterly currents toward North America since World War II before eventually settling on the ocean floor. After the war, explosions from wayward mines resulted in dozens of lost boats and a number of deaths.

On that November day, after hauling back its net, the *Pam Bay*'s skipper, Larry Carlson, informed the Coast Guard station that he thought he had an old mine in its trawl.

One look by the Coast Guard confirmed that what was hanging in the *Pam Bay*'s net, just above the steel stern ramp, was indeed a World War II mine. Fortunately the seas were almost flat calm, keeping the chances of damaging contact between the mine and the steel boat at a minimum.

It was a smooth-skinned magnetic mine—designed to be triggered by an approaching vessel's magnetic field—that American fishermen had obviously seen before as it had a number of bullet holes in it. That was enough to sink the mine to the bottom, where the *Pam Bay*'s trawl caught it, but not enough to detonate it.

What was needed was a way to move the mine far enough away from the *Pam Bay* so that when it was set off, flying metal wouldn't injure the fishermen or Coast Guard personnel.

Enter the *CG 007*, the sacrificial boat. She was quickly removed from the playground, patched up and floated out to the *Pam Bay*, which was off the Chetco River. There, the *CG 007* was hauled up to the *Pam Bay*'s stern ramp where Navy ordnance experts attached a plastic charge to it. The *Pam Bay*'s crew then lowered the mine into the *CG 007* after pulling the string on the cod end at the tapered end of the net.

The *Pam Bay* moved away from the *CG 007* and its mine, the fuse was lit, and ninety seconds later the mine and the *CG 007* were no more. As one Coast Guardsman said, "Thank Christ that's over with."

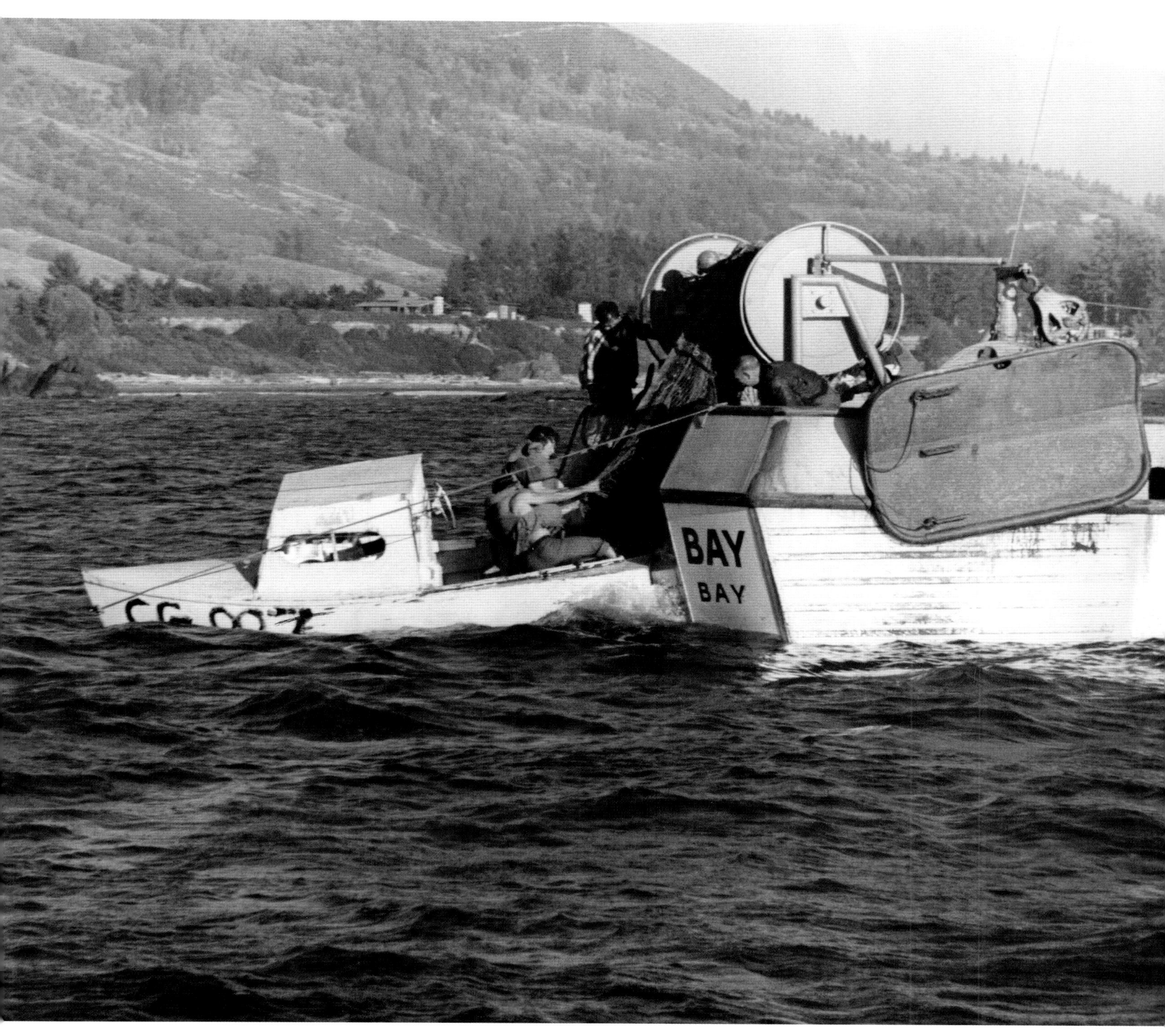

CG 00
BAY
BAY

Rescue by Air

When things get really dicey, it's nice to have an air rescue outfit nearby, as these two photos demonstrate. Below, the salmon tender *Prowler* is going down with 12 tons of salmon onboard on July 28, 1976, as a Navy helicopter lifts both crewmen to safety near tiny Smith Island in the Strait of Juan de Fuca in Washington.

In the opposite photo, the dragger *Arney P* has grounded out on a beach south of Crescent City, California. But that's not people the helicopter is lifting off the *Arney P*, but rather 18,000 pounds of bottom fish, which was then brought to shore and trucked to a nearby processing plant.

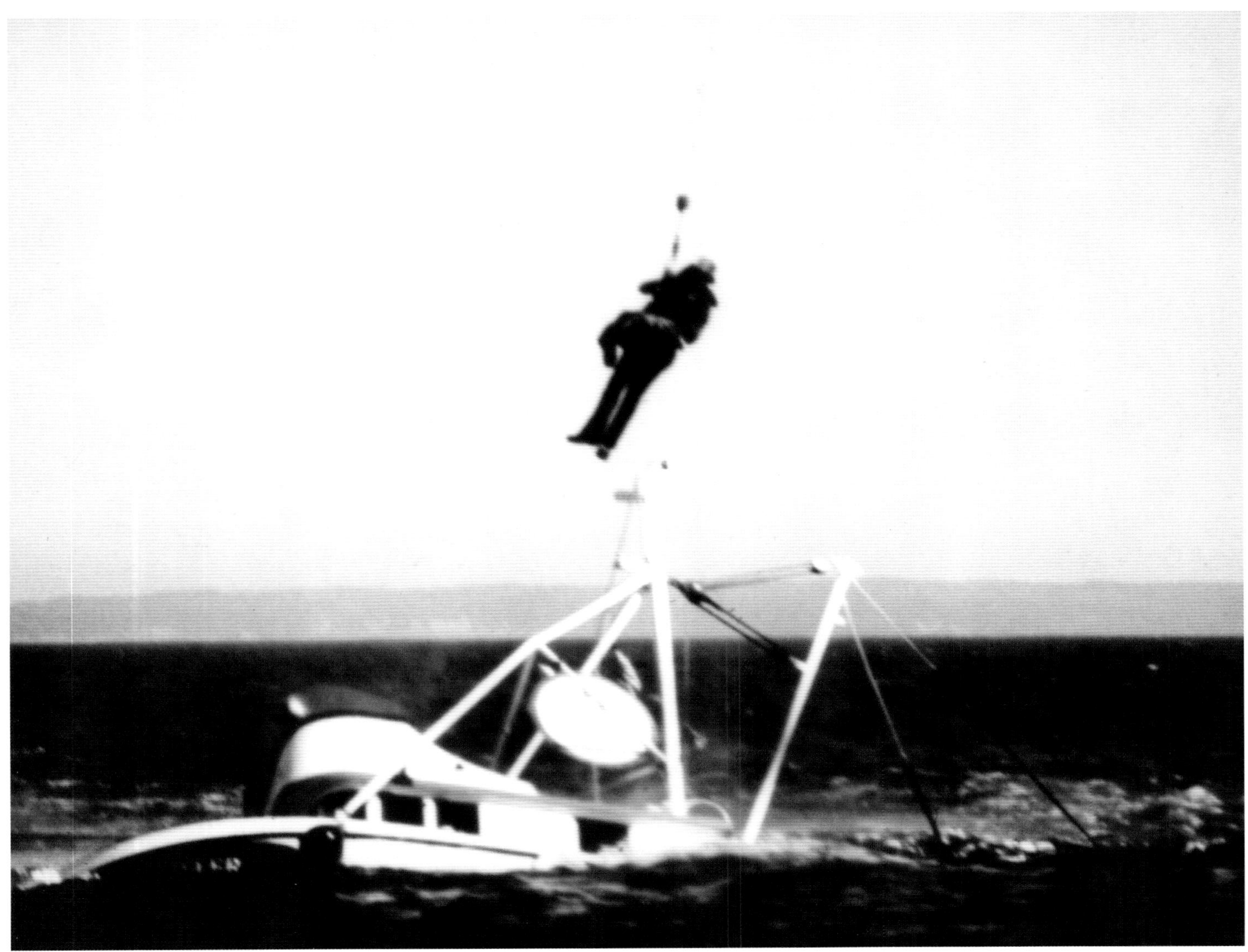

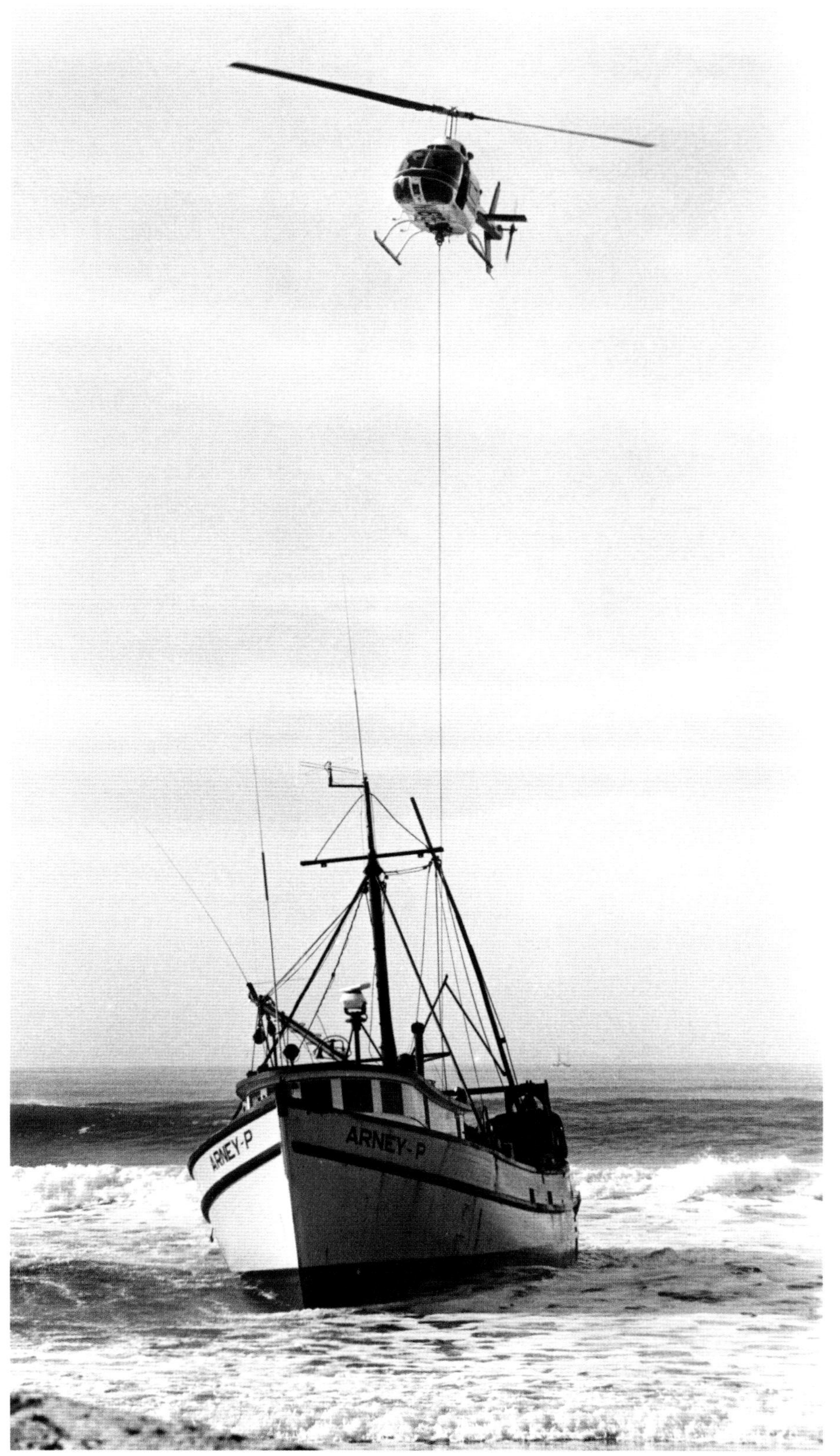

ARNEY·P
ARNEY·P

Shrimper Survival

Looking at this photo of Galveston, Texas, shrimpers tied up to Piers 19 and 20, also known as Fishermen's Wharf, you might think everything is fine. And it should have been. After all, a fisherman's day is stressful enough without having to worry about having a place to tie up when he returns home at the end of a trip. But when your town isn't backing you, it's something you have to worry about. That was the issue facing about 80 Galveston shrimpers in 1978 when all the vessel owners on Piers 19 and 20 received eviction notices because the town was bent on turning their piers into a cargo dock.

But the shrimpers had nowhere else to go—so they fought. A petition with five thousand signatures was presented to the city council requesting an election to decide the pier's fate. It was judged to be invalid. A second petition was circulated, which resulted in an injunction to stop eviction proceedings until an election was held. The election was Galveston's largest ever, with nine thousand people voting three to one to let the shrimpers stay. The shrimpers were given a twenty-year lease with an option for another twenty years.

Pier 19, known as the "Mosquito Fleet Berth," is listed on the National Register of Historic Places and continues to be used by shrimpers. The fleet is whimsically called the Mosquito Fleet because of the shrimp boats' insect-like profiles. The Gulf of Mexico continues to produce bountiful shrimp harvests, and Galveston remains the top commercial fishing port in Texas.

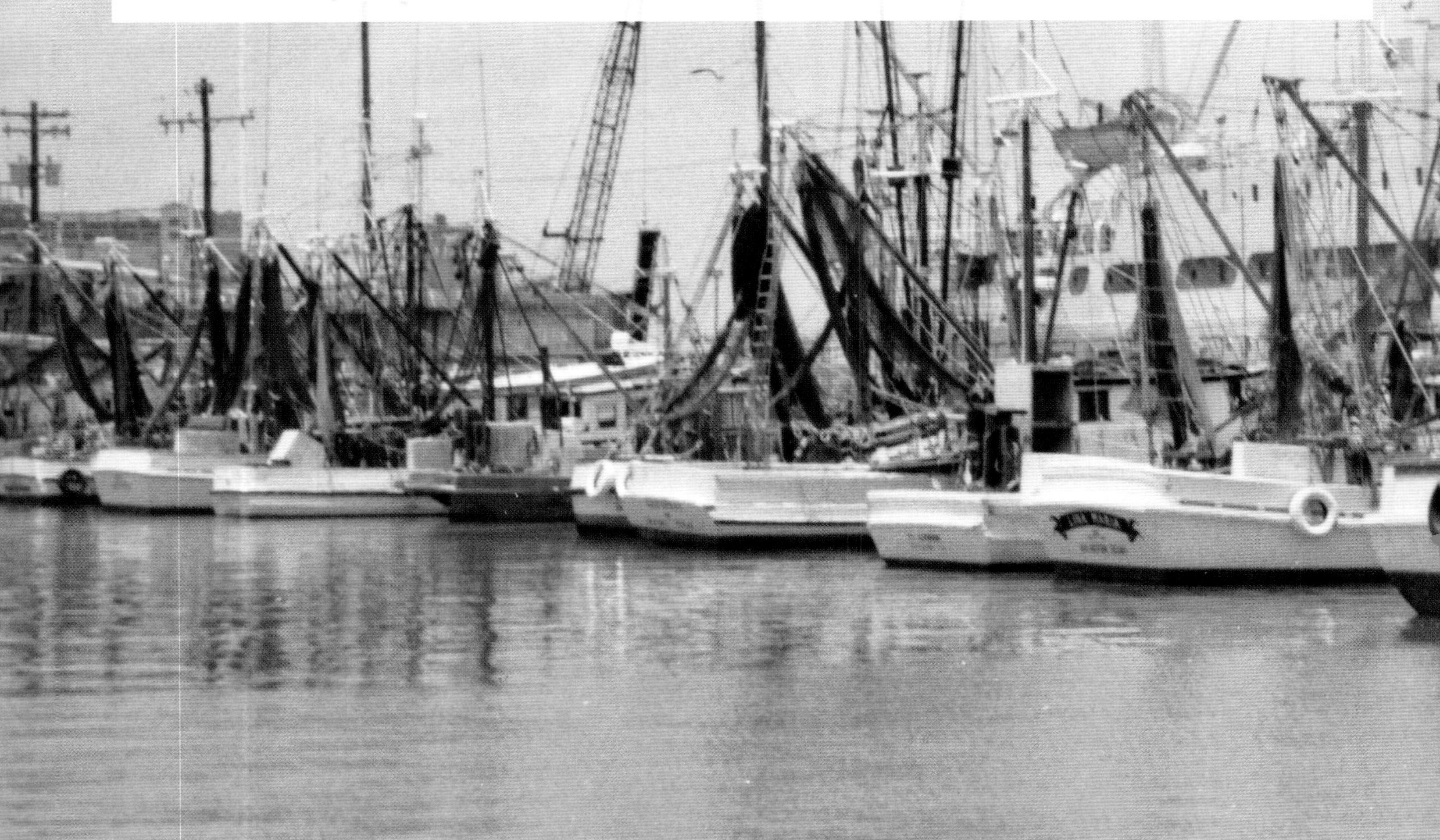

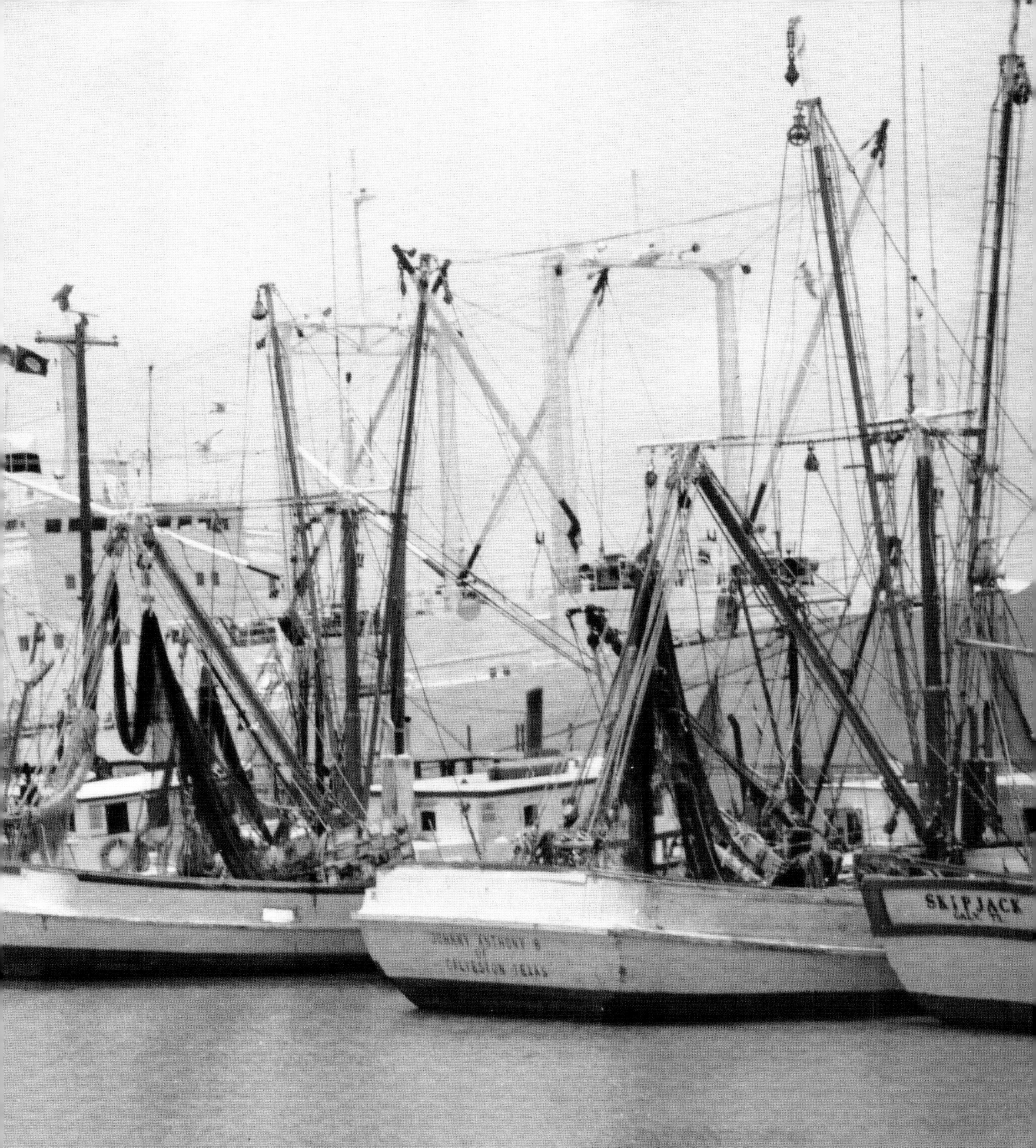

JOHNNY ANTHONY B
OF
GALVESTON TEXAS
SKIPJACK
GALV TX

Double Trouble

The night of December 4, 1972, was not good for either the *Alton A*, a wooden 55-foot Maine dragger, or the 44-foot Coast Guard utility boat that came to its rescue. A fierce snowstorm drove both the *Alton A* and the Coast Guard boat ashore where they ended up pounding on the ledges in Cape Elizabeth at the mouth of Maine's Casco Bay.

The *Alton A* was caught in a rocky crevice and couldn't be floated free. After being holed several times over the ensuing week, her owner abandoned her. The Coast Guard boat's steel hull, however, was better able to endure the pounding. Because it grounded closer to the high-water mark, a crane was able to get close enough to lift the boat ashore and onto a trailer.

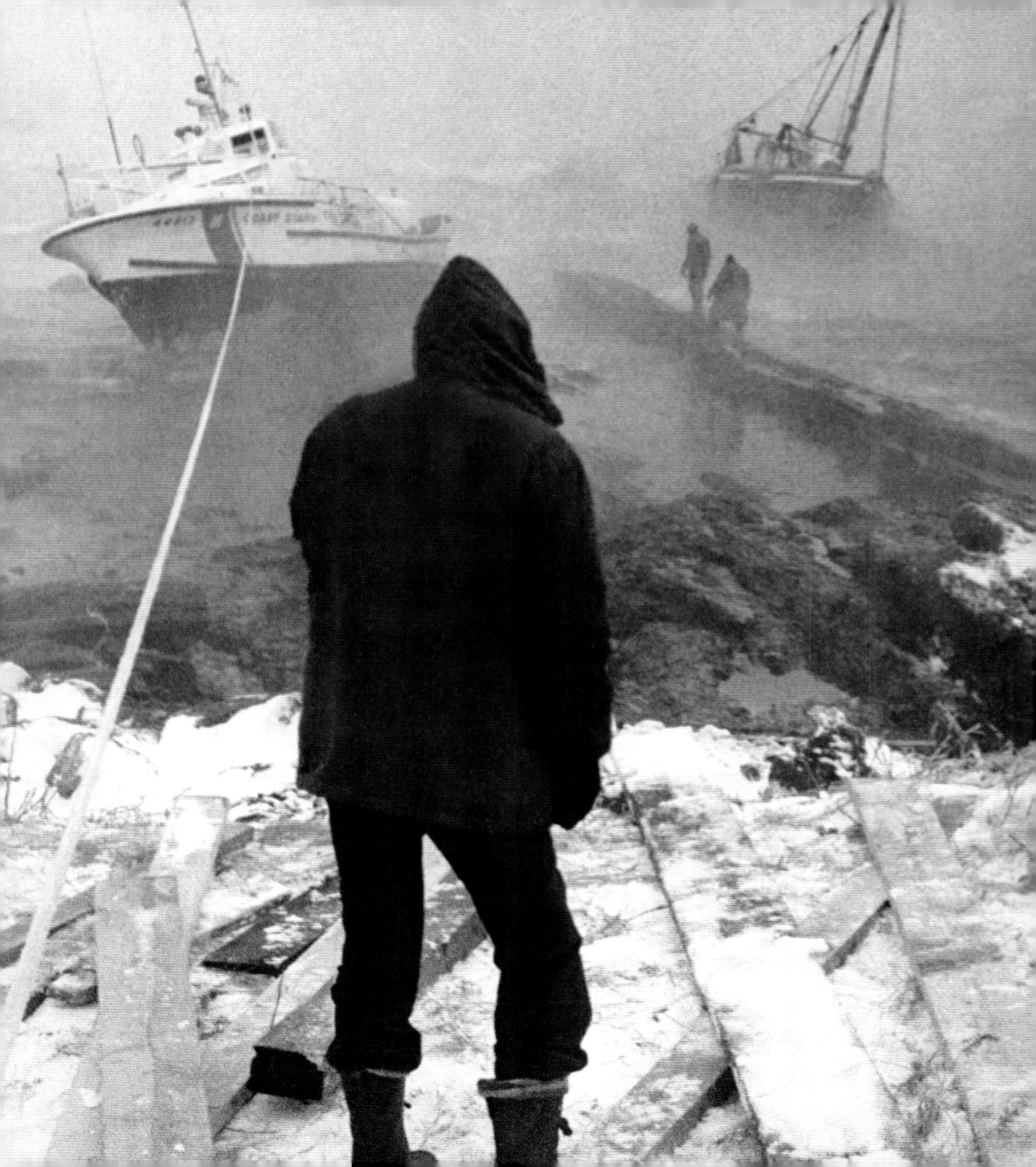

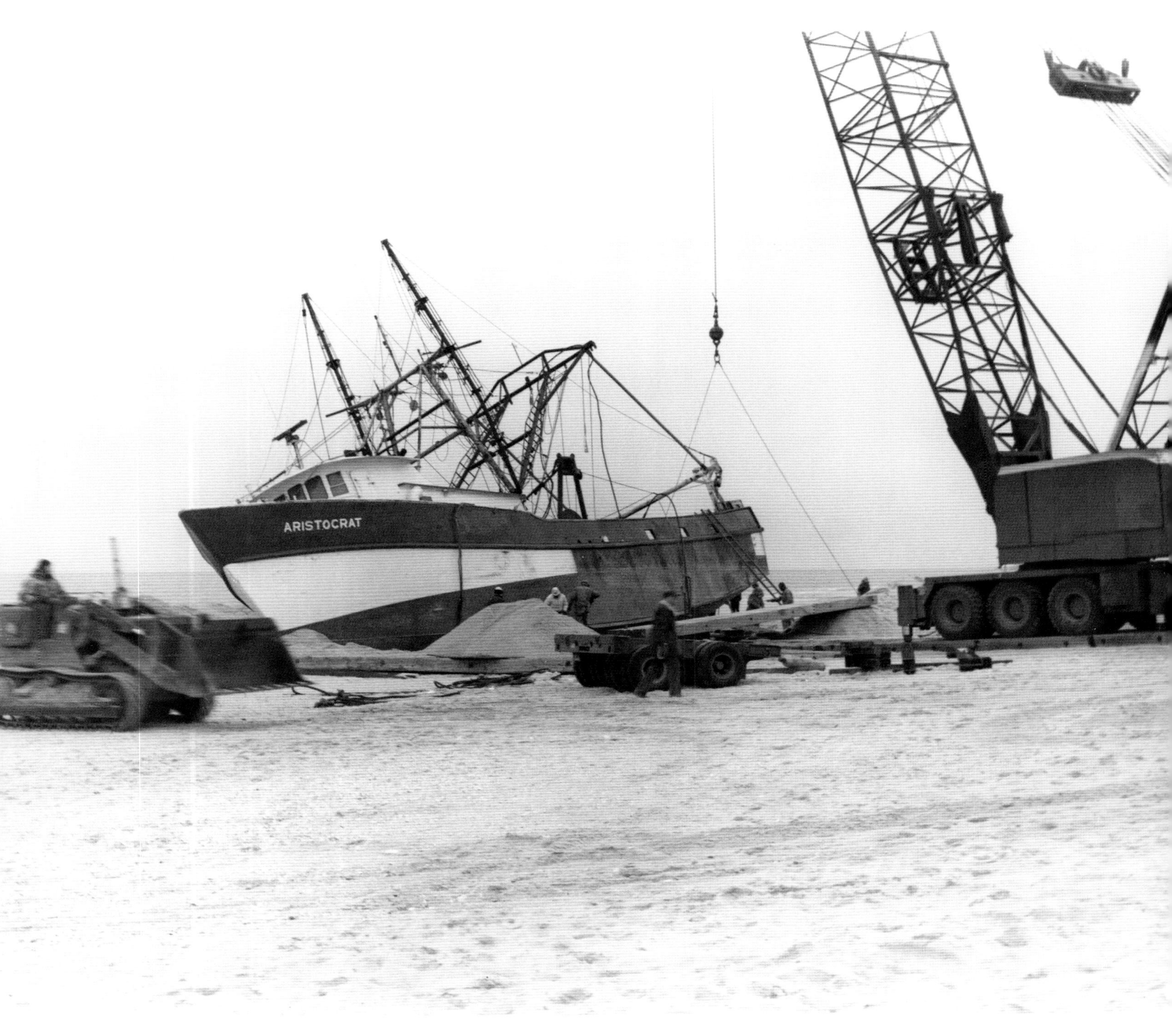
ARISTOCRAT

The Winter it Blew

The 87-foot steel dragger *Aristocrat*, having been tossed on the beach at Point Pleasant, New Jersey, was just one of many casualties in a series of storms that swept the Northeast seaboard in the winter of 1978. Eighty-nine fishing boats were destroyed or severely damaged in Massachusetts that winter. On Cape Ann, hurricane-force winds and 30-foot seas swept away five lobster boats, numerous fish shacks, and hundreds of stored lobster pots.

Three men working the pilot boat *Interport* lost their lives off Sandy Hook, New Jersey in January, and then in February another storm took four more lives when the pilot boat *Can Do* went aground on Coney Island Ledge off Marblehead, Massachusetts, while trying to reach the tanker *Global Hope*. A considerable number of dead lobsters washed up on Massachusetts beaches from Boston to Plymouth. The toll was especially severe along a quarter mile stretch of Nantasket Beach, where about a quarter-million dead lobsters were found.

Sea Lion Feast

Sea lions have insatiable appetites, consuming about 8 percent of their body weight in fish each and every day. Nowhere was that more evident than in the eastern Bering Sea, where some eighty thousand sea lions consumed over 200,000 metric tons of fish—including 20,000 tons of high-priced salmon alone—in 1979. Fishermen blamed sea lions for costing them significant money in terms of lost product and damaged fishing gear.

The driving need to get that next meal is what got this sea lion in trouble. In pursuing that meal, it ended up in the net of a Japanese trawler fishing for yellowfin sole in the eastern Bering Sea. When the net was pulled in, the sea lion was dumped on deck along with the fish that were caught. There's enough fish around this sea lion to satisfy its momentary dietary cravings; he just has to figure out how to get back in the water.

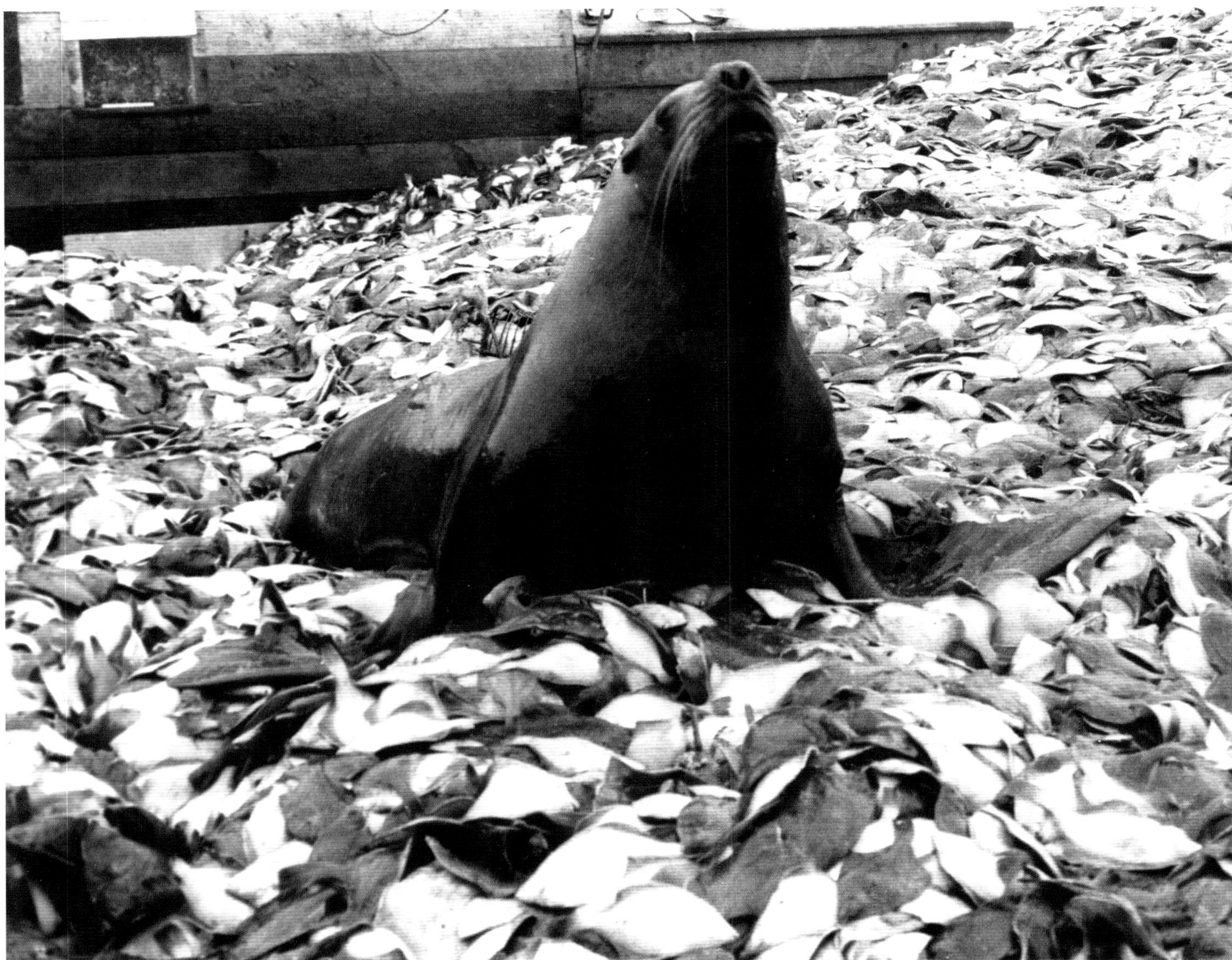

Canada's First Freezer Trawler

The *Martin & Phillip*, Canada's first freezer trawler, lies flat on its side in Dartmouth, Nova Scotia, after a supporting bilge block gave way as it was being hauled out. The introduction of the Norwegian-built 152-foot *Martin & Phillip* marked a significant change in Canada's fishing industry, which had been reluctant to acknowledge the offshore fisheries that other countries were taking advantage of could be profitable. In fact, the Canadian government didn't authorized freezer trawlers for ground fisheries until the end of 1979.

The *Martin & Phillip* could freeze her catch at sea and spend more than three weeks away from port at a time, which other Canadian trawlers were not capable of. The Martin *& Phillip* made her maiden trip on January 15, 1980 and returned with 425,000 pounds of cod and grey sole—headed, gutted, and frozen in blocks. While being hauled out the following month for some work on its propeller shaft tube, a bilge block collapsed and the boat fell sideways through the bottom of its cradle, ending up at a sharp angle against a wharf.

The *Martin & Phillip* remained there for seven weeks until engineers and shipyard workers got her back in the water on Easter weekend. Then there was a three-week inspection. The boat, of course, wasn't fishing all that time, making the owner—who was also the captain—quite unhappy. He figured he had lost between $300,000 and $400,000 in fish. The *Martin & Phillip* was back on the fishing grounds in early May.

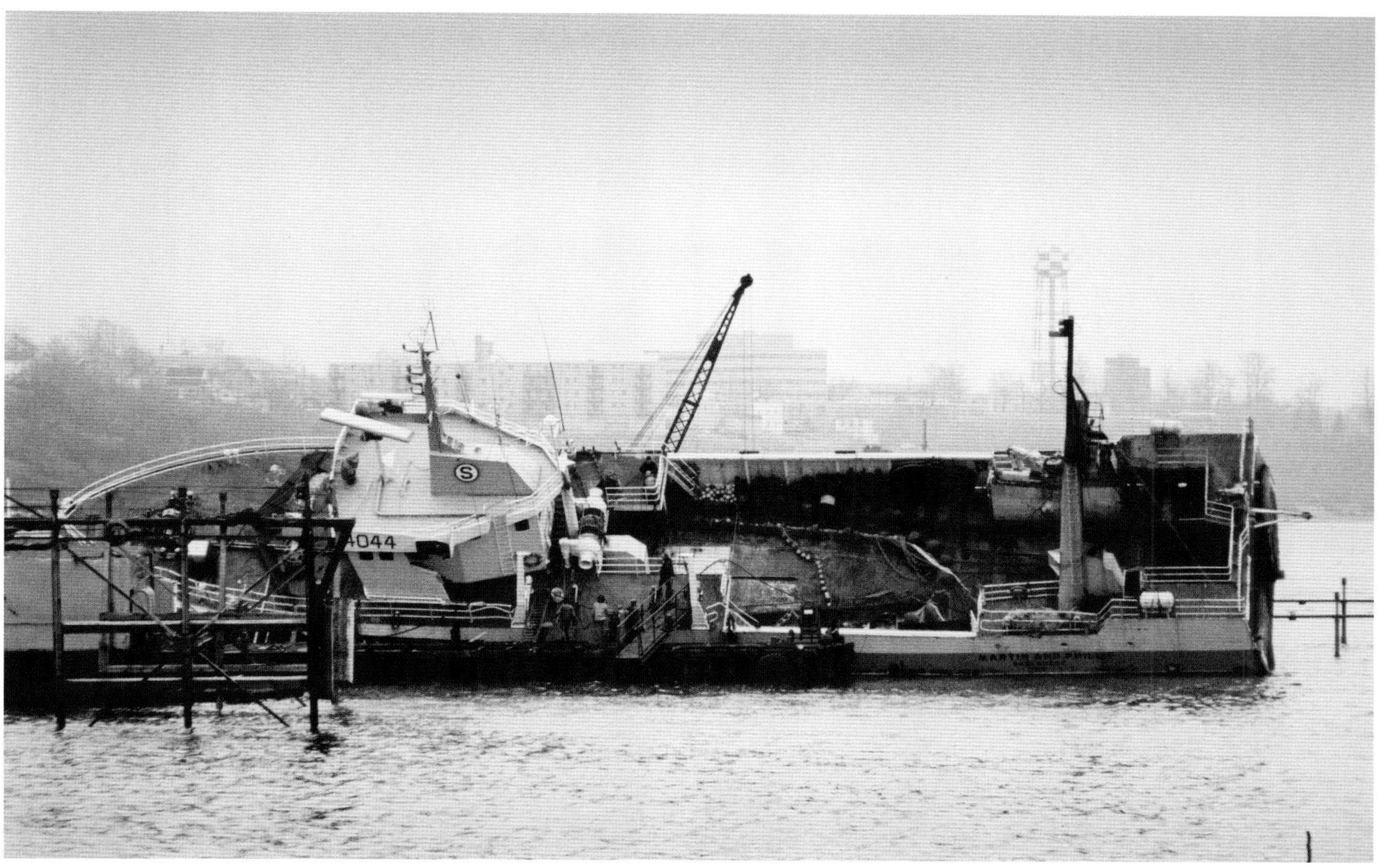

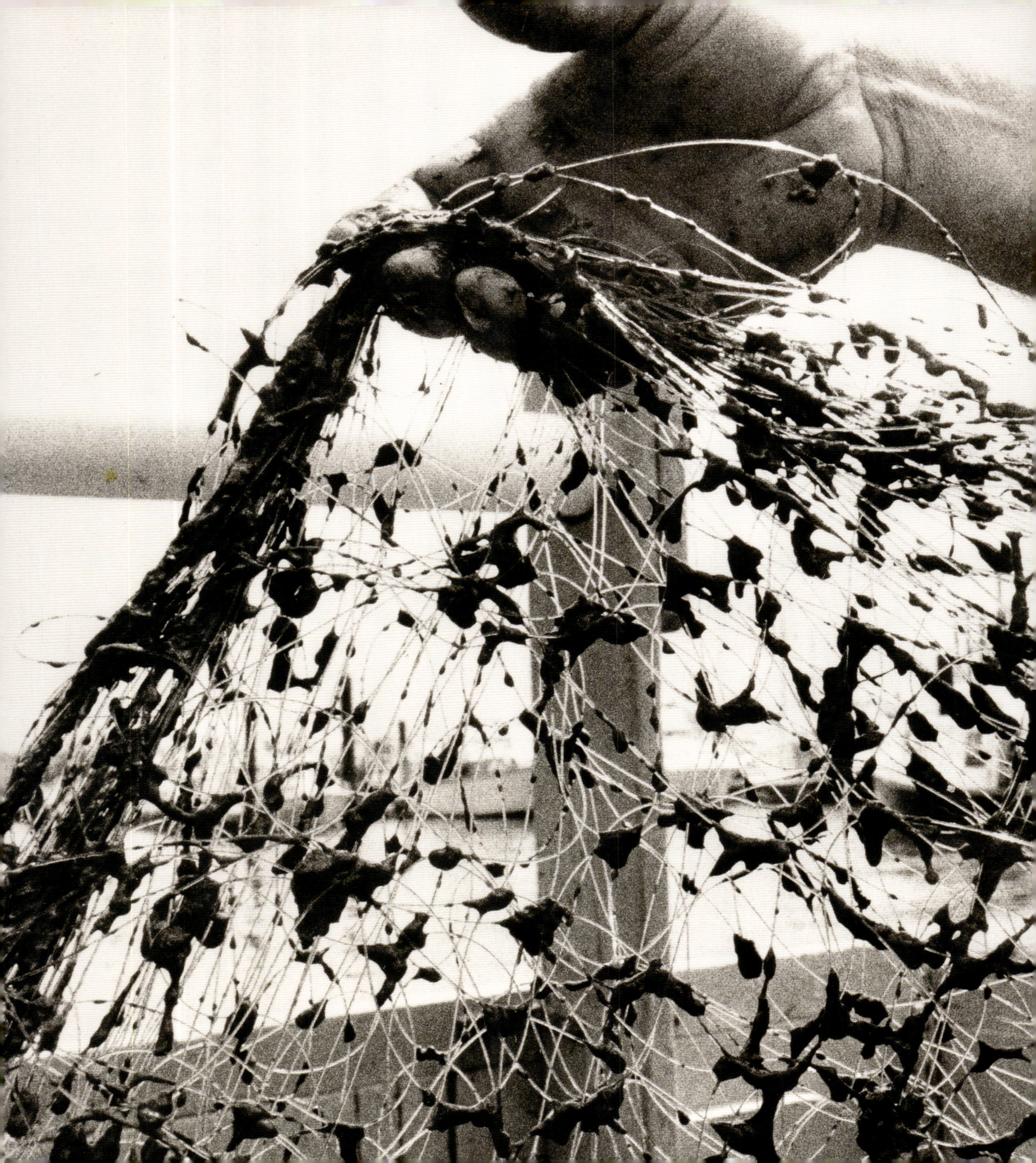

Sea Snot

"It's like someone took a truck load of chocolate pudding and dumped it all over your boat." That's how one Maine gillnetter described the mess that was threatening to ruin New England's gillnet fishery in the early 1980s. But if it was chocolate pudding at least you could eat it. You couldn't eat the muddy, gooey, brown slime known as "sea snot" that showed up at the end of 1981 and was still decimating the fishery a year later.

Gillnets covered with the slime did not fish well. They might sink to the bottom or be so clogged that fish deemed them something to be avoided—thereby driving down the catch rate and the money fishermen were making. In one case, crewmen on a Portland, Maine gillnetter made only $50 each after eight weeks fishing. On Cape Ann, Massachusetts, a conservative survey estimated a gillnetter's losses to be between $250,000 and $500,000 that year.

Scientists who examined the slime couldn't fully agree with certainty as to its identity. Some thought it was a kind of jellyfish deemed responsible for a much smaller outbreak in the mid-1970s, but that wasn't a unanimous opinion. What was agreed upon is gillnetters would never be able to make up what was lost. "All those trips are gone for good," is how one fisherman summarized the lost season.

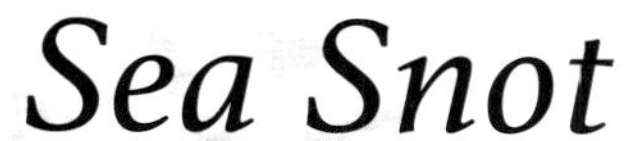

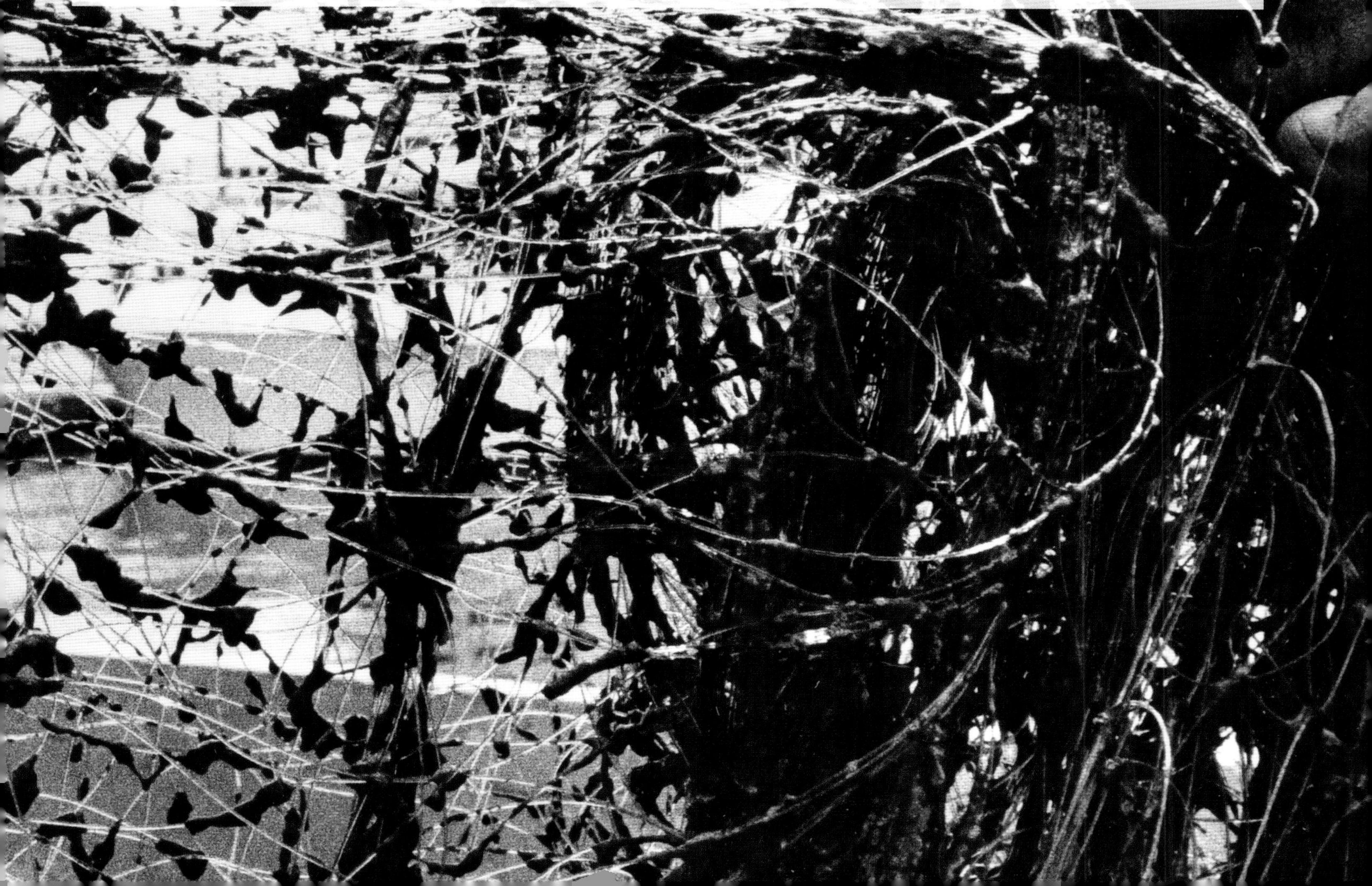

Greenpeace Goes After Driftnets

Greenpeace activists used a small inflatable in 1983 to harass this Japanese driftnetter in the Bering Sea and draw attention to their campaign to outlaw driftnetting. The vessel was one of approximately eight hundred high-seas driftnetters from Japan, Taiwan, and Korea fishing the North Pacific for neon flying squid and deploying up to thirty miles of monofilament driftnets per vessel. That earned driftnets the moniker "walls of death" for their deadly impact on marine life.

High-seas driftnetting began after the United States extended its Exclusive Economic Zone two hundred miles out from its shores in the late 1970s, putting hundreds of Japanese, Taiwanese, and Korean salmon vessels out of work in the North Pacific. They then discovered large schools of neon flying squid beyond the EEZ and quickly turned them into the world's largest single fishery. But driftnets drew outrage when it became obvious they caught many other species—including marine mammals, turtles, seabirds, and fish.

Greenpeace was among the environmental groups that spent years highlighting the perils of high-seas driftnet fishing by documenting driftnetters killing seabirds and porpoises, and by using small inflatable boats, like the one shown, to prevent the setting of nets. The international attention Greenpeace drew to driftnets resulted in the U.S. government banning Japanese fishing vessels from the Bering Sea and eventually contributed to a 1992 United Nations moratorium on driftnet fishing.

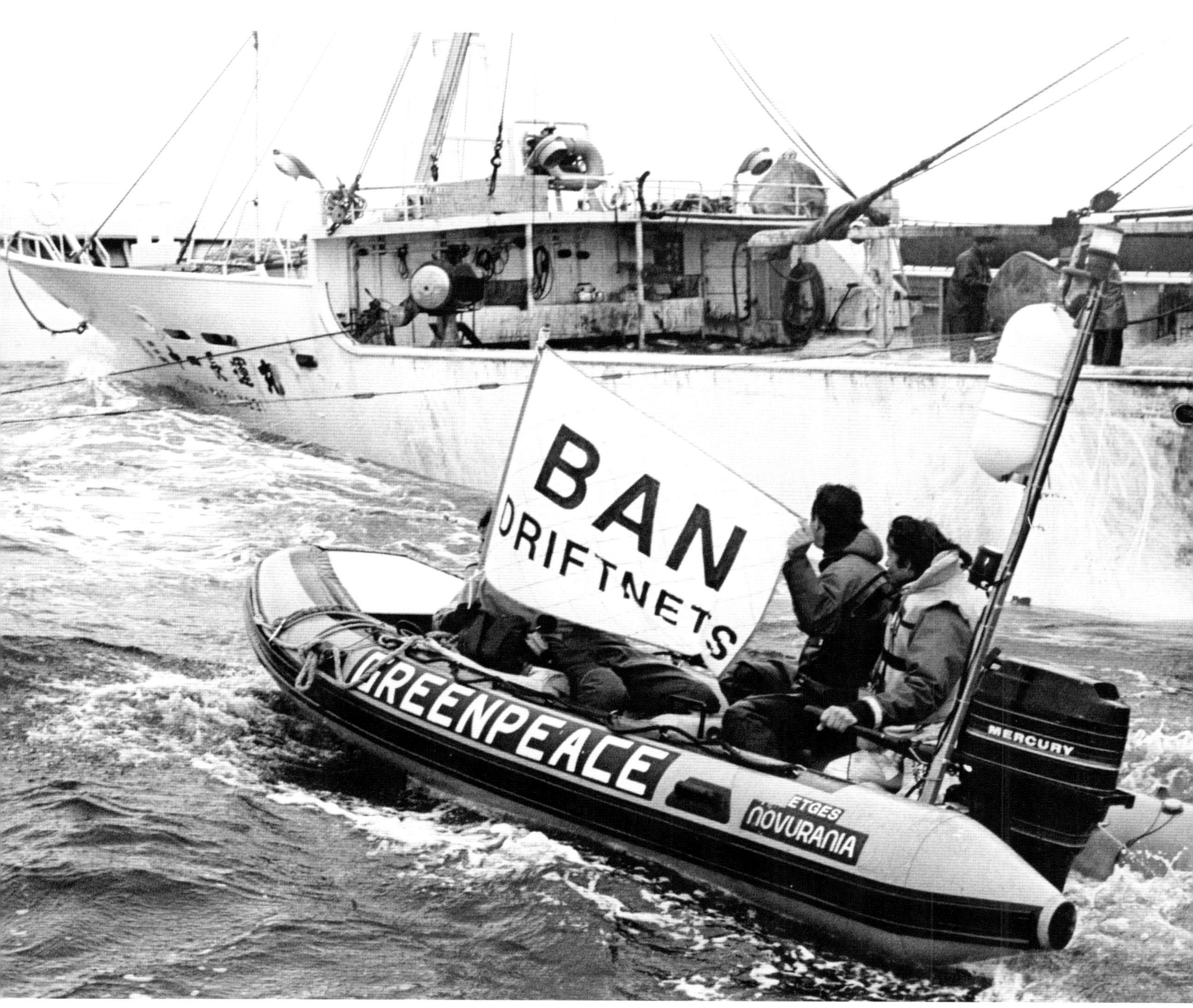

BAN
DRIFTNETS
GREENPEACE
MERCURY
ETGES
NOVURANIA

Deadly Collision

A fisherman reached out with a harpoon and tapped the hull. The response from inside the capsized boat was strong but then turned weaker and weaker—and then only silence.

In the predawn darkness of September 5, 1996, some ten miles northeast of Gloucester, Massachusetts, the tug *Houma* was towing an empty 272-foot barge from New York to Maine. About an hour away, the 45-foot *Heather Lynn II* with three fishermen aboard had been fishing for tuna. For one of them, it was his first trip.

The tug's crew saw the *Heather Lynn II*, based in Newburyport, Massachusetts, coming at a distance. As it became obvious the tuna boat was headed in their direction, the *Houma*'s crew tried communicating by radio. When that didn't work and with the distance between the two boats rapidly decreasing, the tug's crew activated a siren and shined a spotlight on the approaching *Heather Lynn II*. But nothing worked, and the fishing boat struck the *Houma*'s towing cable. The *Heather Lynn II* capsized, trapping the captain and his two crewmen. Before divers could arrive, all three drowned.

The *Heather Lynne II* was considered a star in the Newburyport fleet. Twenty years later, in September 2016, the Fishermen's Memorial in Newburyport was rededicated to pay tribute to the *Heather Lynne II*'s crew: Captain Jeffrey Hutchins, Kevin Foster, and John Lowther as well as other two fishermen, Sean Cone and Daniel Miller, who died when *Lady Luck* sank on January 31, 2007. The book *Dead Men Tapping: The End of the Heather Lynne II* by Kate Yeomans, examined the tragedy.

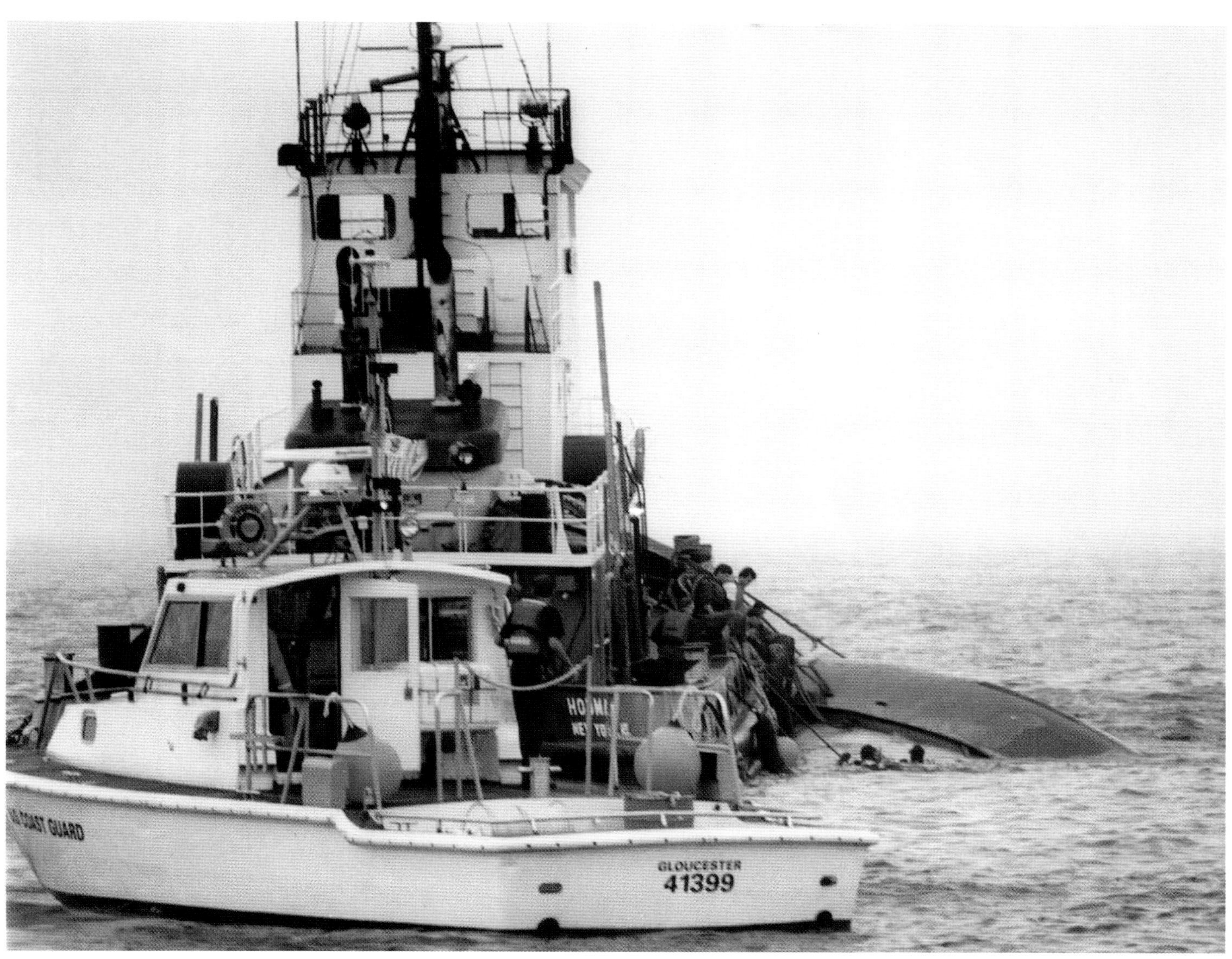
U.S. COAST GUARD
GLOUCESTER
41399

About Michael Crowley

Michael Crowley spent several years working on halibut longliners in the Gulf of Alaska and the Bering Sea. He has also worked as Contributing Editor and Field Editor for *National Fisherman* and as a correspondent for *WorkBoat* magazine, specializing in stories related to new vessel construction and new gear. He lives in Maine.

About the Penobscot Marine Museum

Since 1936, Penobscot Marine Museum has been sharing an ever-expanding collection of stories and histories from Maine's coastal communities spanning centuries. Located in Searsport, Maine, the museum has a campus of historical homes and buildings that display and share art, objects, photos, documents, and small boats. In-person visitors explore Maine's working waterfronts through hands-on exhibits, historical artifacts, fine art, and a research library. Online visitors join lectures and workshops broadcast free to the public, and also search historical databases of the museum's collection, which contains more than 500,000 photos, objects, and documents. All of the Penobscot Marine Museum offerings spread the stories of the tight-knit communities of Mainers whose lives and livelihoods have long been sustained on or by the sea. More information is available online at penobscotmarinemuseum.org.